# EU Accession Dynamics and Conflict Resolution

## Catalysing Peace or Consolidating Partition in Cyprus?

NATHALIE TOCCI

ASHGATE

Published by
Ashgate Publishing Limited
Gower House
Croft Road
Aldershot
Hampshire GU11 3HR
England

Ashgate Publishing Company
Suite 420
101 Cherry Street
Burlington, VT 05401-4405
USA

Ashgate website: http://www.ashgate.com

**British Library Cataloguing in Publication Data**
Tocci, Nathalie
    EU accession dynamics and conflict resolution : catalysing
    peace or consolidating partition in Cyprus?
    1.European Union - Cyprus 2.Partition, Territorial
    3.Conflict management - Cyprus 4.Cyprus - Politics and
    government - 1960-
    I.Title
    956.9'304


**Library of Congress Cataloging-in-Publication Data**
Tocci, Nathalie.
    EU accession dynamics and conflict resolution : catalysing peace or consolidating
partition in Cyprus? / by Nathalie Tocci.
        p. cm.
    Includes bibliographical references and index.
    ISBN 0-7546-4310-7
    1. European Union--Cyprus. I. Title: European Union accession dynamics and conflict
resolution. II. Title.

    HC240.25.C93T63 2004
    956.9304--dc22

                                                    2004011848

ISBN 0 7546 4310 7
Printed and bound by Athenaeum Press, Ltd.,
Gateshead, Tyne & Wear.

# Contents

# List of Figures, Tables and Maps

# Preface

Since 1993, the European Commission and the governments of EU member states and of the Republic of Cyprus have raised the expectation that Cyprus' EU accession process would act as a catalyst for a settlement of the island's conflict. Yet throughout the 1990s the divisions between the positions of the principal parties widened. While in the late 1980s and early 1990s the parties had negotiated on the basis of UN proposals for a bi-zonal and bi-communal federation, after 1993 negotiations were stalled and the Turkish Cypriot side rejected federal proposals and advocated the establishment of a confederation instead. In addition, the 1990s witnessed an escalation of tensions in the Eastern Mediterranean, between Greece and Turkey, as well as between Greek Cypriots and Turkish Cypriots. Cyprus' accession process appeared to catalyse unwittingly a consolidation rather than a settlement or resolution of the conflict.

Substantive negotiations were re-launched only in 2002. The 2002 direct talks were intended to reach an agreement before the December 2002 European Council meeting, that would have invited Cyprus and nine other candidate countries to join the Union. Despite the publication of the comprehensive 'Annan Plan', the talks failed to reach an agreement due to the rejection by the Turkish Cypriot side. The divided Cyprus signed the Treaty of Accession in April 2003.

Again direct talks re-started in February 2004, as a last-ditch attempt to secure the reunification of the island through a separate referendum before Cyprus' EU entry. Yet this time due to an overwhelming rejection by the Greek Cypriot leadership and public in the referendum, the Greek Cypriots joined the EU on 1 May 2004, leaving Turkish Cypriots, who instead had accepted the UN Plan, on the other side of the divide.

This study analyses the inter-relationship between the evolution of the conflict and the development of relations between the conflict parties and the EU in the context of enlargement. More specifically it focuses on the linkages between the Cyprus-Greece-Turkey triangle on the one hand and the EU-Cyprus/EU-Turkey nexus on the other. What explains the negative developments in the conflict during the course of the 1990s, concomitantly with the progress in Cyprus' EU accession process? Why did negative developments seem to reverse by the turn of the century? In particular, what impact did Cyprus' as well as Turkey's accession process have on the increased prospects for reunification in 2002-04? And finally why did the formidable efforts to secure an agreement before May 2004 ultimately fail?

If EU actions and decisions had a significant albeit often unintended impact on the conflict, what explains the conduct of the Union? Was the failure of the 'catalytic' effect the product of a misguided EU strategy or were events the result of the very absence of a strategy? This book shows that the problem was precisely that the Union was not a monolithic actor with a consistent and comprehensive strategy to catalyse a settlement through accession. The flaws in the 'catalytic effect' are intricately related to and explained by the nature of the EU as a foreign policy actor(s). In the case of Cyprus, one member state, namely Greece, based its policies and positions on a consistent strategy. However, Greece was also a principal party to the conflict, and as such its strategy was not that of an impartial third party. The other member states, with the exception of the UK, had no strategy to catalyse a settlement through accession. Apart from Greece, no member state was willing to see a more active EU involvement in conflict resolution.

This is not to say that the EU framework in the context of accession could not have generated important incentives for an agreement in Cyprus. Indeed, the EU framework could have provided an alternative context within which to address the basic needs of the principal parties. Inclusion in a multi-level system of governance in which sovereignty is shared rather than exclusive, in which borders are permeable, and in which freedoms are secured while cultural and historical specificities are respected, could have added a constructive new dimension to conflict resolution efforts.

Hence, the potential for conflict settlement and resolution within the EU framework did not materialise yet due to the deficiency of the EU as a foreign policy actor. By analysing in depth the case of Cyprus, this book casts a different light on the problems involved in mobilizing the EU's multi-level framework of governance in the field of external relations, particularly in situations of active or latent crisis, typical of ethno-political conflicts.

*Rome, May 2004*

# Acknowledgements

This book would not have been possible without the valuable advice of William Wallace. Special thanks also to Michael Emerson, Bruno Coppieters, Heinz Kramer and Kevin Featherstone and my colleagues in CEPS for their constant help and support during these years. I would also like to thank the Economic and Social Research Council, the Frank Educational Fund, the Central Research Fund of the University of London and the Turkish Foreign Policy Institute. Finally, my gratitude goes to my family and all my friends and colleagues in Cyprus, Greece and Turkey, to whom this book is dedicated.

*Pity the nation divided into fragments,*
*each fragment deeming itself a nation*

*Khalil Gibran*
*The Garden of the Prophet*

# Political Party Spectrum

**Greece**
ND          Nea Demokratia (conservative)
PASOK       Pannelion Socialistikon Kinima (socialist/social democratic)

**Republic of Cyprus**
AKEL        Anorthotikon Komma Ergazomenou Laou (left)
EDI         Enomenoi Democrates (liberal)
DIKO        Democratico Komma (nationalist centre-right)
DISY        Democraticos Synagermos (centre-right)
KISOS       Kinima Sosialdemocraton (nationalist centre-left)
            Previously:
EDEK        Enie Democratiki Enosis Kyprou (nationalist centre-left)
NO          Neoi Orizontes (nationalist extreme right)

**Turkish Republic of Northern Cyprus**
BDH         Barış ve Demokrasi Hareketi (centre-left)
ÇABP        Çözüm ve Avrupa Birliği Partisi (liberal)
CTP         Cumhuriyetci Türk Partisi (centre-left)
DP          Demokrat Parti (nationalist centre-right)
TKP         Toplumcu Kurtuluş Partisi (centre-left)
UBP         Ulusal Birlik Partisi (nationalist centre-right)

**Turkey**
ANAP        Anavatan Partisi (liberal)
CHP         Cumhuriyetçi Halk Partisi (nationalist centre-left)
DSP         Demokratık Sol Parti (nationalist centre-left)
DYP         Doğru Yol Partisi (nationalist centre-right)
MHP         Milliyetçi Hareket Partisi (nationalist extreme right)
AKP         Adalet ve Kalkınma Partisi (Islamic democratic/conservative)
            Previously:
FP          Fazilet Partisi (Islamic)
            Previously:
RP          Refah Partisi (Islamic)

# Chapter 1

# Introduction

*'What satisfies their fears is what increases our fears, and so we have this*
*paradoxical situation that unless we can find a way in which the fears of both*
*communities are put at rest, it would be extremely difficult to find a solution to the*
*Cyprus problem'*
(Glafcos Clerides quoted in Coughlan, 1992, p.93)

In July 1990 the Republic of Cyprus applied for EC membership on behalf of the whole island. Since 1993, the Commission, the member states and the Greek Cypriot government have raised the expectation that the accession process would catalyse a resolution of the conflict on the island. The 1993 Commission Opinion claimed that the accession process would 'help bring the communities on the island closer together' (Commission, 1993, paragraph 46). Particularly with the launch of accession negotiations, the 'catalytic effect' argument was frequently reiterated in official speeches and documents. In February 1997, Commissioner Hans Van der Broek declared that 1997 would witness a final breakthrough in Cyprus: 'why should this year be different? The difference is that the Union has offered Cyprus membership, and that prospect could be the key that helps unlock a solution to the Cyprus problem' (Commission, 1997a).

Behind these statements lay the expectation that EU conditionality in the context of enlargement would generate new incentives to reach a negotiated agreement. The assumption of EU actors throughout the 1990s was that the accession process and conflict resolution efforts under the aegis of the UN would proceed in parallel. Parallel processes would accelerate Cyprus' path to the Union.

Yet as the accession process progressed during the 1990s, the divisions between the principal parties widened. The prospect of a consolidated partition on the south-eastern borders of an enlarged EU became increasingly likely at the turn of the century. The 2002-04 negotiations finally seemed to offer the opportunity for a final breakthrough. Yet with the rejection of the UN-proposed 'Annan Plan' by the Greek Cypriot community on 24 April 2004, one week later the divided island joined the EU. If it were to last, the resulting 'europartition' could further separate the peoples of Cyprus, it could represent a major stumbling block in the emerging Greek-Turkish rapprochement and it could exacerbate the problems in Turkey's own path to full membership.

Why, contrary to official expectations, did the accession process fail to catalyse the reunification of Cyprus? Did it offer any such prospects? Were EU policies the product of a misguided strategy? Or was the failure of the 'catalytic effect' the result of empty rhetoric compounded by the very absence of a consistent

1

strategy? In turn what are the implications for the EU as a foreign policy actor? To what extent is the Union capable of mobilizing its multi-level framework of governance in the field of external relations, particularly in situations of active or latent crisis typical of ethno-political conflicts?

In attempting to answer these questions, this book first explores the inter-relationship between the conflict and relations in the EU-Cyprus-Greece-Turkey quadrangle from 1988 to 2003. EU actors did not expect to catalyse a settlement by replacing the UN as the official mediator in Cyprus. Rather they expected the accession process to complement the UN's mediation efforts by altering the incentive structure underlying the frozen conflict. Incentives would alter as a result of EU-related 'carrots' and 'sticks' that would be conditional on progress in the peace process. This approach required a clear and consistent EU-strategy based on a careful assessment of the conflict and its structure. Its successful implementation also depended on close collaboration between the UN and the EU.

Scratching beneath the surface, the 'catalytic effect' expectation was ridden with fundamental flaws. First, member governments neglected the fact that the Turkish and Turkish Cypriot sides viewed the Union as structurally biased against them, and were sceptical of Cyprus' EU accession process initiated and conducted exclusively by the Greek Cypriot side. Second, EU actors overlooked the reasons motivating the Greek Cypriot drive for membership, reasons that were inherently linked to their position in the conflict and in conflict settlement efforts. Finally and most critically, member governments misjudged the complex make-up of the principal parties, each of which included different players aiming to achieve radically different outcomes. As such, the incentives for some players perversely acted as disincentives to others. On several occasions and most dramatically at the culminating moment of the UN's peace efforts in 2004, the accession process contributed to strengthening the hand of those wishing to stall a solution.

The flaws in the 'catalytic effect' are intricately related to and explained by the nature of the EU as a foreign policy actor. The problem was that the Union was not a monolithic actor with a consistent and comprehensive strategy to catalyse a settlement through accession. One member state, namely Greece, based its policies on a consistent strategy. However, Greece was also a principal party to the conflict, and as such its strategy was not that of an impartial third party. The other member states, with the exception of the UK, had no strategy to catalyse a settlement through accession. The British government, as guarantor power and UN Security Council member, did pay limited consistent attention to Cyprus. However it did so through its bilateral relations with the principal parties and its close collaboration with the UN Secretariat. The other member states were largely uninterested, paying only sporadic attention to the conflict. With the exception of Greece, no member state was willing to see a more active EU involvement in conflict resolution, and all were content with the exclusive UN role in mediation. This also entailed that up until 2001, there was minimal interaction between UN mediators and Commission officials negotiating Cyprus' accession to the Union.

This is not to say that the EU framework in the context of accession could not have generated important incentives for an agreement in Cyprus, by providing an alternative context within which to address the basic needs of the principal parties.

Inclusion in a multi-level system of governance in which sovereignty is shared rather than exclusive, in which borders are permeable, and in which freedoms are secured while cultural and historical specificities are respected, could have added a constructive new dimension to conflict resolution efforts. In addition, EU accession could have eased the economic ills of northern Cyprus. This would have halted the flow of emigration of Turkish Cypriots from Cyprus, and reduced their dependence on Turkey. Finally EU-Turkey ties, which since 1996 included Turkey's participation in the EU customs union and since 1999 Turkey's inclusion in the accession process, represented another key element of a win-win solution.

In tackling these questions, this study draws on the insights in the conflict and peace literatures and in particular theories of negotiation and mediation in inter or intra-state conflicts. At first sight the focus on international mediation may appear misplaced in the current context, given that the UN, and not the EU, was the official mediator in the conflict. The EU collectively was not a mediator in Cyprus; nor were the member governments or the Commission in close contact with UN mediators up until late 2001. In addition, the difficulties of the EU to act as a coherent, let alone single, actor in the field of foreign policy raises the critical question of whether the Union had the capability of mediating in the conflict.

Nonetheless, insights from the conflict settlement and resolution literatures provide useful theoretical instruments. Although the EU collectively did not (and perhaps could not) mediate in Cyprus, EU actors agreed in assuming that the accession process created the scope for the effective use of leverage and conditionality towards the principal parties. As argued in the conflict settlement literature, the use of leverage and conditionality is typical of mediation, and principal mediation in particular. Like principal mediation, EU policies towards Cyprus and Turkey affected the incentive structure underlying the conflict. Criticism of the 'conflict settlement' school can instead contribute to the analysis of whether and how the EU framework could have generated additional positive incentives for a settlement, transformation and resolution of the conflict.

## Negotiation and Conflict Settlement between Principal Parties

In order to understand the nature and dynamics of mediation let us begin with an analysis of negotiation as a method of conflict settlement between principal parties. Who are the principal parties to a conflict? Principal parties are those with direct stakes in the conflict. However the assessment of the value of the stakes may differ between the different actors operating within the broad categories of 'principal parties'. Following Robert Putnam, this study highlights the importance of differentiating between the positions and interests of leaders and those of the constituents in a negotiating context (Putnam, 1988). At the domestic level, interest groups, acting independently or in coalitions, press governments and politicians to adopt particular positions. Leaders who negotiate in conflict lie at the crux between their domestic constituents and the external negotiating setting. In some instances, leaders may have fewer interests in solving a conflict than the people, if they enjoy advantages that would be lost in the event of a settlement. In these cases, an agreement may be elusive even if it would satisfy in principle the demands of the population it is intended for. On other occasions, leaders may wish but may be unable to move ahead of their constituents towards a settlement. Particularly in cases in which the constituents do not suffer from acute immediate costs from the status quo and populist nationalist language is predominant in public discourse, leaders may be unable to take the risks entailed in a settlement. In such instances, while being bolstered by a tough domestic constituency, leaders may fail to reach an agreement altogether.

Bearing these issues in mind, let us turn to the method of negotiation. Negotiation occurs when two or more principal parties acknowledge a conflict between them and appreciate that their aims cannot be realized through unilateral action. Negotiation is thus a mechanism for conflict settlement that can take place when the parties feel that they have common interests (integrative bargaining) as well as conflictual zero-sum interests once the Pareto frontier is reached (or redistributive bargaining). When relations are either purely cooperative or purely conflictual, there is no scope for negotiation. Scope for compromise in negotiation can exist either because principal parties have different goals with respect to a common problem, or because they attach different values to commonly desired objectives.

Negotiation occurs along the bargaining range, or the range in which the win-sets of the principal parties overlap. This includes all points of agreement which both parties prefer to their 'security point' or their 'Best Alternative to a Negotiated Agreement' (BATNA) (Fisher and Ury, 1991). The BATNA represents each party's limit after which non-agreement becomes preferable to a negotiated settlement. In Figure 1.1, the bargaining range includes all points along and within the Pareto frontier bounded by the dotted lines showing the respective parties' BATNAs. All agreements within these boundaries are mutually beneficial to all parties. They are the points where the win-sets of the principal parties overlap. BATNAs need not be fixed over time. They are likely to alter with changing evaluations of agreement and non-agreement, changing expectations and possibly changing goals as well.

Within the bargaining range there are numerous potential agreements. A process of strategic interaction in the light of imperfect information determines the exact point of agreement along the Pareto frontier. The concept of relative bargaining strength is of fundamental importance in determining at which point agreement is reached.

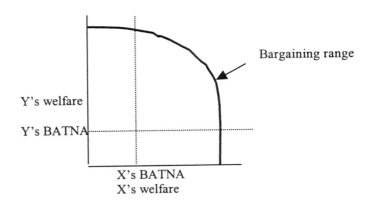

**Figure 1.1    The Bargaining Range**

But to state that relative bargaining strength determines the negotiation outcome is little more than a tautology. What exactly determines balance in a negotiation setting? Habeeb defines relative bargaining strength as 'relative power'. He argues that relative power is determined by aggregate structural power, issue-specific power and behavioural power (Habeeb, 1988). Aggregate structural power is given by the general resources (economic, military, demographic and political) available to a negotiating party.

However, what often appears to be more important than general resources is issue-specific power, i.e., the parties' strength in their bilateral relations in the context of the conflict in question. This depends on the levels of dependence and interdependence of the parties, the value they respectively attribute to the issues at stake, their control over the situation, and their BATNAs. The higher a negotiating party's BATNA, the more advantageous an agreement it is likely to secure. The party that stands to lose most from non-agreement (i.e., the party with the lower BATNA) instead gains the least from a settlement.

Yet the importance of relative bargaining strength is a matter of perception as well as reality. This is what Habeeb defines as behavioural power determined by communication strategies and tactics. During negotiations parties seek to discover each other's relative strength by distinguishing enduring positions and underlying needs from temporary bluffs. Each party tries to give the opponent the impression of the highest possible relative strength through the use of communication tactics. Each party aims to create the perception of a high BATNA and attempts to lower that of the opponent. But the excessive use of strategic misinformation can lead to failure in negotiations by creating the misperception of an excessively narrow bargaining range, in cases when mutually beneficial deals would be possible.

Another critical element of strategic bargaining, related both to behavioural power and to issue-specific power, is the use of threats and promises (Hopmann, 1996). Negotiating parties attempt to alter the relative balance of bargaining strength through the use of threats and promises. A threat is a conditional statement by A to B stating that if B does not behave in A's preferred way a punishment or the withdrawal of a reward will follow. A promise is a conditional statement by A to B stating that if B behaves in A's preferred way a reward or the withdrawal of a punishment will follow. The success of threats or promises depends both on their credibility and on their relative value to the recipient compared to the incremental value of his or her preferred course of action. Credibility in turn depends on the recipient's perception of the donor's capacity and willingness to carry out the declared commitment.

In Cyprus, negotiations between the leaderships took place because no principal party could achieve its aims through unilateral action. Given Turkish/Turkish Cypriot *de facto* control of northern Cyprus, Turkey's superior military strength and strategic significance, and its ensuing relations with the US and European countries, Greece and the Greek Cypriots were unable to alter unilaterally the status quo. They could not reunite the country and regain control of Greek Cypriot land and property in the north. Turkish Cypriots in turn could not achieve communal security and self-determination in a stable and prosperous environment given the non-recognition of their state. Similarly, Turkey could not attain its strategic objectives unilaterally, while retaining international legitimacy and the support of Western powers. Greece and the Greek Cypriots had higher international legal standing because of the status of the Republic of Cyprus as the only internationally recognized authority on the island. They used their standing to prevent any form of recognition of the Turkish Cypriot state. Hence, the need for negotiations.

The bargaining range converged on discussions of federal-confederal models, territorial readjustments, the return of refugees, economic redistribution and external guarantees. Through a federal-confederal arrangement, the Turkish Cypriots could enjoy some form of self-determination without independent statehood. The Greeks and Greek Cypriots could achieve the reunification of the island. Turkey instead could ensure that the island was not dominated by Greeks. Yet separate Turkish Cypriot self-government on the one hand required territorial redistribution on the other, given the disproportionate share of territory controlled by Turkish Cypriots relative to their size. This in turn would allow a proportion of Greek Cypriot refugees to return to their homes under Greek Cypriot rule. The return of the rest of the refugees, as well as the extent of liberalization of the freedoms of movement, settlement and property, would then be subject to negotiations along the bargaining range. Negotiations would also determine the precise role of external guarantors and peacekeepers, and the economic redistribution from the south to the north.

However, the BATNAs of the principal parties have been high. As such, the incentives to move away from the status quo have been relatively low (given the narrow bargaining range). In the past, the parties attempted to reduce each other's BATNA. Hence for example the Greek/Greek Cypriot attempts at hampering trade and tourism in northern Cyprus. Both parties also engaged in unilateral actions (or threats) to raise their own BATNA. Turkish Cypriot attempts to seek recognition from the Organization of the Islamic Conference is a case in point. Most relevant to this study was the Greek Cypriot logic behind its EU membership application and its use of the accession process as a means to alter the status quo by strengthening its BATNA, weakening that of its adversary and achieving particular gains through unilateral action (such as the filing of cases to the European Court of Human Rights on the return of refugees). For many years, the Turkish side reacted with threats of integration between Turkey and northern Cyprus. As will be argued over the course of this study, both approaches significantly hampered the negotiation process throughout the 1990s.

## Mediation: Roles and Characteristics

Mediation has been broadly defined as 'a process of conflict management related to but distinct from the parties' own efforts, where the disputing parties or their representatives seek assistance, or accept an offer of help, from an individual, group, state or organization to change, affect or influence their behaviour, without resorting to physical force or invoking the authority of law' (Bercovitch, 1992, p.7). This general definition can encompass different roles and functions of mediation to be carried out by different actors. Mediation includes a wide range of activities provided these are non-coercive and non-binding (hence, the distinction between mediation as non-binding and arbitration as a legally binding activity). What are these roles and activities and who are they carried out by?

Mediator roles have been separated into communication, formulation and manipulation (Touval and Zartman, 1989). These different roles may be carried out by the same or by different actors. The mediator as communicator and formulator has also been described as the pure mediator, while the mediator as manipulator is often defined as a principal mediator.

The role of the mediator as communicator is that of facilitating communication, identifying interests and issues, changing perceptions, and persuading principal parties to increase flexibility and understanding. The mediator acts as a passive conduit and a repository of information, aims and perceptions. By doing so, it uncovers the bargaining range and attempts to create empathy which in turn facilitates an agreement. Despite differences, the mediator as communicator can also engage in consultation and conciliation. Consultation helps the parties diagnose issues and re-conceptualize their relations and their conflict by viewing each other as collaborators tackling a joint problem. Conciliation provides additional communication links, lowers tensions and encourages direct interaction.

The mediator can also act as a formulator. Here the mediator provides good offices, establishes protocol and procedures, structures an agenda, suggests plans for face-saving de-commitments, draws up a formula for negotiation and actively introduces new ideas and proposals.

Finally, the mediator can act as a manipulator, i.e., the third party can engage in principal mediation. In this case the mediator adopts a structural role in negotiations. The manipulator negotiates directly with the conflict parties, thus changing negotiations from a dyad into a triad (unless the mediator forms a coalition with one of the parties). At times, the principal mediator may actually become the main negotiating partner of the conflict parties. A three-way bargaining situation may arise whereby party A negotiates directly with the mediator who in turn negotiates directly with party B. Hence, in the case of principal mediation the difference between principal and third party roles may blur if not cease to exist. The mediator attempts to enhance the incentives for an agreement by altering the payoff structure of the bargain. He/she does so through influence and leverage, discussed in detail below. The mediator as manipulator often retains links with the conflict parties even following a settlement, normally as a provider of continuing benefits such as security guarantees.

It is widely believed that the pure mediator should be impartial (Young, 1968). A mediator is impartial (not necessarily neutral) when it has no connection with the conflict parties and has no direct or indirect interests in the conflict. Impartiality allows the mediator to gain the confidence and trust of the conflict parties, which allows him/her to act as a repository of information, proposals and perceptions. The mediator can thus induce an agreement by uncovering the bargaining range and making new proposals. In reality complete impartiality is rarely if ever present. Particularly in cases of international organizations' involvement in secessionist conflicts, full impartiality is almost impossible, given the international system's natural aversion to secession and the recognition of new states. This is indeed the case of the OSCE's involvement in secessionist conflicts in the former Soviet Union and the UN's involvement worldwide, not least in Cyprus.

Authors concentrating on the role of principal mediation argue that the most critical characteristic of the mediator is his/her acceptability rather than impartiality (Touval and Zartman, 1989, p.122). In so far as the role of the principal mediator is not as easily separable from that of the conflict parties, impartiality is a condition that almost by definition cannot be met. Acceptability however is key to the success of principal mediation. And acceptability hinges on the extent to which the principal parties believe that the mediator is capable of bringing about a more desirable outcome. In some instances, impartiality is the main determinant of acceptability. But this is not necessarily so. A party may accept the role of an unfavourably biased mediator if it believes the mediator can exert influence on the opponent precisely in virtue of the bias. The most frequently quoted examples of this are the role of Henry Kissinger in the Middle East, the role of Algeria in mediating the Iranian hostage crisis and the Soviet mediation in the conflict between India and Pakistan. Precisely because of the third party's connection with one principal party, the other party accepted him/her as mediator.

The EU accession process affected significantly the dynamics of the Cyprus conflict, altering the incentives to reach an agreement. However, the precise role of the EU cannot be easily pinpointed because of its nature. It is thus important to disentangle the various actors within the EU in order to assess the overall role of the Union. The next chapter discusses at length the actors in the Cyprus conflict. Nonetheless, two examples will be cited here to give a flavour of the complex role of the Union.

Member state Greece was a principal party to the conflict. Although after 1974 its interests were mainly to support the Greek Cypriot cause, Greece, as guarantor state, remained a principal party. This does not exclude the fact that the Greek government at times also played third party functions, influencing the positions of the Greek Cypriot leadership in negotiations. The PASOK government's support for the UN Plan in 2002-03 indeed bolstered the stance of the former Greek Cypriot leadership that appeared willing to conclude a deal on the basis of the Plan.

The UK, due to its historical responsibilities, contributed to mediation efforts with fluctuating intensity and generally outside the EU framework. However, in certain respects, and particularly those which relate to the future of the British military bases in Cyprus, the UK was also a principal party in negotiations. The 2002-3 negotiations on the island highlight the blurring distinction between the UK's principal and third party roles. In February 2003, the UN presented the third version of the Annan Plan for the reunification of Cyprus. One of the proposed elements was the transfer of approximately fifty percent of the territory of the bases predominantly to the Greek Cypriot side. The cessation of territory was intended to facilitate an agreement on the territorial aspect of the conflict. As such, the British role fluctuated between that of third party and principal party.

While acknowledging the multi-faceted nature of the EU, this study focuses on its actual and potential role in principal mediation. Yet due to the EU's complex nature, which included both principal and third party attributes, it is important to determine at the outset that the EU was not a neutral or impartial actor in Cyprus. Particularly over the course of the 1990s, it became an integral element of the dynamics of the conflict. Greece and the UK were EU member states, while both Cyprus and Turkey enjoyed institutionalized relations with and aspired to join the Union. As such, the EU, while technically remaining a third party, was certainly not an impartial one. Yet the EU's partiality did not alone affect its acceptability in the eyes of the principal parties. Had both principal parties perceived the third party's role as offering the potential for a more desirable outcome, its role as an insider could have been viewed as an asset rather than a liability in peace efforts.

## Principal Mediation

Having reviewed the different forms of mediation, let us concentrate on principal mediation, which is of particular relevance to this study. This is for two main reasons.

First, because of the potential desirability of principal mediation in the Cyprus conflict. Principal mediation is most appropriate in conflicts which are deadlocked in a stage of segregation because the conflict parties are relatively content with the status quo. This appeared to be the case in Cyprus, particularly at the level of the leaderships. The BATNAs of the leaderships were relatively high and the resulting bargaining range was too narrow. Since 1974, the Turkish Cypriot leadership enjoyed an unprecedented *de facto* status and secured, together with Turkey, the physical and communal security of its people. It was reluctant to forego these gains for unsubstantiated promises of political equality. The Greek Cypriot leadership instead benefited from undiluted sovereignty, and many leaders (and citizens) were unwilling to relinquish these gains for an effective sharing of sovereignty in a loose federal structure. In such circumstances, the principal mediator could increase the incentives for a settlement, by raising both the gains from agreement (shifting out the Pareto frontier) as well as the costs of no agreement (reducing the BATNA).

Second, a discussion of conditional threats and promises appears to be particularly relevant in the case of EU external relations in general and EU-Cyprus relations in particular. Particularly over the last decade and in the process of the fifth enlargement, the EU developed its policies of conditionality as a means to induce domestic change within the candidate countries (Smith, 1999; Grabbe, 2001). The offer of full membership has been the most powerful form of conditional reward on offer by the Union. In the case of Cyprus, the EU accession process, and the use of conditionality that it entailed, presented sticks and carrots to the conflict parties.

But what are the conditions for effective principal mediation? The notions of influence and leverage are key to success. While all mediators can exert some form of leverage, principal mediation relies on influence and leverage in his/her role. The mediator exerts leverage to increase the gains from an agreement and the costs of no agreement. This can be done in two ways. The mediator may shift his/her weight in order to create an (old or new) balance between the conflict parties and thus facilitate an agreement as opposed to a unilateral victory. When there is a significant imbalance between the conflict parties, these may be reluctant to engage in meaningful negotiations. The stronger party may feel it can achieve its aims unilaterally, while the weaker party could feel that a settlement would entail total submission. The same is true when the relative strength of one side is growing. In these circumstances, the party whose strength is growing is reluctant to negotiate, expecting a continuing rise, while the weakening party fears an unfavourable deal (Lall, 1966, p.150).

In these circumstances, the principal mediator can shift his/her weight creating a situation in which the strength of the upper hand starts slipping and that of the underdog starts rising (Zartman, 1989). The mediator may feel it necessary to create a situation of perceived parity of bargaining strength or movement towards parity. This may entail having to temporarily exacerbate a stalemate in order to ultimately yield a settlement. In Cyprus, for those who believed that the Turkish and Turkish Cypriot sides were the stronger parties in the conflict, EU sticks (such as the banning of Turkish Cypriot exports to the EU) were viewed as a means to shift the conflict towards greater parity in bargaining strength. To those who viewed the conflict through different lenses and emphasized the relative Greek Cypriot advantages stemming from international recognition, EU sticks to the Turkish Cypriots were viewed as counterproductive to peace efforts.

Alternatively, the mediator can add side-payments to negotiations thereby increasing the prospects for an integrative bargain. In extreme situations deals are struck more because of the prospect of receiving side-payments than because of the substantive issues of the deal itself. Side-payments can be conditional or non-conditional. Conditionality is a strategy whereby a reward is granted or withheld depending on the fulfilment or non-fulfilment of an attached condition. Conditionality is not necessary for the effectiveness of an incentive and can be used in different ways. A positive incentive may be provided unconditionally and demands for policy changes can be made subsequently, when trust between the mediator and the principal party has increased. Alternatively, conditionality can be applied at different stages, and not exclusively at the time of delivery of the side-payments. The latter is particularly true of the EU accession process, where depending on the depth and speed of domestic reform, EU institutions determine when and whether to give the green light to the different stages along the accession process (Grabbe, 2001).

Side-payments in the form of threats and promises can take a variety of forms, including aid, trade, investment, security guarantees and membership of an international organization. Their aim is generally that of creating incentives for settlement by altering the negotiating range. The bargaining range changes because of altered expectations of the mediator's future actions (see Figure 1.2). Through threats the principal mediator raises the costs of non-agreement and thus reduces the value of the BATNA. Through promises the mediator increases the expected gains from a deal (or reduces the costs of the concessions) and therefore raises the bargaining range by pushing outwards the Pareto frontier. Post-settlement guarantees may also serve as a useful promise in so far as mutual distrust in the implementation phase may be a major hindrance to reaching agreement.

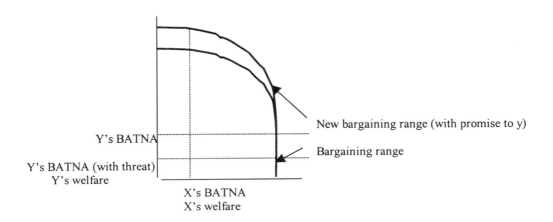

**Figure 1.2      Shifts in the Bargaining Range**

However, while the apparent impact of threats and promises on the bargaining range may be identical, there are important differences between the two, both in terms of their nature and in terms of their effect (Cortright, 1997; Dorussen, 2001). Positive incentives may provide advantages to the donor as well as to the recipient. This can increase the credibility of the promise. However it can also reduce its credibility when the delivery is supposed to be conditional on the principal party's compliance with the mediator's demands. In the case of economic sanctions, the effectiveness of a threat decreases or disappears if the recipient finds alternative suppliers. While positive incentives can be effective through unilateral action, sanctions often hinge on multilateral efforts, unless the affected party is highly dependent on a single supplier. However, promises as opposed to threats can create dependence, requiring the persisting involvement of the mediator to sustain peace. While the threat may generate resentment and nationalistic reactions and thus reduce goodwill and flexibility, a promise is more likely to induce cooperation. However, a promise may be perceived as a sign of appeasement and fail to induce moderation. Another important issue concerns the extent to which the principal mediator can mobilize sufficient resources to offer valuable and credible side-payments to all parties. This is particularly important because a promise to one side may be viewed as a threat to the other. Finally, the relative value of a mediator's threat or promise is also critical. Equally important is the objective value of the cost or benefit and the subjective perception of it by the recipient. If the recipient feels it can live without the incentive or sanction, the incentive strategy would fail and simply result in an additional cost to the mediator.

Ripeness is a useful concept when attempting to discern the conditions for effective mediation. A conflict is ripe for resolution when the circumstances of a conflict change, thereby increasing the likelihood of a negotiated settlement. Ripeness can occur in the event of a 'mutually hurting stalemate', i.e., a sufficiently painful situation which cannot be unilaterally altered by the principal parties (Touval and Zartman, 1989, p.125). This tends to require a change in the power balance in favour of the weaker party. Alternatively, ripeness is created when parties are confronted with a precipice, i.e., when parties realize that matters have deteriorated or are about to do so. An expected precipice creates ripeness also by setting a deadline for change.

Ripe conditions may emerge due to a contextual change. There may be a change in the domestic environment within a principal party, such as a change in leadership or a deterioration in the economy inducing leaders to raise their popularity through a foreign policy success (Stedman, 1991). Ripeness can also emerge from changes in the international environment. An international change could make conflict parties natural allies and thus foster a more cooperative atmosphere in negotiations. An external crisis can harm negotiations by increasing cognitive rigidity, disrupting communication and inducing a shift of attention to other issues. Alternatively a foreseen crisis can create a deadline for a settlement. However the resulting deals may be sub-optimal. This phenomenon has been referred to as the 'musical chairs' effect (Zartman and Berman, 1982). While the music is playing the parties place themselves in the best possible position, ready to stand still when the music suddenly stops. But the way in which they ultimately stop and reach an agreement may be inherently unstable as well as unfair.

Ripeness is not necessarily the product of coincidental changes in the domestic and international environment, but can also be cultivated. This idea is particularly relevant in cases when conflicts are protracted because principal parties develop vested interests in the status quo. Principal mediators may cultivate ripeness through the use of threats or the creation of an impending deadline. However, while applied leverage can make a stalemate hurting, in order for short-term decisions to stick, it is necessary for the agreements to be sufficiently attractive. A threat alone rarely contributes to a lasting solution. It must be complemented by the positive exercise of influence, which goes beyond the mere lifting of the sticks (Zartman and Aurik, 1991, p.181).

Several examples from the history of the Cyprus conflict discussed in Chapter 3 can be used to illustrate this argument. In 1960 an agreement was reached largely through external pressures on the Greek Cypriot leadership. The threat of the 1958 Macmillan Plan, and Greek dependence on the US, induced Archbishop Makarios to accept the 1959-60 compromises. The agreement however was inherently unsatisfactory to the Greek Cypriots, explaining its early death in 1963. In 1964 the US deterred Turkish military plans by threatening not to defend Turkey in the event of a Soviet attack in defence of the Greek Cypriots. The threat succeeded in its short-term intent to deter war. However, it did not raise incentives to reach a settlement. In the longer term, it reduced Turkish dependence on the US and induced a Turkish-Soviet rapprochement, which a decade later favoured the Turkish military intervention on the island.

Several decades later, did the EU accession process generate the incentives to shift progressively and durably from a low to a high welfare equilibrium? Collective EU decisions concerning Cyprus emphasized the positive effect of conditional side-payments to the principal parties deriving from EU accession. But to what extent did the accession process raise the incentives to reach a durable agreement? Were the gains and losses entailed in accession sufficiently valuable? To what extent were the threats and promises conditional and credible? Were unconditional promises viewed as a form of appeasement and partiality? Did the deadline of accession generate the conditions for a 'hurting stalemate'? How did these new conditions interact with domestic dynamics within the conflict parties? Did European threats generate hostility and nationalistic reactions or did sticks and carrots strengthen the hand of the most conciliatory forces in society?

## Criticizing the Conflict Settlement Approach

The discussion above falls within a conflict settlement approach. The underlying assumption of conflict settlement scholars is that while conflict cannot be resolved easily it can be managed with the (re) creation of stable balances. Conflict is generated over objective issues deriving from a scarcity of resources or incompatible goals. Thus attempting to eradicate conflict is often an exercise in futility. It would also be undesirable, in so far as conflict is viewed as a motor for progress. What is desirable is to minimize the costs of conflict in terms of violence and disorder. This is achieved through a rational process of negotiation between principal parties, that aims to reach a new (or return to an old) balance through a compromise agreement. Mediators, preferably representing strong (and not necessarily impartial) powers with the necessary skills and resources to exert leverage, aim to yield speedier agreements. They do so by shifting the balance of bargaining strengths and thus generating incentives to settle.

This approach has been criticized by advocates of conflict resolution for its inadequacy and superficiality in dealing with the sources and causes of conflict. It may lead to cease-fire or settlement, but fails to encourage conflict transformation and resolution, an aim which is both desirable and possible. It attempts to manage conflict by eliminating excessive violence and instability. The conflict itself remains intact (Kleiboer, 1996, p.382).

In John Burton's view, conflict is not endemic in human nature, but arises under specific socio-economic structures in which basic human needs (BHN) are frustrated (Burton, 1990a). These include both ontological needs (such as physical security, participation and redistributive justice) and subjective psychological needs (such as recognition or stimulation). BHN are universal, permanent and essential to the fulfilment of the 'humanness' in man. Hence, unlike interests, BHN are non-negotiable. When BHN are frustrated the premises for conflict emerge. Actual conflict may then either erupt or remain latent depending on the specific political and socio-economic circumstances on the ground.

Burton believes that BHN are not in short supply (Burton, 1990b). In fact their fulfilment is mutually reinforcing. The more secure is A, the more security will B enjoy. What may be mutually incompatible are particular 'satisfiers', expressed through bargaining positions. It is the strategy (or type of satisfier sought) which leads to conflict. For example, within most ethno-political conflicts, the drive for secession is not an end in itself. The underlying basic needs are those of communal security and self-determination. The means through which the smaller community often seeks to satisfy these needs are positions (satisfiers) on independence or confederalism. Yet these chosen satisfiers give rise to or entrench the conflict with the metropolitan state. The latter, normally representing the larger community, seeks to retain its territorial integrity in order to satisfy its own security and identity needs. It refuses to go beyond provisions for local autonomy or federalism. Hence, the persisting conflict.

Conflict is thus intended as the incompatibility of subject positions (Diez, Stetter and Albert, 2004). These subject positions include the articulation of objective goals through the lenses of subjective interests and identities. While basic needs are objective, chosen satisfiers are not. Bargaining positions are a result of subjective attitudes, perceptions, recollections and experiences, which can distort the rational pursuit of objective needs (Kelman, 1997).

Given that BHN are non-negotiable, the objectives sought (i.e., the fulfilment of BHN) remain unaltered. But the means through which BHNs are pursued (satisfiers) can be changed to give way to creative win-win solutions. Altering the chosen satisfiers requires a re-conceptualization of relations between principal parties. Third parties can facilitate this quest. But in stark opposition to the roles of principal mediators, third parties intervene to assist the peace process, playing a reactive and supportive role (Curle, 1995). The mediator should be impartial and should not impose solutions. He/she should help the parties find an acceptable outcome themselves, by eliminating misconceptions and other obstacles to communication. Mediators should empower the mechanisms for indigenous peace-building, rather than prescribe ready-made solutions (Lederach, 1997).

Critical theorists have mounted a further critique of the 'traditional' literature. They view both conflict settlement and conflict resolution approaches as wanting (Fetherston, 2000). In different ways, both engage in conflict management, without challenging the underlying systems generating conflict. The conflict settlement school does so explicitly. It accepts a given power configuration and attempts to conserve it by managing conflict. But also the conflict resolution school fails to deliver resolution through its exclusive focus on subjective processes.

The focus on perceptions and impartial mediation suggests that underlying structures generating conflict are left untouched. Impartiality entails that in the light of a clear imbalance of bargaining strength between the parties, the mediator contributes to the preservation of the status quo rather than its change Conflict resolution efforts can solve, re-solve and re-resolve the same conflicts through a re-conceptualization of relations. But the objective roots of conflict are not tackled. This is not to say that the transformation of perceptions is not important. Simply, that alone is insufficient. The aim should be that of transforming and resolving conflict by questioning existing structures and modes of social relations (Featherston and Parkin, 1997).

Yet many of the concerns of critical thinkers were already integrated in the work of structuralists such as Johan Galtung in his analysis of structural violence (Martinelli Quille, 2000). In a seminal article, Galtung elaborated the concept of violence, distinguishing between intentional, manifest, physical and personal violence as opposed to unintended, latent, psychological and structural violence that inhibits human self-realization (Galtung, 1969). Structural violence implies violence which is inbuilt in the system, characterized by inequality, underdevelopment, repression and alienation. Structural violence does not follow the common 'subject-verb-object' pattern. There is no subject involved, whose intentions and actions are to be blamed and punished. Furthermore, the violence is often latent, silent, not readily observable, but creeping under the surface, ready to emerge at any point in time.

The elimination of structural violence is of fundamental importance to the quest for peace. Negative peace can be achieved with the elimination of personal violence, through a well-functioning legal deterrent system. But the attainment of positive peace, through the eradication of structural violence, is much more arduous. Positive peace can only be achieved through structural change, i.e., by redressing power relations. In this respect, these arguments give almost as much importance to underlying structures as conflict settlement approaches do (Groom, 1990; Hoffman, 1987).

Critical theories may indeed be too 'critical' of the conflict resolution analysis. Proponents of the conflict resolution approach do focus on structural conditions that generate violence. Yet, while their analysis pays due attention to both objective and subjective elements of conflict, their prescriptive component focusing exclusively on subjective elements may be over-idealistic. The concept of compatible BHN leads Burton and others to concentrate predominantly on the need to alter subjective attitudes through problem-solving workshops and third party consultation. The argument is that with the alteration of subjective factors, objective conditions would also change. But this automatic link may not always exist. As such, the prescriptions of the conflict resolution school often fail to address objective structures, even if structures are acknowledged as being critical to the quest for positive peace.

## Re-conceptualizing Principal Mediation

The prescriptions of both the conflict settlement and conflict resolution schools are found wanting. Traditional realist prescriptions focus exclusively on achieving a settlement through the aid of resourceful mediators. The focus here is on objective power and interests. Conflict resolution theorists instead focus on subjective elements and call for integrative solutions achieved through the re-conceptualization of relations. Yet these approaches need not be mutually exclusive, but can be, on the contrary, highly complementary. Three reasons support the thesis of complementarity.

First is the changing mix of objective and subjective elements across the different stages of conflict. Conflicts evolve over time, and at each stage a conflict is constituted by a different mix of objective and subjective elements (Keashley and Fisher, 1996). In so far as different methods of mediation are more adequate in dealing with objective or subjective components of conflicts than others, the choice of third party roles should vary over time according to the objective-subjective mix. In the initial discussion and polarization stages, third party conciliation and consultation may help to facilitate communication and prevent the emergence of substantive conflict. In the stages of escalation and de-escalation, pure mediation can deal with the substantive issues at stake, by formulating proposals, providing information and good offices and persuading the parties to negotiate. In the segregation and destruction phases of conflict, principal mediation together with peacekeeping may best tackle the conditions of conflict. When agreement cannot be found because parties are content with the status quo or because there are insufficient resources to address all needs, principal mediation may also be appropriate.

Objective and subjective elements may not only vary over time, but at any given moment different aspects of the conflict may include different objective-subjective mixes (Bloomfield, 1995). Hence, different techniques may be required simultaneously as well as sequentially to tackle different aspects of conflict.

Second, conflict settlement and resolution efforts can be mutually reinforcing. All-encompassing conflict resolution can only gain momentum once a negotiated settlement is reached. The role of grass-roots initiatives is of fundamental importance. But particularly in the case of intra-state secessionist conflicts with blockaded frontiers and segregated communities, grass-roots activities can only become widespread once elites negotiate an agreement. Conflict settlement thus should not be viewed as an alternative, but rather an indispensable complement to conflict resolution activities. Likewise conflict resolution efforts should both cultivate ripeness before a settlement and consolidate peace once an agreement is reached. Particularly after a first agreement is reached, conflict resolution activities are key to re-conceptualize relations and thus sustain peace.

Finally, principal mediation together with third party consultation may aid the search for alternative solutions. The BHN literature stresses the importance of basic needs attained through a reformulation of subjective attitudes. Nonetheless, the belief that win-win satisfiers will emerge automatically provided subjective elements are altered may be wishful thinking. Some conflicts are indeed characterized by seemingly zero-sum alternatives and scarce resources. Changes in subjective conditions cannot resolve conflicts alone. Innovative solutions require the alteration of objective realities as well. Furthermore, particularly at the level of elites, conflict often persists not only because of mutual misconceptions. In many conflicts, while the populations may suffer from the status quo, their leaderships have vested interests in them. Leaders may be relatively content with a stalemate, and as such they will lack the political will to reach an agreement. In such cases, it is imperative for third parties to cultivate ripeness by altering realities and in turn inducing the top-level to settle.

The need to cultivate ripeness through a variety of third party activities appears particularly relevant in the case of Cyprus. In the light of stalemate, the potential roles of the UN and the EU were highly complementary. The UN pure mediators could facilitate negotiations and propose solutions that also satisfied the parties' BHN by accounting for the specific advantages provided by EU accession. EU actors in turn could have made careful conditional use of their sticks and carrots to raise the incentives of the principal parties to converge on the UN's proposals. These third party roles could have been complemented further by grass-roots bi-communal activities, aimed at preparing the ground for reunification by re-conceptualizing relations and building inter-communal trust.

Furthermore, EU policies of conditionality could have two types of effect on the Cyprus conflict, the first contributing more towards short-term conflict settlement and the second to medium and long-term conflict transformation and resolution. Principal parties could alter their bargaining positions favouring a settlement as a rational re-calculation of costs and benefits affected by EU conditionality. However, the very fact of being subject to EU conditionality over the longer term could give rise to a deeper process of societal change (Borzel and Risse, 2000). EU conditionality entails the participation of elites in EU structures. Through participation in or close contact with the EU institutional framework, parties may come to alter their substantive beliefs, visions and purposes. They may also alter their preferred 'ways of doing things' and codes of action (i.e., preferring negotiation and compromise over unilateral actions and brinkmanship). Subsequently they will alter their chosen strategies and tactics. This is what Checkel has defined as a process of 'complex learning'. It occurs when 'agents, in the absence of obvious material incentives, acquire new values and interests; their behaviour in turn, comes to be governed by new logics of appropriateness' (Checkel, 1999, p.90).

But how exactly could the EU accession process have altered positively the context of the Cyprus conflict? What kind of policies could EU actors have adopted to increase incentives for a solution? Could these policies have generated ripeness in a manner that would have encouraged a UN-mediated win-win solution satisfying the parties' BHN?

Theory cannot give precise answers to these questions. It can only provide rough guidelines concerning the aims and methods of third party activities. Principal mediation can be useful at particular stages of a conflict; it can cultivate ripeness and the political will to settle. Yet not all principal mediation aiming to reach a settlement is conducive to conflict resolution and transformation. It is not necessarily desirable to use any conditional threat or promise to create political will. This was Fisher's well-articulated critique of Henry Kissinger's role as mediator following the 1973 Arab-Israeli war (Fisher, 1981). Kissinger used all conditional carrots that were readily available to yield an already likely agreement between Egypt and Israel. He effectively engaged in direct negotiations with Israel, buying concessions from the latter by offering significant military aid. Israel's objective became to reap the maximum military and economic assistance from the US rather than to achieve peace with Egypt. Kissinger succeeded in his short-term aim, but paid little service to the deeper aim of conflict transformation and resolution in the region. On the contrary, he militarized the region further, hindering peacemaking and preparing the ground for subsequent wars.

Creating political will and enlarging the pie in order to facilitate its carving-up can thus be highly detrimental in the long term. Principal mediation is complementary to conflict resolution efforts if it motivates without coercing the parties to settle and if it increases incentives to engage in peaceful change (rather than to reap unrelated gains). Furthermore, principal mediation should employ its resources to facilitate the search for adequate satisfiers, which are not mere compromises, but which address BHN and trigger the mechanisms for conflict transformation. The incentives provided must strive to address the roots of conflict and address the parties' fundamental needs. Only in such instances would principal mediation facilitate integrative solutions paving the way for conflict transformation and resolution.

In the case of Cyprus, did EU actors do the most to present additional frameworks and resources which could have facilitated the search for alternative satisfiers and thus an integrative agreement on the island? Or did they overemphasize the potential effect of conditional threats and carrots that were only indirectly related to the issues at stake in the conflict and thus to its potential settlement and resolution?

Having set out the principal theoretical tools used in the following chapters, let us conclude with a brief exposition of the structure of this book. Chapter 2 introduces the main actors in this study, including both the principal parties and the third party actors in the conflict. While the main body of the book is devoted to the analysis of the interaction between these actors, Chapter 2 provides the background of the nature of these players and their changing interests and positions over time.

Chapter 3 reviews the history of the conflict from the 1930s to 1988, when Cyprus and the EC launched a political dialogue. The chapter recounts the views and actions of the principal parties and the most relevant external actors over the decades. Rather than attempting an explanation of the conflict as such, Chapter 3 seeks to highlight the principal reasons for its enduring stalemate. It argues that particularly since 1974, failure to reach an agreement was due to the relatively high BATNA of the principal parties, particularly as perceived by their leaderships. The persisting stalemate was also driven by the formulation of absolute and mutually incompatible satisfiers, centred on notions of absolute sovereignty and statehood.

Chapters 4 and 5 argue that up until late 2001, EU-Cyprus-Turkey relations in the context of enlargement affected critically and negatively the evolution of the conflict. The changes in the rhetoric and the actions of the principal parties, and the Turkish and Turkish Cypriot sides in particular, were directly linked to developments in relations with the EU. The nature of the carrots and sticks offered by the Union, and the manner in which they were conditionally offered, had counterproductive effects on the dynamics of the conflict. Rather than aiding the search for alternative satisfiers, the accession process contributed to entrench Turkish Cypriot positions. Furthermore in its policies of conditionality, EU actors neglected or underestimated the extent to which Greek Cypriot positions also hindered the peace process. They did so by raising the perceived Greek Cypriot BATNA, without inducing a re-conceptualization of traditional satisfiers. These two chapters also analyse the re-launch of the peace process in 2002 until Cyprus' EU accession on 1 May 2004. How, why and to what extent had the factors inducing a deterioration of the conflict over the 1990s been reversed by 2002-04?

Did the expected 'catalytic effect' fail because it was based on a misguided strategy? Or did it rather fail because of the absence of a coherent EU strategy based on a collective analysis of the expected responses of the principal parties? The 'catalytic effect' rested on the assumption that the EU, not unlike a principal mediator, would alter the incentives underlying conflict. Yet the EU did not (and perhaps could not) act as a single and coherent actor. Chapter 6 explores the actors and factors that determined EU actions or inactions towards the conflict. What was the role and relative importance of member state interests or lack of interests, institutional settings and external developments in determining the EU's 'default strategy' towards the conflict and EU accession? EU policies were the product of the complex inter-relationship between internal EU factors and external developments and expectations. These factors predominantly interacted by reinforcing each other over the course of the 1990s, and as such crystallizing the Union's 'non-strategy' towards Cyprus. Only by the turn of the century did countervailing forces, operating in a constructive direction, begin to have some impact on EU policies. However, these changes came too little and too late and as such they could not prevent the consolidation of partition as the divided Cyprus entered the Union.

But could the EU framework in the context of accession have positively affected conflict resolution efforts? Chapter 7 analyses whether and what the EU framework, with its institutions and policies, could have offered to alter the dynamics of the conflict. Could the prospect of accession to a multi-tier system of governance have increased the incentives of the principal parties to reach a mutually agreed solution? Were the Turkish and Turkish Cypriot sides (as the parties sceptical of EU membership) aware of these realities? Could the EU framework have accommodated the concerns deriving from Turkey's exclusion from the Union?

By way of conclusion, Chapter 8 inserts the findings of this study within the context provided both by the conflict and peace literatures and by the literature on EU foreign policy. What do the conclusions drawn in this study tell us about the formulation and conduct of European foreign policy and in particular about the EU as a third party actor in ethno-political conflicts? One of the most interesting lessons drawn is that when faced with a typical foreign policy problem such as an ethno-political conflict, a traditional state actor is often far more effective at mobilizing its resources, given the greater simplicity in its policy-making process. The complexity of a multi-level framework, like that of the EU, instead creates critical obstacles to effective external action. Yet the resources offered by a non-nation state framework are precisely those which created the potential for a win-win agreement in Cyprus. In other words, while being potentially of greater value, the EU's framework cannot be easily exported through coherent and consistent external action *because* of its very nature.

## References

Bercovitch, J. (1992), 'The Structure and Diversity of Mediation in International Relations', in J. Bercovitch and J.Z. Rubin (eds.), *Mediation in International Relations - Multiple Approaches to Conflict Management*, Macmillan, London, pp.1-29.

Bloomfield, D. (1995), 'Towards Complementarity in Conflict Management: Resolution and Settlement in Northern Ireland', *Journal of Peace Research*, Vol.32, No.2, pp.151-164.

Borzel, T. and Risse. T. (2000), 'When Europe Hits Home: Europeanization and Domestic Change', *European Integration Online Papers*, Vol.4, No.15, http://eiop.or.at/eiop/texte/2000-015.htm

Burton, J. (ed.) (1990a), *Conflict: Human Needs Theory*, Macmillan, London.

Burton, J. (1990b), 'Unfinished Business in Conflict Resolution', in J. Burton and F. Dukes (eds.), *Conflict: Readings in Management and Resolution*, Macmillan, London, pp.328-335.

Checkel, J. (1999), 'Norms, Institutions and National Identity in Contemporary Europe', *International Studies Quarterly*, Vol.43, No.1, pp.83-114.

Commission of the European Communities (1993), *Opinion on the Application for Membership from Cyprus*, COM (93) 313, EC Bulletin 6-1993, Brussels.

Commission of the European Communities (1997a), *Press Release*, Speech 97/45, Hans Van der Broek Speech at the North Cyprus Young Businessmen Association, Reuter Briefing, 27 February 1997, Brussels.

Cortright, D. (1997), 'Incentives and Cooperation in International Affairs', in D. Cortright (ed.), *The Price of Peace: Incentives and International Conflict Prevention*, Carnegie Corporation of New York, Rowman and Littlefield, New York, pp.3-20.

Coughlan, R. (1992), 'Negotiating the Cyprus Problem: Leadership Perspectives from Both Sides of the Green Line', *The Cyprus Review*, Vol.4, pp.80-100.

Curle, A. (1995), *Another Way - Positive Response to Contemporary Violence*, Jon Carpenter, Oxford.

Diez, T., Stetter, S. and Albert, M. (2004), 'The EU and the Transformation of Border Conflicts', *EUBorderConf Working Papers*, No.1, January 2004.

Dorussen, H. (2001), 'Mixing Carrots with Sticks: Evaluating the Effectiveness of Positive Incentives', *Journal of Peace Research*, Vol.38, No.2, pp.251-262.

Fetherston, A.B. (2000), *From Conflict Resolution to Transformative Peace Building: Reflections from Croatia*, Working Paper 4, University of Bradford, Bradford.

Fetherston, A.B. and Parkin, A.C. (1997), 'Transforming Violent Conflict: Contributions from Social Theory', in L.A. Broadhead (ed.), *Issues in Peace Research 1997-98*, Department of Peace Studies, University of Bradford, pp.19-57.

Fisher, R. (1981), 'Playing the Wrong Game', in J.Z. Rubin (ed.), *Dynamics of Third Party Intervention, Kissinger in the Middle East*, Praeger, New York, pp.95-121.

Fisher, R. and Ury, W. (1991), *Getting to a Yes - Negotiating an Agreement without Giving In*, Random House, London.

Galtung, J. (1969), 'Violence, Peace and Peace Research', *Journal of Peace Research*, Vol.3, pp.167-192.

Grabbe, H. (2001), 'How does Europeanization Affect CEE Governance? Conditionality, Diffusion and Diversity', *Journal of European Public Policy*, Vol.8, No.6, pp.1013-1031.

Groom, A.J.R (1990), 'Paradigms in Conflict: The Strategist, the Conflict Researcher and the Peace Researcher', in J. Burton and F. Dukes (eds.), *Conflict: Readings in Management and Resolution*, Macmillan, London, pp.71-98.

Habeeb, W.M. (1988), *Power and Tactics in International Negotiation: How Weak Nations Bargain with Strong Nations*, John Hopkins University Press, Baltimore.

Hoffman, M. (1987), 'Critical Theory and the Inter-Paradigm Debate', *Millennium Journal of International Studies*, Vol. 16, No.2, pp.231-250.

Hopmann, T. (1996), *The Negotiation Process and the Resolution of International Conflicts*, University of South Carolina Press, Columbia.

Keashley, L. and Fisher, R. (1996), 'A Contingency Perspective on Conflict Interventions: Theoretical and Practical Considerations', in J. Bercovitch (ed.), *Resolving International Conflicts - the Theory and Practice of Mediation*, Lynne Rienner, Boulder, Colorado, pp.235-261.

Kelman, H.C. (1997), 'Social-Psychological Dimensions of International Conflict', in I.W. Zartman and J.L. Rasmussen (eds.), *Peacemaking in International Conflict, Methods and Techniques*, US Institute of Peace Press, Washington D.C., pp.191-237.

Kleiboer, M. (1996), 'Understanding Success and Failure in International Mediation', *The Journal of Conflict Resolution*, Vol.40, No.2, pp.360-389.

Lall, A. (1966), *Modern International Negotiation: Principles and Practices*, Columbia University Press, New York, London.

Lederach, J.P. (1997), *Building Peace: Sustainable Reconciliation in Divided Societies*, US Institute of Peace Press, Washington D.C.

Martinelli Quille, M. (2000), *A Response to Recent Critiques of Conflict Resolution: Is Critical Theory the Answer?*, Copri Working Paper, Copenhagen.

Putnam, R. (1988), 'Diplomacy and Domestic Politics: the Logic of Two-Level Games', *International Organization*, Vol.42, No.3, pp.427-460.

Smith, K.E. (1999), *The Making of EU Foreign Policy, The Case of Eastern Europe*, Macmillan, London.

Stedman, S. (1991), *Peacemaking in Civil War: International Mediation in Zimbabwe 1974-1980*, Lynne Reinner, Boulder, Colorado.

Touval, S. and Zartman, I.W. (1989), 'Mediation in International Conflict', in K. Kressel, D.G. Pruitt and Associates (eds.), *Mediation Research, the Process and Effectiveness of Third Party Intervention*, Jossey-Bass Publishers, San Francisco, pp.115-137.

Young, O. (1968), *The Politics of Force: Bargaining during International Crises*, Princeton University Press, Princeton, New Jersey.

Zartman, I.W. and Aurik, J. (1991), 'Power Strategies in De-escalation', in L. Kriesberg and S.J. Thorson (eds.), *Timing the De-escalation of International Conflicts*, Syracuse University Press, Syracuse, New York, pp.152-181.

Zartman, I.W. (1989), *Ripe for Resolution, Conflict and Intervention in Africa*, OUP, Oxford.

Zartman, I.W. and Berman, M.R. (1982), *The Practical Negotiator*, Yale University Press, New Haven.

# Chapter 2

# The Actors in the Cyprus Conflict

*'There is no magic way of accommodating the maximum demands of one side*
*while at the same time accommodating the maximum demands of the other'*
(Kofi Annan, UNSG, 2004c)

This chapter introduces the main actors in this study, including both the principal parties to the conflict and the main external players. In doing so, it analyses the nature of these actors, as well as their respective positions concerning or affecting the conflict.

In the case of Cyprus, the Greek Cypriot and Turkish Cypriot communities, Greece and Turkey were the principal parties to the conflict. The interests of Turkey and the Turkish Cypriots on the one hand and Greece and the Greek Cypriots on the other, largely although not entirely overlapped. As such, although it would be inappropriate to refer to four separate and independent sides to the conflict, the differences in the positions of the communities and their respective 'motherlands' must be accounted for.

The main external players were the EU, the US and the UN. The UN Secretary General was the official mediator in the conflict since the outbreak of inter-communal violence in 1963. The US, as global superpower and UN Security Council member, affected the dynamics of the conflict, both through its relations with Turkey and through its role in mediation efforts.

Most critically, this chapter attempts to discern the different actors within the EU, whose positions shaped EU policy towards the region. In this respect, the roles of member states Britain and Greece were particularly relevant, together with the passivity of the other member states. The interaction between these positions determined the role of EU institutions, and the Commission in particular.

## The Greek Cypriot Community: Players and Positions

The Greek Cypriots seek the reunification of Cyprus and the prevention of a recognized secession of northern Cyprus, or its annexation to Turkey. They seek the greatest possible restoration of the status quo ante, i.e., that pertaining before the 1974 partition of the island. Within a reunified island, they call for a fair and fully functioning arrangement in terms of territorial distribution and government structures. Most Greek Cypriots accept that the Turkish Cypriots would be granted more than minority rights. However, the vast majority rejects an interpretation of the 'political equality' between the two communities as meaning the full (or close) numerical equality between the Greek Cypriot majority and the Turkish Cypriot minority (in 1960, the demographic balance was approximately 82:18). The Greek Cypriots also insist on the liberalization of the 'three freedoms', i.e., the freedom of movement, settlement and property. They also call for the recognition and implementation of the right of return of displaced persons. Finally, they demand security arrangements guaranteeing Cyprus against Turkish expansionism and aggression.

While most Greek Cypriots share these basic aims, there is a wide array of political views in southern Cyprus. Nationalism within the Greek Cypriot community, and subsequently positions on the conflict, historically took two different forms: Hellenocentrism or Greek Cypriot nationalism and Cyprocentrism, or Cypriot nationalism (Mavratsas, 1997; Papadakis, 1998; Stavrinides, 2001). Greek Cypriot nationalists emphasized notions of Greekness in the Cypriot identity, and up until the 1974 partition they gathered around the banner of *enosis*, i.e., union between Greece and Cyprus. Since 1974, Greek Cypriot nationalists, while no longer advocating *enosis*, emphasized the Greekness of Cyprus in the context of an independent republic that would be organically linked to Greece. Variants of this ideology were espoused by the Democratic Party (DIKO), the extreme right New Horizons (NO), the socialists (EDEK/KISOS), the Greek Orthodox Church, as well as by elements in the moderate right, namely the Democratic Rally (DISY).

On the other side of the political spectrum, Cypriot nationalists emphasized the *sui generis* nature of the Cypriot identity, shared by both Greek and Turkish Cypriots, as well as the de-ethnicized or civic elements of identity based on common economic, social and political interests. Their political ideology emerged after 1974. They imagined a shared history of inter-communal coexistence and amity. Turks, and not Turkish Cypriots, were viewed as the 'enemy'. Cypriot nationalists strongly supported the reunification of Cyprus and its independence from external interference. This also included independence from Greece, whose irredentism and ethno-nationalism was seen as partly responsible for the events of 1974. Since 1974, variants of Cypriot nationalism were espoused by the leftist Reformist Workers' Party (AKEL) and the liberal United Democrats (EDI). However, it should be noted that the historically moderate AKEL has toughened its stance since the turn of the century.

Apart from the marginal and extreme right-wing New Horizons, after 1974 all political parties in the south accepted the principle of a federal settlement. However, most Greek Cypriot nationalists considered a federation as a major concession made in view of the skewed balance of power in the region in favour of Turkey. A federation was not viewed as just; it was simply considered necessary to secure a 'realistic' outcome. As such, the differences between the positions of 'Hellenocentric' exponents were more due to different assessments of what could be realistically achieved. They were not clear-cut differences in ideology towards a settlement.

Successive Greek Cypriot governments accepted the concept of a bi-communal and bi-zonal federation in the aftermath of 1974. Yet while accepting the idea of a federation, the Greek Cypriot leadership had in mind a specific federal solution. The federation would be tightly integrated, the territory of the northern province would be significantly reduced, the freedoms to move, settle and acquire property would be respected throughout the island and the security of the federation would be guaranteed from all unilateral interventions. As argued by Mavratsas, although the leadership officially embraced the notion of a federation: 'with a closer look, one realizes that emphasis upon the alleged Greekness of the island certainly contradicts the idea of federation and the ethnic coexistence that it implies, and may lead one to question the sincerity of its official acceptance by the Greek Cypriots' (Mavratsas, 1997, p.728).

Another important qualification is the difference between the views of the Greek Cypriot public and of some elements in the political elite. Since 1974, the Greek Cypriot public has been persuaded by its governments, civil society and media elites, of the moral and legal superiority of the Greek Cypriot cause. The political class never invested in arguing to the public the need, let alone the desirability, of a true compromise solution with the Turkish Cypriots. As such, the differences between the demands of the leaders and the public's expectations have been stark, particularly when past leaderships appeared more willing to make the necessary compromises to reach a negotiated agreement. The electoral defeats of moderate George Vassiliou in 1993 to the (then) more hard-line Glafcos Clerides, or the 2003 defeat of Clerides to the tougher Tassos Papadopoulos are both cases in point. Particularly interesting were the appeals in favour of the UN Plan made during the referendum campaign by former leaders such as Clerides and Vassiliou. The appeals for the first time explicitly stated that a compromise solution with the Turkish Cypriots was desirable as well as realistic. Yet they came too late and were largely unheard by 76 percent of the Greek Cypriot voters who rejected the UN Plan. Persuaded by its current leadership, the majority of the Greek Cypriots believed they could secure a more favourable agreement in future.

On the constitution, the Greek Cypriot side insisted that a federation would emerge through the dis-aggregation of the existing Republic of Cyprus (RoC) and thus the reintegration of the Turkish Cypriot community into the state structures. Any other solution, including the establishment of a new state, would have entailed the recognition of the self-declared Turkish Republic of Northern Cyprus (TRNC). The State of Cyprus would represent all Cypriots and have single sovereignty, international personality and citizenship. The federated entities would have limited powers and would not enjoy sovereignty as such.

In the 1989 proposals of the National Council, the Greek Cypriot side accepted the idea of political equality (RoC, 1989). There would be a Greek Cypriot President and a Turkish Cypriot Vice-President. In the Council of Ministers, there would be seven Greek Cypriot and three Turkish Cypriot members. In the Supreme Court there would be an equal number of Greek and Turkish Cypriots. There would be a bi-cameral legislature in which the upper house would represent the equality of the two provinces and the lower house would represent the equality of all citizens. However, when compared to the UN's positions, let alone to the Turkish Cypriot positions, the Greek Cypriot side espoused a narrow meaning of political equality. Bi-communal participation was accepted to the extent that it would not hinder the unity and workability of the state, and it would reflect the demographic balance. Hence, elections would not be based on separate electoral rolls but on a single unified list. Legislative and executive decisions would be taken largely on the basis of majority vote. There would be concurrent powers shared by the federal level and the provinces, effectively increasing the potential for hierarchical relations between the two levels of government. The Greek Cypriot side held that political equality would be guaranteed by establishing a 'symmetric' federation, i.e., the two provinces would have identical powers. Yet the competences reserved for the provinces were limited to welfare, religion, personal status, education and culture. These were the same competences that the 1960 Constitution already had reserved for the separate communal chambers.

The fundamental difference in the Greek Cypriot positions after 1974 therefore appeared to be in their acceptance of a territorially based federation, i.e., the acceptance of bi-zonality. The leadership accepted that the northern province would exceed the 1960 population and the land ownership share of the Turkish Cypriots (approximately 18.5 percent). Nevertheless, they expected a considerable reduction in the territory controlled by the Turkish Cypriots. Territorial readjustments would also allow Greek Cypriot displaced persons to return to their properties under Greek Cypriot administration. In 1992, the leadership accepted the 'Ghali map' as a basis for discussion (UNSG, 1992b). This map provided for a reduction of northern Cyprus to 28 percent of the land, returning Morphou (western coast) and Varosha (eastern coast) to Greek Cypriot control. Figures privately mentioned by Greek Cypriot officials ranged from 28 percent to 24 percent.[1]

However, while accepting the concept of bi-zonality, the Greek Cypriot leadership called for the full respect of individual rights and freedoms. All Greek Cypriot displaced persons should be allowed to exercise their right of return to northern Cyprus and receive compensation only if they chose to renounce their former properties. At most, the leadership was prepared to discuss a gradual implementation of these rights due to 'practical difficulties'. Apart from the right of return, the 'three freedoms' of movement, settlement and property should be fully liberalized. Over time, this would erode if not eliminate the principle of bi-zonality.

On security questions, the Greek Cypriot side proposed a demilitarization of the island. This would include the withdrawal of all foreign troops, and most notably the 35,000-45,000 Turkish troops stationed in northern Cyprus. There would be no unilateral rights of intervention, preventing a repeat of the Turkish attack of 1974. On the contrary, there would be international guarantees against foreign interventions. In the 1989 proposals, the Greek Cypriot side also called for the withdrawal of all Turkish settlers from northern Cyprus and their repatriation to Turkey. The settlers were considered a security threat, given they 'artificially' altered the demographic balance on the island and harmed its 'Cypriot' identity.

---

[1] Private interviews with Greek Cypriot officials and negotiators, Nicosia, March 2002, July 2003.

Finally, turning to the question of EU accession, full membership has enjoyed the overwhelming support of both the public and the political class in southern Cyprus throughout the 1990s. When in 1988 the PASOK government in Greece attempted to persuade the Greek Cypriot government to apply for full membership, the latter refused. In 1988, President George Vassiliou was in power with the leftist party AKEL, which rejected accession both due to the economic liberalization and the abandonment of the non-aligned movement that it entailed. By 1990, all political parties along the Hellenocentric-Cyprocentric and left-right political spectrums endorsed the goal of full membership. The vast majority of the public shared the same views, with opinion polls constantly reporting over 80 percent support for EU membership throughout the 1990s and 2000s. The following chapters will delve into the reasons for this overwhelming support.

**The Turkish Cypriot Community: Players and Positions**

The Turkish Cypriots seek political equality with and prevention of domination by the larger Greek Cypriot community. They also call for the highest degree of self-rule and physical separation from the Greek Cypriots (at least for a limited period of time). They call for Turkey's involvement in Cyprus' security, in view of their underlying mistrust of other foreign involvement. However, beyond these general basic aims, there are wide divisions within northern Cyprus (Bertrand, 1999; Suvarierol, 2001). The Turkish Cypriots are divided between the nationalist camp, that up until the December 2003 elections was consistently in power, and the centre-left, which in recent years has also embraced the liberal business community and many civil society groups.

The nationalist camp emphasized the ethnic differences between Greeks and Turks and the impossibility of the two communities living together. It equally stressed the commonality between Turkish Cypriots and Turks and the organic links between the Turkish Cypriot community and 'motherland' Turkey. According to the nationalists, there are no Cypriots as such, other than the wild donkeys in the Karpass peninsula, as sarcastically put by Rauf Denktaş. The history of 1963-74, i.e., when the 1960 constitutional arrangements collapsed and ethnic violence erupted on the island, is flagged both as evidence of the endemic incompatibility between Greeks and Turks, as well as the justification for rejecting an integrated federal solution. The 1974 Turkish military intervention is considered as irrefutable proof that the Turkish Cypriots need, and only need, Turkish guarantees for their security. Many critics of the nationalist camp doubt its commitment to a new partnership on the island, arguing that nationalists are content to preserve the status quo, in which the Turks and Turkish Cypriots *de facto* accomplished their historic goal of *taksim*, or partition.

Aside from President Denktaş, the two major parties in the nationalist camp are the National Unity Party (UBP) led by Derviş Eroğlu and the Democrat Party (DP) led by Serdar Denktaş. As Table 2.1 shows, apart from the 2003 elections, the UBP and DP have consistently won the lion's share of the vote since 1976. Since partition, Rauf Denktaş has been the leader of the Turkish Cypriot community and of the *de facto* state in the north.

The centre-left parties and large sectors of civil society, while recognizing the important differences between Greek Cypriots and Turkish Cypriots, equally emphasized the differences between Turks and Turkish Cypriots. As such, they opposed the immigration of mainland Turks to the north, arguing that the different political, cultural and economic background of the settlers 'dilutes' the Turkish Cypriot identity of the north. The centre-left, while sharing the same understanding with the nationalist camp of the community's basic aims, has been more flexible about its chosen satisfiers. It argued that Turkish Cypriot aims could be achieved within the confines of a federal settlement. A federation would guarantee maximum Turkish Cypriot self-rule and minimum interference of both Greek Cypriots and Turkey from internal Turkish Cypriot affairs. The two main parties on the centre-left were the Communal Liberation Party (TKP) led by Mustafa Akıncı and the Republican Turkish Party (CTP) led by Mehmet Ali Talat. During the 2003 parliamentary campaign, the TKP formed an alliance with the smaller leftist parties transforming into the Peace and Democracy Movement (BDH). The liberal business community created a third party in favour of EU membership and a solution (ÇABP).

**Table 2.1          Election Results in Northern Cyprus (seats)**

|          | 1976 | 1981 | 1985 | 1990 | 1993 | 1998 | 2003 |
|----------|------|------|------|------|------|------|------|
| UBP      | 30   | 20   | 24   | 34   | 17   | 24   | 18   |
| DP       |      |      |      |      | 15   | 13   | 7    |
| TKP/BDH  | 6    | 13   | 10   | 5    | 5    | 7    | 6    |
| CTP      | 2    | 6    | 12   | 7    | 13   | 6    | 19   |
| Other    | 2    | 1    | 4    | 4    |      |      |      |

Before analysing the negotiating positions of the Turkish Cypriot leadership, two important provisos need to be borne in mind. First is the degree of independence of the Turkish Cypriot regime from the Turkish establishment. The nationalist camp, and Rauf Denktaş in particular, has enjoyed extremely close links with the Turkish establishment, which in Cyprus is embodied by the Turkish armed forces and the Turkish embassy. The Turkish Cypriot government would not take any key decisions without Ankara's consent. Particularly in view of the non-recognized status of the TRNC, the latter could not survive without Turkey's political and economic support. However, it would be mistaken to view Rauf Denktaş merely as a puppet in Ankara's hands. The Turkish Cypriot leader, having retained power longer than any Turkish politician, enjoyed considerable support and respect in Turkey, particularly amongst the military and the nationalist civilian establishment. Furthermore, to the extent that Denktaş shared similar views with Turkish nationalists, the key question is not so much one of relative influence of one on the other, but rather one of relative strength between the conservative/nationalist camp and the progressive forces in Turkey and north Cyprus incorporated. In this respect, Denktaş added much weight to the strength of the former against the latter.

Second is the degree of representativeness of the Turkish Cypriot leadership. Up until the last parliamentary elections, presidential and legislative elections consistently brought to power exponents of the nationalist camp. While the proper functioning of the democratic process in northern Cyprus may be debated, up until 2002 there had been rare expressions of public discontent against the regime in the north. This dramatically changed in 2002-03. The widespread disapproval of Rauf Denktaş's tough stance was manifested through the mass demonstrations in northern Cyprus during the winter of 2002-03, the ensuing parliamentary election results in December 2003, and the Turkish Cypriot referendum outcome in 2004, where 65 percent of the community voted in favour of the UN Plan despite the adamant opposition of their leader.

With these important provisos in mind, let us turn to the negotiating positions of the leadership since 1974. Over the course of the 1990s Turkish Cypriot positions changed, in particular with the rejection of a federal settlement in favour of a confederal one in 1998. But in so far as these changes were linked to the ongoing EU accession process, discussed in the next chapters, this section presents the negotiating positions before the accession process began.

Beginning with the constitution, the Turkish Cypriots called for separate sovereignty as a means to ensure their political equality. Objecting to the legitimacy of the RoC, the Turkish Cypriot leadership held that a solution should emerge from the 'present realities' on the island. This meant that the federation would be a new state established through the aggregation of the Greek and Turkish Cypriot separate states.

The Turkish Cypriots called for a loosely federalized Cyprus, in which the federal level would enjoy select sovereign competences accorded to it by the sovereign cantons. In other words, the sovereignty of the federal level would emanate from that of the two cantons. Within the centre, the political equality between the two communities would be institutionalized through the greatest possible numerical equality, rotation and unanimity in decision-making. Hence, the President and the Vice-President as well as the Foreign Minister, the Governor of the Central Bank and the Minister of Finance would rotate between Greek Cypriots and Turkish Cypriots. There would be equal numbers of Greek Cypriots and Turkish Cypriots in the Council of Ministers. The President and Vice-President would have veto rights and the Council would decide on the basis of unanimity. Elections would be carried out through separate communal lists. The two cantons would have extensive competences and would be responsible for the implementation of specific federal competences as well. The cantons could also conclude independent international treaties with third states, as long as these did not contradict the general foreign policy orientation of the federation.

Turning to territory, the leadership accepted the notion of territorial readjustments but stated that it was only willing to consider a map entitling the Turkish Cypriot canton to 29 percent plus of the island's territory. The map presented in 1992 by UN Secretary General Boutros Ghali, providing for a Turkish

Cypriot zone of approximately 28 percent, was rejected on the grounds that it would displace approximately 37,500 Turkish Cypriots. Denktaş also opposed the idea that Morphou would be returned to the south, on the grounds that the Morphou plains provided the Turkish Cypriots with their main agricultural land and water aquifer.

On questions of rights and freedoms, the leadership agreed on the freedom of movement throughout the island, but objected to the full liberalization of the freedoms of property and settlement. It argued that security imperatives called for at least temporary restrictions to the inter-mixing of the two communities. The leadership therefore demanded that for those Greek Cypriots who wished to settle and acquire property in the north, there should be a 'moratorium' of time after which their applications would be considered. Following the moratorium, there would be a 'ceiling' of Greek Cypriots allowed to settle in the north. Return would also be regulated by specific provisions. For example, refugees would not be allowed to return to their properties if these were occupied by homeless or displaced persons, if they had been altered or converted to public use, if they were occupied by war veterans, or if they were located in potential 'hotspots'. Property claims from 1963-74 would then be settled through a global communal exchange between the two cantons. Compensation would be based on the current value of their lost properties.

The leadership supported a retention of the 1959 Treaties of Guarantee and Alliance. It viewed with scepticism Greek Cypriot proposals for demilitarization, and insisted on the retention of Turkish forces in Cyprus. It also emphasized the need for an external balance between Greece and Turkey. As such, it opposed membership of international organizations unless both Greece and Turkey also participated.

Connected to this, the leadership was highly sceptical of Cyprus' EU accession. Both the President and the two nationalist parties accepted EU membership as an objective in theory. But their support was conditional on first reaching a settlement protecting the political equality of the Turkish Cypriots, as well as on Turkey's own membership that would ensure the respect of the external balance of power. The opposition parties, the business community and a large section of the population held different views. Both TKP and CTP actively campaigned for EU membership before Turkey if necessary but after a settlement. Dominant civil society groups also supported EU membership after a solution, including both unions and the business community. Opinion polls also revealed a high, qualified support for EU membership. A 1997 poll showed that 94.5 percent of Turkish Cypriots supported membership. However an overwhelming majority of these supporters only preferred accession either after a solution (42 percent), or together with Turkey (42 percent) (COMAR, 1997). These results changed dramatically in 2003, when 77.4 percent supported membership after a solution, but only 18.7 percent supported membership together with Turkey.[2]

---

[2] Report presented during: *Cyprus' EU Accession and the Greek-Turkish Rivalry,* Conference organized by Yale University, 4-6 April 2003.

## Turkey: Players and Positions

In its support for the Turkish Cypriots, Turkey has specific security concerns which go beyond the welfare of the Turkish Cypriot community. Turkey supports the political equality of the Turkish Cypriots, it calls for a balance between the roles of Greece and Turkey in the Eastern Mediterranean, and demands a role in Cyprus' security arrangements.

Lying behind these views on Cyprus is the 'Sevrès syndrome' still prevalent in Turkey's political and security culture. Large segments of Turkish policy-makers were suspicious that European powers, in the legacy of the Sèvres Treaty after World War I, were inclined to dismember Turkey by collaborating with hostile neighbours, such as Greece. As such, preventing Cyprus from falling into Greek hands, and thus becoming the 'dagger' pointing at the Turkish mainland was considered an utmost priority. Cyprus was commonly described as a natural 'aircraft carrier' or 'control tower' protecting Turkey against hostile Greek designs.[3]

While the Turkish establishment unanimously viewed Cyprus as key to Turkish security, the same unanimity of opinion did not exist when it came to the European Union and EU membership. Again, this lack of consensus was linked to the underlying mistrust of European countries and their intentions. As far as Cyprus' EU membership was concerned, to the extent that Turkish policy-makers viewed the Union as being inherently hostile to Turkey, Cyprus' accession before Turkey was considered as 'losing Cyprus'.[4]

Regarding Turkey's own EU membership, views were even more complex. Prior to the launch of Turkey's accession process in 1999, all Turkish officials could easily pay lip-service to the goal of membership. Since then, Ankara has been called to prove that it is equally committed to EU membership as it is to the fulfilment of the Copenhagen criteria. Indeed, as European demands for reform rose, so did resistance against reform in Ankara. For example, MHP leader Devlet Bahceli argued that '(w)e strongly oppose the notion that we should fulfil every demand of the EU to become a member or we have to enter the EU at any cost' (Bahceli, 2002). National pride was used as a major weapon, as eurosceptics accused europhiles of displaying a 'lack of confidence in the nation, the Republic, the institutions, ... everything called Turkish' (Aktan, 2002).

Effective opposition to EU membership, or rather to the reforms necessary to attain it, was high amongst the nationalist right and the nationalist left, and existed in both the civilian and the military establishments. Some right-wing nationalists preferred to establish closer links to Turkic Eurasia than to see Turkey's full

---

[3] Interviews with Turkish officials and politicians, Ankara and Istanbul, February and May 2002.
[4] In an editorial, journalist Ilnur Cevik stated: 'If Turks really believed that they would be a member of the Union in a not too distant future, then both the Cyprus problem and the problems with Greece could be solved. But no one believes that will ever happen and thus everyone looks at the issue as "our interests and our security" and not "the interests and security of the whole Union"' (Cevik, 2001).

integration with Western Europe. Others, such as National Security Council Secretary General Tuncer Kılınç (in March 2002) hinted at alternatives such as Russia and Iran. Traditional Kemalists in the political and military establishments objected to the erosion of sovereignty entailed in the renunciation of competences to 'Brussels'. Others were more inclined to pursue Turkey's Western orientations through closer ties with the US. The US was traditionally far readier to recognize Turkey's geostrategic importance and downplay the need for domestic reforms.

Determining the relative strength of these underlying forces in Turkey is beyond the scope of this chapter. It remains unclear whether europhile or eurosceptic forces will gain the upper hand, and the way in which their relative strengths will fluctuate over time. Nevertheless, suffice it to say that highly EU-sceptic forces existed and overlapped with the most intransigent voices on the Cyprus conflict. To these actors, Turkey's EU accession process was viewed as a threat to Turkey's Cyprus policy. Furthermore, an intransigent position on Cyprus added another welcome obstacle in Turkey's EU path, dampening the momentum for what some viewed as threatening domestic reforms. In other words, a non-solution in Cyprus perversely was viewed more as an externally given opportunity to cool down EU-Turkey relations, than as a threat to Turkey's foreign policy goals (Brewin, 2000, p.192).

### Greece: Players and Positions

Greece's position in the Cyprus-Greece-Turkey-EU quadrangle was highly complex, due to its double role as principal party to the conflict, and member state of the EU, influencing EU policies towards Cyprus and Turkey.

From 1974 to 1981, following the restoration of democracy in Greece, Prime Minister Constantine Karamanlis (New Democracy) took a low profile on Cyprus and concentrated on Greece's accession to the EC. The post-1974 ND doctrine was 'Cyprus decides, Greece supports' (Tsardanidis and Nicolau, 1999). Cyprus was no longer considered a direct Greek foreign policy problem. All ambitions of *enosis* evaporated with the collapse of the Greek junta. Furthermore, the government believed that the partition of the island was temporarily irreversible, both due to the skewed military balance between Greece and Turkey, and because of the unwillingness of Western powers to actively promote a reversal of the status quo. As such the Greek government simply supported the inter-communal talks on the island. At the same time, it pursued vigorously its EC accession between 1975 and 1981. In doing so, its logic was primarily security driven. Following the 1974 war and the collapse of the military junta, Karamanlis was determined to protect Greek security interests both by consolidating the nascent democracy and by enveloping it into the Western security system. The reactivation of Greece's NATO membership and Greece's entry into the EC were the means to achieve these aims (Valinakis, 1994).

With the election of Andreas Papandreou's socialist PASOK in November 1981 both logics were seriously questioned. In 1981 PASOK represented an extreme form of populist catch-all party thriving on a nationalist, anti-Western, anti-capitalist and anti-imperialist rhetoric. Its foreign policy language was highly ideological, and as such not amenable to negotiation and compromise. In terms of its Cyprus policy, the government pursued an aggressive internationalization strategy as a means to restore the status quo ante on the island. Internationalization was pursued primarily within the framework of the UN, where Papandreou sought the denunciation of Turkish policies and the Turkish Cypriot 'illegal pseudo state'. The government also pressed for the EC's condemnation of Turkey and used its relative advantage as an EC member state to block financial aid to Turkey.

PASOK exploited the EC framework to advance its national interests and expected solidarity from the Community. Yet the Greek socialists felt no need to show solidarity towards it. Its problems within the EC were of two different orders. First, PASOK was ideologically sceptical of European integration, viewing it as a Western capitalist project subjugated to American imperialism. Second, its strong ideological language contrasted sharply with the mode of EC decision-making, based on intricate bargaining, alliance-building and compromise (Ioakimidis, 1999).

In the 1977 election campaign, Papandreou opposed EC membership. In the 1981 campaign, PASOK's tone remained highly polemical, as Papandreou proposed a referendum on the re-negotiation of Greece's terms of accession. Although Greeks never voted in a referendum, Papandreou's antagonistic attitude towards the EC persisted. In February 1982, the government sent a memorandum to the Commission demanding a review of the terms of reference for Greece's membership. In addition, PASOK openly diverged with the other member states over key foreign policy questions, ranging from the Arab-Israeli conflict to relations with the Soviet Union to, naturally, relations with Turkey. Up until the mid-1980s, Greece made almost indiscriminate use of its veto power to block consensus in European Political Cooperation (EPC). PASOK portrayed to the Greek public its intransigent positions as the courageous defence of Greek national interests against the will of the powerful member states. Success was judged by the degree of distinctiveness from others (and subsequent isolation), rather than by the effectiveness of policies. These attitudes led to the poor results of the first Greek Presidency in January-June 1983 (Tsakaloyannis, 1985 and 1996).

Largely due to economic factors, by 1985-86 PASOK had undergone a significant U-turn in its attitudes towards the Community. By the mid-1980s, Greece was facing acute economic problems with the devaluation of the drachma and quantitative trade restrictions. The economic rescue was coming neither from the Soviet Union nor from the Arab world, but rather from the EC. Following the submission of the Greek memorandum, the Commission disbursed substantial financial assistance in February 1983. In March 1985 with the adoption of the IMF stabilization programme, Greece received over 2 billion ECUs in financial assistance from the Commission through the Integrated Mediterranean Programmes. Moreover, with the southern enlargement of the 1980s, the Community moved towards a greater emphasis on social cohesion in the framework of the 1986 Single European Act. Structural funds and cohesion policy led to a significant net rise in EC financial assistance to Greece, from 0.6 billion ECUs in 1982 to 2.5 billion ECUs in 1992 (Kazakos, 1994). Consequently, public support for EC membership rose from 38 percent in 1981 to 73 percent in 1991 (Tsakaloyannis, 1996).

Political and security considerations also affected PASOK's positions. The rise to power of socialist administrations in southern Europe (i.e., Bettino Craxi in Italy, Francois Mitterand in France, Felipe Gonzalez in Spain and Manuel Soares in Portugal) allowed PASOK to find its place more comfortably in the European family and forge coalitions with member states sharing similar political views and national interests. Furthermore, the weakening of the USSR by the mid-1980s decreased the appeal of the Soviet bloc as a credible alternative to West European integration. Finally, the rising European attention to security questions, with the 1984 reactivation of the West European Union (WEU), came at a propitious moment for Greece, given the heightened tensions with Turkey over the Aegean in 1987. Indeed, Greece's ratification of the Maastricht Treaty was made conditional on the WEU's acceptance of its full membership. By the mid-1980s, the vision of the EC as a security community, capable of protecting Greece through political and economic rather than sheer military power, started seeping into PASOK's ideology. Greek vetoes were used more selectively and reserved primarily to EC-Turkey relations.

In the late 1980s, the PASOK government also actively encouraged the accession of Cyprus to the Community. It argued that the accession process should be pursued and completed irrespective of a political settlement. Accession was viewed as the most effective means of internationalizing the problem, and thus seeking a more active international and more specifically European involvement in conflict resolution.

PASOK's return to power in 1993, and most critically the replacement of the late Andreas Papandreou with moderate Costas Simitis in 1996, marked a fundamental shift in the Greek government's positions with respect to the EU, to Turkey and to EU-Turkey relations. First, the Simitis governments were outspokenly pro-European, integrationist and multilateralist. Domestically, PASOK was countered by an equally pro-European opposition, led by Costas Karamanlis since March 1997. Second, in 1999 and particularly after the replacement of Theodoros Pangalos with George Papandreou as Foreign Minister, the government's attitudes towards Turkey and EU-Turkey relations radically transformed. Since the summer-autumn of 1999 Greek Foreign Minister Papandreou spearheaded a rapprochement with Turkey that, whilst cautious, is comparable to that of the 1920s between Mustafa Kemal Atatürk and Eleftherios Venizelos. In its attitudes towards Turkey's EU membership, the PASOK government also shifted from advocating 'conditional sticks' to pressing for 'conditional carrots'. The days of outright Greek obstructionism in the early 1980s gave way to a complete reversal of Greek attitudes, as Greece became Turkey's principal spokesman in the Union. In August 1999, George Papandreou stated that: 'Greece not only wants to see Turkey in the EU, it wants to be pulling the cart of a European Turkey' (Papandreou, 1999). As the following chapters will argue, by September 2002 this was becoming increasingly the case. At the time of writing (May 2004), the New Democracy government, in power since March 2004 under

Costas Karamanlis, has not visibly reversed PASOK's foreign policy vis-à-vis Turkey and EU-Turkey relations.

Greece's socialization into the EU's ethos and mode of operation was certainly a crucial factor explaining this turnaround in the government's positions. A related explanation is Greece's growing sense of security within the Union.[5] Since 1981, EC/EU membership gradually imbued the Greek state and society with a sense of security which increasingly enabled policy-makers to rationally assess the country's security interests. Greece's interests have always been to engage in gradual rapprochement with its considerably larger and militarily stronger neighbour, and to encourage Turkey's transformation into a country that would no longer pose a threat to Greece. As put by Papandreou 'contrary to popular belief, it is in Greece's interests to see Turkey, at some point, in the EU, fulfilling European standards, rather than having it in continual conflict and tension with the bloc' (Papandreou, 1999). But only with the growing maturity of Greek democracy and the sense of reassurance within the European 'security community', was the government able to rationally assess Greek interests and act accordingly.

**The UK: Role and Positions**

As a former colonial power, the role of the UK is intricately linked to developments in Cyprus since the emergence of the conflict in the early 20th century. Following the establishment of the Republic of Cyprus, the UK remained involved in the affairs of the island due to its two sovereign military bases of Dhekelia and Akrotiri, its role as guarantor power, and its permanent seat on the UN Security Council. In addition, since the eruption of violence on the island in 1963-64, and particularly in the aftermath of the 1974 partition, the UK has become host to an increasing number of Greek Cypriot and Turkish Cypriot immigrants.

Since its accession to the EC in 1973, the UK, contrary to Greece, has been of the view that the EC/EU should keep out of the conflict and conflict resolution efforts. The UN Secretariat alone should be responsible for mediation. Notwithstanding, the UK has supported Cyprus' EU membership, particularly since the mid-1990s. Its positions were driven by a set of overlapping considerations. The UK Foreign Office appreciated the problems involved in the direct involvement of the EU in mediation, without seeing any tangible benefits.

On the one hand, British governments were concerned that strategic ally Turkey would reject the EU's involvement in the conflict, in view of Greece's status as a member state and Turkey's non-membership. Turkey's rejection would have complicated the UN Secretary General's mediation efforts. On the other hand, the Union's direct involvement was unlikely to add positive momentum to the peace process. The actors involved in seeking a solution already did so outside the

---

[5] Foreign Minister George Papandreou at a speech in Vouliagmeni, Athens, on 8 September 2002. The same argument was made in interviews with Greek Foreign Ministry officials, Athens, March 2002.

confines of the EU. Both the UK and the US as permanent members of the UN Security Council conducted their bilateral foreign policies towards the conflict in collaboration with each other and the UN Secretary General. Indeed, the close contact between the UK Foreign Office and the UN Secretariat was evident in 1999-2003, when UK Special Representative Lord Hannay worked closely with the UN team led by Alvaro de Soto. Finally, the UK's reluctance should be viewed in the context of its wider scepticism towards the EU, and the importance it attached to the retention of an independent British foreign policy, not least towards a strategically-positioned island on which it held two sovereign military bases.

The UK's strong preference for the UN rather than the EU in mediation did not entail its rejection of Cyprus' EU accession. On the contrary, since the mid-1990s, Britain has actively supported Cyprus' full membership. While encouraging the participation of the Turkish Cypriots in accession negotiations (in 1998), and stating its preference for a settlement before membership (up until 2004), the UK never voiced serious objections to the ongoing accession process. Its support for Cyprus' membership was due to its belief that the accession process would create new incentives for a solution. The UK supported accession in view of the Greek Cypriot government's drive for membership and its acceptance that this would not jeopardize the status of the British bases. Indeed, while in 2004 Cyprus acceded to the Union, the two military bases remained extra-EU territory.

## The Other Member States and the Commission: Positions towards Cyprus and Turkey

Excluding Greece and the UK, the member states did not have strong specific interests in the conflict. The member states were generally supportive of the UN's efforts to reach a settlement. A solution would increase stability in the neighbouring Eastern Mediterranean and would encourage peace between strategic ally Turkey and member state Greece. Some member states were marginally more concerned with the conflict than others. France, as a permanent UN Security Council member, and Germany, in view of its strong ties to Turkey, paid occasional attention to the conflict. However, like the UK, when France or Germany turned to the conflict, they did so outside the confines of the EU. With the exception of Greece, no member state was keen to see an active EU involvement in conflict resolution. Neither did the member states have strong enough interests to play an active role, nor did they wish to jeopardize their delicate relations with Turkey by doing so.

As such, despite the development of a structured relationship between Cyprus and the EC in 1972 through an Association Agreement, the member states avoided any interference in the conflict. Since 1974, the member states have considered the conflict to be an internal dispute between the two communities, which only called for the independent involvement of member states Greece and Britain. After 1974, the member states downgraded the conflict from the EPC agenda. The Community no longer considered itself an 'intermediary', but rather an 'advisor' engaged in 'friendly action' towards the problem in support of the UNSG's efforts. A Council

Working Group dealing with Cyprus was established, but the problem was never the subject of high level political discussions. In 1970-87, the member states made twelve EPC declarations on Cyprus, out of a total of 299 declarations (Pijpers, 1990, p.184). Each declaration merely stated the Community's commitment to the independence, sovereignty and territorial integrity of the island and called for reunification in accordance with UN resolutions.

Throughout the accession process, the member states persisted in paying sporadic attention to Cyprus. None, apart from Greece, had a consistent well-thought-out strategy to settle the conflict through EU accession. The member states were keen to see a settlement prior to accession, given their reluctance to import a bitter ethno-political conflict within the Union. Furthermore, a settlement would have strengthened the EU's image as a community of peace and reconciliation. EU actors also had an interest in preventing a clear-cut two-state solution, that would have complicated the task of absorbing the island into the Union. However, this did not entail an increased willingness to actively promote an agreement. The same reasons of the 1970s and 1980s were cited for justifying European neglect. The member states were aware that Turkey would not accept an active European role in conflict mediation. Furthermore, the UN's involvement justified the EU's non-involvement. The member states claimed that there was a 'division of labour' between the Commission and the UN. While the former dealt with accession, the latter attempted to mediate a settlement.[6] Indeed, the Council did not mandate the Commission to deal with the conflict, but only to negotiate accession with Cyprus. Until the late 1990s, there was minimal contact between Commission officials and UN mediators. Contact increased over the course of 2002-04, when Commission officials informed the UN Secretariat on how to reconcile a settlement with EU membership. The assumption behind this approach was that accession and conflict settlement were separate and independent issues. As the next chapters argue, the member states neglected how the accession process fundamentally affected the conflict and the parties' perceptions of the Union.

Member state attitudes and positions towards Turkey were far more complex. European countries had several inter-linked interests in good relations with Turkey. Turkey's geostrategic position, its key role in NATO, its strong relationship with the US and its large and growing market called for strong ties with Ankara. The presence of large Turkish immigrant communities in Germany, Holland and Belgium was cause for concern, which also reinforced the imperative not to alienate Turkey. In addition, the US constantly exerted pressure on EU member states to take due account of Turkey's importance. This pressure was felt particularly by those member states (Britain, Italy, Denmark and Holland as well as Spain during the Popular Party rule) that attributed utmost importance to strong transatlantic relations. Finally, particularly in the aftermath of the 11 September 2001 attacks in New York and Washington, the argument that Turkey's EU inclusion would refute the alleged thesis of a 'clash of civilizations' between the 'West' and 'Islam' also gained increasing salience.

---

[6] Interview with Commission official, London, May 2002.

This did not entail that the member states had a concerted strategy concerning the future development of the Union's relations with Turkey. Up until 1999, the member states had not addressed the issue of Turkey's full EU membership. To date, despite the fact that in December 1999 the European Council defined Turkey as a candidate to EU accession, there is not yet a consensus within the Union concerning the question of Turkey's full membership.

The official reasons for such scepticism were the serious flaws in Turkey's partial democracy and economic system. The Commission's successive Progress Reports since 1998 indicated Turkey's diminishing yet still fundamental political and economic problems. Turkey's torture cases, constrained freedoms of expression and association, repression of cultural and religious diversity, skewed military-civilian balance, capital punishment, border disputes, economic inequalities and volatile monetary system, seriously and negatively affected European views of Turkey's full membership prospects. The member states and the Commission argued that the Copenhagen criteria had to be met before Turkey could become a full member state and that the political criteria should be fulfilled in order for Turkey to begin accession negotiations. If the Union were to accept Turkey as a full member in its current state, its own credibility would be impaired, as it would be grossly failing to respect its own standards.

Yet other unspoken factors also explained the reluctance of both EU governments and societies to accept the idea of Turkey's full EU membership. These factors have weighed in particularly heavily when conservative or Christian Democratic parties have been in power. Turkey's demographic growth would entail that it would soon represent the largest EU member state, with evident implications on voting rights and representation in EU institutions. This raised concerns particularly to the extent that member states did not believe that Turkey would share their same '*esprit communautaire*'. The country's size and location would entail that the largest member state would fall beyond the geographical borders of the European continent and would result in a Union bordering the volatile Middle East (Syria, Iran and Iraq) and Caucasus (Georgia, Armenia and Azerbaijan). Turkey's low level of economic development would entail significant redistribution of EU funds towards Anatolia and away from the current recipients and the future CEEC members. It would also mean that while economic disparities persisted, Turkey's EU membership could induce accelerated Turkish immigration to wealthier member states, such as Germany, Belgium or the Netherlands, which already host sizeable Turkish minorities. Least noble of all, and to varying degrees underlying all of the above-mentioned concerns, was the reluctance to integrate a country with an allegedly 'different' culture and religion.

## UN Peacekeeping and Mediation

The UN has been involved in Cyprus since 1964 when, following the outbreak of inter-communal violence, the first UN peacekeepers (UNFICYP) were sent to the island (Richmond, 1998). UNFICYP has remained on the island since then, with its mandate being renewed on a six-monthly basis. Due to the need to respond to inter-communal violence in 1964, the UN continued to recognize the legitimacy of the RoC, despite the absence of Turkish Cypriots from its structures. By doing so, it set the precedent then followed by the entire international community. In 1983, UN Security Council Resolution 541 indeed condemned the Turkish Cypriot unilateral declaration of independence.

Since 1964 the UN Secretary General has provided good offices for negotiations between the principal parties. The Secretary General's Assistants have acted as the official mediators between the parties and on several occasions have brought forward bridging proposals to settle the conflict. Since UNSC Resolution 367 (1975), UN proposals have been made within the framework of a solution based on an independent, sovereign, bi-communal and bi-zonal federation. Efforts in this direction were particularly intense both between the late 1980s and the early 1990s and in 2002-04.

The UNSG's bridging proposals since the late 1980s have essentially sought a compromise by splitting the differences between the positions of the two communities. The new constitution would establish a single bi-zonal and bi-communal federation, and would be approved by separate referenda by the two communities. The proposals outlined a rough division of competences between the two levels of government, allowing for largely self-governing federated states. At the federal level, the numerically smaller Turkish Cypriot community would be sufficiently represented, so as to embody the political equality of the two communities at the centre. The questions of refugee return and the 'three freedoms' would be resolved through a mixture of return principally through territorial adjustment, compensation and exchange. Modified versions of the Treaties of Guarantee and Alliance would remain in force.

**The US: Role and Positions**

The US's role in the Cyprus conflict has been the product of its status as global superpower with key interests in the Eastern Mediterranean and the Middle East, and as a permanent member of the UN Security Council. The US has always been a strong supporter of Turkey's integration into Europe. A 'European Turkey' was historically considered the strongest guarantee that the vital NATO ally would remain firmly anchored to the 'West' and would not drift into dangerous alliances with the 'East'. This reasoning remained equally relevant both during and after the Cold War. Subsequent American administrations have pressed EU member states to be more conciliatory towards Turkey, attempting to impress upon them Turkey's geostrategic significance. In doing so, they downplayed the relevance of a strict adherence to the Copenhagen political and economic criteria.

America's positions on Cyprus throughout the 1990s tended to be a function of its assessments of Turkey's geopolitical importance and its interests in stability in the Eastern Mediterranean, a region at the periphery of the strategic Middle East. In practice, this entailed supporting Cyprus' EU accession and encouraging efforts for a settlement under the aegis of the UN. However since 1974, the US has paid decreasing attention to the substance of a settlement and has rather played a supporting role to the work of the UN Secretariat. More than other European actors, US administrations raised awareness about the need to avert crisis in the region in the event of accession prior to a settlement. Again, their proposed solution was to encourage closer EU-Turkey ties.

This chapter introduced the main actors of this study, outlining the main features of these players, as well as their positions towards the principal questions affecting the conflict. In particular, positions towards a settlement of the conflict, the European Union, and the EU accession of both Cyprus and Turkey are key to the underlying questions of this book. What this chapter has not done is to assess the dynamic interactions between these actors and their positions. These interactions will be analysed in detail over the course of the following chapters, as they are key to understanding the overall outcomes.

The discussion above also introduced the complex role of the European Union as an actor, by discerning the principal players within the Union that determined EU policies towards Cyprus and Turkey. By so doing, it has touched on the key problems of the EU as a foreign policy actor due to the Union's non-monolithic nature, a key question explored over the course of this book. In this respect, the Cyprus conflict provides a critical example of how EU external action, while often being viewed externally as the product of an integrated and coherent decision-making process, is rather the result of the interaction of disparate internal actors with differing agendas and positions.

## References

Aktan, G. (2002), 'New Consensus', *Turkish Daily News*, 4 March 2002.
Bahceli, D. (2002), quoted in 'Bahceli Toughens on EU and its Domestic Supporters', *Turkish Daily News*, 4 March 2002.
Bertrand, G. (1999), 'Vingt-cinq Ans Après, Où en est la Partition de Chypre?', *Les Etudes du CERI*, No.59, SciencesPo, Paris.
Brewin, C. (2000), *The European Union and Cyprus*, Eothen, Huntingdon.
Cevik, I. (2001), 'Denktaş emerges as Peace Maker', *Turkish Daily News*, 23 November 2001.
COMAR (1997), Poll conducted in Northern Cyprus on EU Accession, on 23 November 1997. Results re-published in *Kibris*, 21 October 1998.
Ioakimidis, P. (1999), 'The Model of Foreign-Policy Making in Greece: Personalities versus Institutions', in S. Stavridis, T. Couloumbis, T. Veremis and N. Waites (eds.), *The Foreign Policies of the EU's Mediterranean States and Applicant Countries in the 1990s*, Macmillan, London, pp.140-170.
Kazakos, P. (1994), 'Greece and the EC: Historical Review', in P. Kazakos and P. Ioakimides (eds.), *Greece and EC Membership Evaluated*, Pinter, London, pp.1-10.
Mavratsas, C. (1997), 'The Ideological Contest between Greek Cypriot Nationalism and Cypriotism 1974-1995', *Ethnic and Racial Studies*, Vol.20, No.4, pp.718-737.
Papadakis, Y. (1998), 'Greek Cypriot Narratives of History and Collective Identity: Nationalism as a Contested Process', *American Ethnologist*, Vol.25, No.2, pp.149-165.
Papandreou, G. (1999), interview in *The Guardian*, 13 September 1999.
Pijpers, A. (1990), *The Vicissitudes of European Political Cooperation*, CIP-Gegevens Koninkluke Bibliotheek, Leiden.

Republic of Cyprus (1989), 'Outline Proposals for the Establishment of a Federal Republic and for the Resolution of the Cyprus Problem', Submitted on 30 January 1989, Appendix 20 in *The Cyprus Problem, Historical Review and the Latest Developments,* April 1999, Information Office, Republic of Cyprus, Nicosia.

Richmond, O. (1998), *Mediating in Cyprus,* Frank Cass, London.

Stavrinides, Z. (2001), *Greek Cypriot Perceptions on the Cyprus Problem,* available on http://website.lineone.net/~acgta/Stavrinides.htm

Suvarierol, S. (2001), 'La Question de l'Adhésion de Chypre à l'Union Européenne et le Problème de la République Turque de Chypre-Nord', *CEMOTI* (Cahiers d'Études sur la Méditerranée Orientale et le Monde Turco-Iranien), No. 31, Janvier-Juin 2001, pp.163-188.

Tsakaloyannis, P. (1985), 'Greece's First Term in the Presidency of the EC: A Preliminary Assessment', in C. O'Nuallain (ed.), *The Presidency of the European Council of Ministers,* Croom Helm, London, pp.101-118.

Tsakaloyannis, P. (1996), 'Greece: The Limits to Convergence', in C. Hill (ed.), *The Actors in Europe's Foreign Policy,* Routledge, New York and London, pp. 186-207.

Tsardanidis, C. and Nicolau, Y. (1999), 'Cyprus Foreign and Security Policy: Options and Challenges', in S. Stavridis, T. Couloumbis, T. Veremis and N. Waites (eds.), *The Foreign Policies of the EU's Mediterranean States and Applicant Countries in the 1990s,* Macmillan, London, pp.171-194.

United Nations Secretary General (1992b), *Summary of the Current Positions of the Two Sides in Relation to the 'Set of Ideas',* 11 November 1992, S/24472 English, New York.

United Nations Secretary General (2004c), 'Secretary General, in Message to Cypriot People, says Reunification Plan will Determine Destiny of Divided Island', SG/SM/9264, 21 April 2004.

Valinakis, Y. (1994), 'Security Policy', in P. Kazakos and P. Ioakimides (eds.), *Greece and EC Membership Evaluated,* Pinter, London, pp.199-214.

# Chapter 3

# The Emergence and Persistence of the Cyprus Conflict

*'Cyprus is small,' he said, 'and we are all friends, though very different'*
(Durrell, 1958, p.74)

Since the emergence of the conflict, all of the parties manifested a reluctance to create, operate or re-establish a unified independent Cyprus where Greek Cypriots and Turkish Cypriots would peacefully coexist on the basis of a shared understanding of the relationship between the two communities. The parties held mutually incompatible views on the means by which they could satisfy their fundamental needs. These means concentrated on absolutist notions of statehood and sovereignty, military power and balance. This argument is elaborated by reviewing the history of the island between the emergence of the conflict in the 1930s and the 1988 initiation of a political dialogue between the Republic of Cyprus and the European Community.

**The Ancient History of the Island**

The first significant evidence of civilization in Cyprus can be traced back to the Myceneans during the 14th century BC. Since then the strategically positioned Eastern Mediterranean island was subject to successive raids, invasions and occupations. The Assyrians, the Egyptians, the Persians, the Romans, the Arabs, the English Crusaders, the French Lusignans and the Venetian traders all controlled Cyprus throughout the centuries of its ancient history. However, invaders principally used the island as a trading or military base and rarely encouraged immigration and settlement. Nor did they attempt to assimilate the local population into their cultures. Up until the 16th century, Cyprus remained almost exclusively inhabited by local Greek-speaking Orthodox Christians.

The Venetians controlled Cyprus from 1489 to 1571. In the latter days of their rule, they fought numerous battles against the Ottomans and ultimately lost the island to the Empire with the fall of Famagusta in 1571. With the Ottoman conquest of Cyprus, the island witnessed a limited inflow of Muslim immigrants. However, due to the system of tribute payment, which varied according to religion, many Christians converted to Islam and subsequently were fully assimilated into the Turkish-speaking community. By 1878 the population of Cyprus consisted of approximately 180,000 Greek Cypriots and 46,000 Turkish Cypriots.

Inter-communal conflict during Ottoman rule never erupted, despite the resentment of the Christian population of the discrimination against them. Tensions between religious communities further increased following the Greek wars of independence in 1821-27 and the development of the Greek *Megali Idea* on the mainland, intended to unify all Ottoman territories inhabited by Greeks. However, inter-communal relations were predominantly characterized by indifference rather than animosity. Due to the Ottoman *millet* system of communal separation in areas such as culture, education and religion, the Christian and Muslim communities of Cyprus by and large conducted separate lives, in parallel neighbourhoods of towns and villages.

Almost six centuries after the departure of Richard the Lionheart, the British returned to Cyprus when they signed the Convention of Defensive Alliance with Sultan Abdul Hamid II in 1878. Under the terms of the treaty, the Ottoman Empire loaned Cyprus to Britain in return for the latter's protection against a possible Russian aggression. In 1925, following the fall of the Ottoman Empire and the 1923 Treaty of Lausanne in which the new Turkish Republic renounced its claims to formerly Ottoman possessions beyond its borders, Cyprus officially became a Crown Colony.

In the late 19$^{th}$ and early 20$^{th}$ centuries, the *millet* system of communal separation was retained. The *millet* system encouraged separate private, social and political lives, with the different religious leaders, i.e., the *mufti*, acquiring political roles. Separation was further encouraged when the British introduced communal voting for separate councils in municipal elections. The British retained and developed the Ottoman system of separation, since it accorded them the role of umpire on the island and thus facilitated colonial rule.

**The Struggle for Independence: 1931-59**

The potential for inter-communal conflict in Cyprus dates back to the period of Ottoman rule and the emergence and consolidation of separate communities. However, the seeds of the dispute were sown during the years of British colonial rule in the 20$^{th}$ century and the years of anti-colonial struggle in the 1930s-1950s. The Greek Cypriot anti-colonial struggle in the form of *enosis* supported by Greece, and the British tactic to counter-mobilize Turkey and the Turkish Cypriots to support its colonial rule, set the scene for one of the most intractable conflicts of the 20$^{th}$ century.

*The Greek and Greek Cypriot Anti-Colonial Struggle for Enosis*

In the 1920s, the Greek Cypriot majority became increasingly dissatisfied with British rule in Cyprus. However, unlike other 20$^{th}$ century decolonization movements, desire for freedom did not result in a demand for independence. Viewing themselves as one people with mainland Greeks, the Greek Cypriots expressed their desire for freedom through *enosis,* or union with Greece, an idea that had already emerged in the 1880s as a development of the Greek *Megali Idea*.

The particular history of Greek nationalism was centred around the annexation of Christian Orthodox territories in the region. As such, *enosis* rather than independence had become the natural aim of the Cypriot decolonization struggle. Any alternative to *enosis*, including self-government, was not regarded as an appropriate expression of self-determination. The Greek Orthodox Church played a key role in this struggle. Indeed the *enosis* struggle actively began in October 1931 when the Bishop of Kition officially demanded union with Greece and by doing so triggered violent riots in Nicosia.

Greece had rhetorically declared Cyprus an inalienable part of its national aspirations in the early 1920s. But due to its catastrophic expedition in Anatolia in 1922 and the ensuing Treaty of Friendship between Mustafa Kemal Atatürk and Eleftherios Venizelos, Athens put at rest its irredentist ambitions during the 1920s and 1930s. In practice, its active involvement in Cyprus did not start until the early 1940s. It initially took the form of diplomatic pressure on Britain. Both during and immediately after the World War II, the Greek government demanded a transfer of Cyprus from Britain to Greece, offering in return military bases on Greek soil. The British responses were non-committal.

While Greece supported the cause for *enosis* through bilateral relations with Britain, the Greek Cypriots, riding on the tide of decolonization trends, reactivated their struggle in the late 1940s and 1950s. In 1948 the Orthodox Church rejected the British Constitutional Plan proposing limited self-government through a Consultative Assembly; and in 1950, backed by the communist party AKEL, it called a plebiscite on the question of *enosis*. Ninety-six percent of the exclusively Greek Cypriot turnout voted in favour. In the light of the plebiscite the Greek Cypriot leadership stepped up its pressure on Greece to support its cause. With the failure of bilateral Anglo-Greek diplomacy, Greece brought the case of Cypriot self-determination to the UN in August 1954 (Stefanidis, 1999). However, the Greek draft resolution was never put to the vote. General Assembly Resolution 814 postponed a decision on the issue.

With the failure of Greek diplomacy, the Greek Cypriot movement resorted to armed struggle. The EOKA (Ethniki Organosis Kyprion Agoniston) fighters led by Georgios Grivas began a guerrilla struggle against the colonial regime. The first EOKA bombs exploded in April 1955. In 1956 EOKA violence intensified after the failure of talks between Alan Lennox-Boyd and Archbishop Makarios III, and the ensuing deportation of the Archbishop to the Seychelles.

By the time of the 1955 London Conference, Greece and the Greek Cypriots were no longer ready to discuss limited self-government. In 1955 Greece rejected Britain's proposal for a more liberal Cypriot government. In 1956 Greece and the Greek Cypriots turned down the Radcliffe Plan which foresaw a Greek-dominated Assembly and guaranteed safeguards for the Turkish community. In the aftermath of Makarios' deportation, nothing short of *enosis* was deemed acceptable.

*The British Reaction to the Enosis Struggle*

Up until the mid-1950s, the British reacted to demands for *enosis* through force and repression. The 1931 riots in Nicosia were crushed by force. With the restoration of order, Britain dealt with Greek Cypriot demands through political repression. They suspended the 1882 Constitution, banned local political parties, banished several bishops and politicians and jailed over 2,000 Greek Cypriot activists. It was not until 1946 that Labour Colonial Secretary, Arthur Creech Jones, finally repealed the illiberal measures of 1931 in favour of a programme of constitutional reform and economic development. However, the 1948 Draft Constitution provided only a limited degree of self-government, through a (Greek) Cypriot majority in the legislative assembly and a British-led executive. Force and repression remained the predominant British tactics until the Tripartite Conference of 1955, when the first, albeit late, accommodating signs were given.

The British did not confront the Greek/Greek Cypriot struggle alone. Their opposition to *enosis* also prevented the expulsion of the Turks/Muslims from Cyprus, as had been the case in former predominantly Orthodox areas of the Ottoman Empire annexed to Greece. The mutual ethnic-cleansing that had automatically 'resolved' the question of inter-religious coexistence in the disintegrating former Ottoman areas was not implemented in Cyprus, due to British presence and British opposition to *enosis*. Yet the British not only allowed the Turkish Cypriots to remain on the island. They actively played the Turkish and Turkish Cypriot cards in their favour (Attalides, 1979; Ertekün, 1981). Internally, the British supported and worked together with the Turkish Cypriot anti-*enosis* struggle. Aware of the potential danger of *enosis* to the Turkish Cypriots, the British encouraged the community's counter-mobilization to serve its own colonial aims. Externally, Britain highlighted Turkey's strategic interests in Cyprus and its aversion to *enosis*. It emphasized Turkey's role in international forums, such as the August 1955 Tripartite Conference in London. This took place within a context of closer Turco-British relations, with Turkey's membership of the Baghdad Pact.

Britain was keen to retain control of Cyprus in the light of its rapidly disappearing colonial possessions in the Middle East. Particularly following the British withdrawals from Palestine (1948) and Suez (1954), the value of Cyprus to the UK greatly increased. Yet in the post-war era, colonial ambitions were no longer considered ethically acceptable. Hence, Britain downplayed the spontaneous Greek Cypriot demand for freedom through *enosis*. In fact it did not invite any Cypriots to the 1955 Tripartite Conference to discuss the future status of the island. Instead, the British highlighted the strategic dimension of the problem and the potential for escalating instability in the event of its departure. British withdrawal would leave a vacuum to be filled by a fierce struggle for control of the island between Greece and Turkey. So the US, fearing a major rift within its sphere of influence in the emerging Cold War configuration, tacitly supported the British position. Particularly after the outbreak of the Korean War, the US, while abstaining from making joint statements with the UK against *enosis*, actively prevented a decisive UN involvement in Cyprus.

*The Turkish and Turkish Cypriot Counter-Mobilization*

Until the mid-1940s, Turkey and the Turkish Cypriots remained largely oblivious to Greek and Greek Cypriot objectives. Up until the mid-20th century the Turkish

Cypriot community was rural, undeveloped and unpoliticized, and it lacked a strong middle class. The population was divided between a small and British-educated elite that cooperated with the colonial rulers in the administration, and a large apolitical peasant class. Turkey was still in its early days of nation-state building. Preoccupied with the momentous task of transforming a heterogeneous, undeveloped and religious population into a homogeneous, Westernized and secular nation, the Turkish Republic was initially unconcerned with Cyprus. Furthermore, until after the World War II there was minimal interaction between Turkey and Turkish Cypriots. Having embarked upon the Kemalist revolution, the modernizing Republic snubbed the backward and religious Turks in Cyprus.

Spurred by the British, Turkish Cypriot concerns about *enosis* grew in the 1940s and particularly after the 1950 plebiscite. Both the Turkish Cypriot elite and the population were still relatively content with British rule. However, well aware of the discriminatory treatment of the Turks/Muslims in former Ottoman areas annexed to Greece, the Turkish Cypriots fiercely rejected *enosis*. 'What was "freedom" for the Greek Cypriots was "enslavement" for the Turkish Cypriots. "Freedom" to the Greek Cypriots was synonymous with *enosis*, whereas this, to the Turkish Cypriots meant neo-colonization and forced exodus from Cyprus' (Ertekün, 1981, p.2.) The persisting British rule and the considerably larger Turkish minority in Cyprus compared to the few thousand Turks in other former Ottoman possessions already annexed to Greece, such as Crete or Thrace, created a qualitatively different situation for the Turkish Cypriots. If the British were to leave Cyprus, the island should be returned to Turkey and should under no circumstance be annexed to Greece.

This spontaneous rejection nurtured by the British led to a British-Turkish Cypriot front against EOKA in the mid-1950s. In 1956 the Turkish Cypriots began countering EOKA through VOLKAN and then in 1957 the TMT (Türk Mukavemet Teşkilatı). These groups cooperated with British forces in resisting *enosis*. As a consequence, the Turkish Cypriots were automatically transformed into the enemies of the Greek Cypriot cause.

Active Turkish political interest in Cyprus began in 1955. This was partly a response to external events, namely EOKA violence and the UN debate on Cyprus. But domestic factors also encouraged Turkey's attention. By the mid-1950s, Turkish Prime Minister Adnan Menderes was beginning to face serious economic problems, with a significant slowdown in growth, rising internal and external imbalances and inflationary pressures. Aiming to distract public attention from internal problems, Menderes turned to the external realm. The government stepped up its nationalist rhetoric on Cyprus. Initially, in the early and mid-1950s Turkey supported a retention of British rule. However, by 1957 Turkey formulated its own counter-position to *enosis: taksim* or partition of the island into Greek Cypriot and Turkish Cypriot zones.

## The Birth of the Republic of Cyprus and the Years of Inter-Communal Violence: 1959-74

By 1957 the principal parties were at loggerheads with each other. The Greek Cypriots and Greece pushed for *enosis*, the Turkish Cypriots and Turkey responded with demands for *taksim*. The British were determined to retain full sovereignty on the island. The path for compromise was cleared with a shift in the British position in late 1957 (Reddaway, 1986). On the advice of the Chief of Staff, the British government was encouraged to abandon the idea of full control over Cyprus and opted for the retention of military bases on the island. The EOKA struggle, the intensifying Greek-Turkish conflict and the changing power configuration in the Middle East spurred Britain to alter its position (Kyriakides, 1968, p.140). This shift gave rise to a third option, first formalized in the 1958 Macmillan Plan; the compromise between *enosis* and *taksim* was independence.

The Framework Agreement was designed in Zurich on 11 February 1959 between the Greek and Turkish Prime Ministers Constantine Karamanlis and Adnan Menderes. The premiers then headed for London, where they joined Selwyn Lloyd and Alan Lennox-Boyd representing the UK and Archbishop Makarios and Fazil Küçük representing the Greek Cypriot and Turkish Cypriot communities respectively. The parties agreed on a basic structure of the new independent Republic of Cyprus, which explicitly ruled out both *enosis* and *taksim* (Article 22). The agreements reserved British sovereignty over the two military bases of Dhekelia and Akrotiri (Article 1).

The parties also signed a Treaty of Guarantee and of Alliance. The Treaty of Guarantee intended to 'ensure the independence, territorial integrity and security' of the Republic of Cyprus and to prevent its 'political or economic union with any state whatsoever' (Article 1). In support of this aim the Treaty gave guarantors Britain, Greece and Turkey the right to intervene in the internal affairs of the island. They could intervene, either jointly or independently, to ensure the respect of the Treaty and to prevent the actualization of *enosis* or of *taksim* (Article 4). The Treaty of Alliance was a defence pact to safeguard the independence and territorial integrity of the RoC (Articles 1 and 2). In its Additional Protocol, the Treaty allowed Greece and Turkey to station 950 and 650 troops respectively on Cyprus. It also entitled extensive British rights in its use of the 99 square miles under its sovereignty.

The Treaty of Establishment set up a bi-communal partnership Republic. Bi-communality was ensured through a detailed and complex arrangement providing for community representation and power-sharing. The executive was governed by a presidential system, with a Greek Cypriot President and a Turkish Cypriot Vice-President elected by the separate communities. The executive would also consist of a Cabinet of ten members. Seven members would be Greek Cypriot and appointed by the President, while the remaining three would be Turkish Cypriot and appointed by the Vice-President. The legislative would consist of a fifty-member House of Representatives elected through separate electoral lists. Communal representation would be determined by a 70:30 ratio. There would be the same ethnic quota in the civil service and the police force. The 2,000 men-strong military would be governed instead by a 60:40 ratio. The judicial system would consist of a Supreme Constitutional Court, a High Court of Justice and lower courts. The Supreme Court dealing with bi-communal constitutional disputes would be composed of one Greek Cypriot, one Turkish Cypriot and one foreign judge. The High Court dealing with offences against the state included two Greek Cypriots, one Turkish Cypriot and one foreign judge. The composition of lower courts depended on the community of origin of the disputants. Separate communal chambers would deal with educational, religious, cultural and personal status matters. The communal chambers were entitled to levy taxes and establish separate courts to administer these competences, and receive direct subsidies from their respective motherlands. Finally, in each of the five largest towns of the island there would be separate municipalities for the two communities.

Several constitutional provisions designed to safeguard the bi-communal nature of the state encouraged inter-communal tension. The Constitution recognized the inhabitants of the island as either Greeks or Turks and spelt out the constitutional provisions to reflect this division. These provisions relied upon the *bona fide* cooperation of the two communities, but did little to encourage it. On the contrary, several rigidly formulated constitutional provisions created the potential for inter-communal conflict and deadlock in decision-making. Indeed by 1963 several issues of contention had emerged.

First, deadlock occurred in the field of fiscal policy, which required separate simple majorities in Parliament (Article 78.2). The Greek Cypriots resented the disproportionate subsidization received by the Turkish Cypriots. By 1960, the Greek Cypriots represented 82 percent, while the Turkish Cypriots constituted 18 percent of the population.[1] Given the lower economic standards of the latter, they demanded a higher share of state expenditure relative to their demographic size. Decision-making was blocked when the Turkish Cypriot parliamentarians refused to vote on tax legislation, which they viewed as imposing unaffordable financial burdens on the poorer community. As of March 1961, the state had no tax law and the two communities proceeded by levying taxes through the communal chambers.

Second, defence policy and the use of the presidential vetoes (Article 50) created inter-communal problems. The Greek Cypriots insisted on a joint army with mixed composition down to the smallest units. Vice-President Fazil Küçük and Defence Minister Osman Örek instead, while accepting a joint army and mixed battalions, insisted on separation at the company level given different cultural and religious habits of the soldiers. Küçük used his veto, and the joint Cypriot army never materialized. In its place, separate communal armed groups reformed.

Third, the establishment of separate municipalities and the need for separate legislative majorities led to conflict and stalemate. Under Article 173 of the Constitution, separate municipalities had to be set up in the five largest towns. The Greek Cypriots resented this provision and in 1962 Greek Cypriot Speaker of

---

[1] According to the 1960 census there were 441,000 Greek Orthodox, 104,000 Turkish Muslims, 3,500 Armenians, 7,000 Maronites and 16,000 others. If Armenians, Maronites and others are included in the Christian Greek Cypriot group, the ratio of Greek Cypriot to Turkish Cypriot was 82:18.

Parliament Glafcos Clerides proposed the unification of all municipalities, which would be staffed according to population ratios in the respective towns. The Turkish Cypriots insisted on the implementation of Article 173. With the absence of the required double majority, the decision on the establishment of separate municipalities was indefinitely postponed.

Some constitutional provisions indeed hindered decision-making in the new Republic. But the workability of the Constitution was never fully tested in practice. The RoC as it was foreseen in 1959 ceased to exist by 1963.

*Greek Cypriot Resentment and the Abrogation of the Constitution*

Almost at the outset, many Greek Cypriots expressed their dissatisfaction with the 1959 agreements, regarding them as a betrayal of the *enosis* cause (Faulds, 1988). In an interview in Nicosia Georgios Grivas described the agreements as 'harmful attempts to enslave the Cypriot people' (New York Times, 30 July 1959). Others, including the first President of the RoC, Archbishop Makarios, viewed the agreements as a tactical move under the given circumstances. Makarios felt the agreements had been imposed on the Greek Cypriots, given the pressures from Greece and the UK. Fearing the implementation of the 1958 Macmillan Plan, which the Greek Cypriots viewed as tantamount to partition, Makarios reluctantly accepted the Zurich deal as a necessary tactic under the given constraints. As reported by the British Colonial Office: 'it seems that Makarios was so alarmed over the possibilities of a partition that he attempted to convey his idea of an independent Cyprus even before October 1 1958, the date when the Macmillan Plan was to go into effect' (British Colonial Office, 1961, p.6).

The Greek Cypriots also contested the legitimacy and workability of the agreements. They argued that the Treaty of Guarantee, which granted the guarantors unilateral rights of intervention, violated the independence of the Republic. The Treaty of Alliance violated the sovereignty of Cyprus, allowing for the stationing of foreign troops on the island. The 1960 Constitution instead violated the self-determination of the Cypriots because it was never ratified by referendum or by Parliament. The costly duplication of positions and functions in the legislature and the executive generated inefficiency. Separate legislative majorities and the presidential veto rights led to deadlock in decision-making. The Greek Cypriots also claimed that Turkish Cypriot officials used the Constitution to purposely jeopardize the workings of the new state, which would in turn encourage Turkey's interference.

But most important, the Greek Cypriots contested what they believed to be the overgenerous concessions granted to the Turkish Cypriot community relative to their size. According to them, the Turkish Cypriots that represented 18 percent of the island's population should have been granted minority rights rather than an almost equal share in government arrangements. In particular, the Greek Cypriots refuted the 70:30 ratio in the executive and the civil service (Article 123). They viewed the ratio as being unfair and implying that under-qualified Turkish Cypriots would enter official positions on the grounds of ethnicity. They felt the constitutional provisions were undemocratic and discriminatory, reflecting international power politics rather than the demographic realities on the island (Kyriakides, 1968, p.143).

Hence, on 3 November 1963 President Makarios presented Vice-President Küçük with a thirteen-point proposal for the amendment of the Constitution. The amendments proposed the abolition of several critical constitutional provisions. These included: the presidential vetoes, the separate legislative majorities, the separate municipalities and the distinctions based on ethnicity made in courts. The package also proposed the re-scaling of ethnic ratios in the civil service, the police and the military according to population ratios. The package undeniably reduced significantly the political equality guarantees of the Turkish Cypriots. The proposal paved the way for a unitary state in which Turkish Cypriots enjoyed individual rights and minority communal rights.

The proposal was officially made on the grounds of the unworkability of the Constitution. The package was entitled 'Suggested Measures for the Removal of Causes of Friction between the Two Communities'. But after only three years of the Republic's existence, Makarios' evaluation of the Constitution's unworkability and his ensuing actions were, as put by former President Glafcos Clerides, 'premature' (Clerides, 1989b, p.24). In reality the amendments were motivated by the deep resentment against the 1960 Constitution. An extract from Clerides' memoirs is worth quoting in full:

> An honest evaluation of the situation during the period 1960-63 divorced from propaganda tendencies would lead to the conclusion that, with the exception of the provisions for separate majorities in voting tax legislation, there was no need to press for constitutional amendments, and that such a move was premature, that it was made before bridges of confidence were built between the two communities, and that it was prompted by the resentment the Greek Cypriots felt over the excessive rights granted to a minority and the need felt by Makarios to vindicate himself against the constant accusations made by his opponents of capitulation both on the issue of *enosis* and on that of minority rights (Clerides, 1989a, p.130).

Resentment did not emerge in 1962-63. It existed back in 1959-60 when the documents were signed. Makarios had never fully endorsed his role as a statesman of a bi-communal republic. As an Archbishop and in the context of the formerly Ottoman Eastern Mediterranean, Makarios remained the national leader of his religious community. The aims of Greek Cypriot nationalism and of its leader Makarios remained *enosis*. The British House of Commons Select Committee on Foreign Affairs shared this reading in its report of 2 July 1987, which stated that: 'both before and after the events of 1963, the Makarios government continued to advocate the cause of *enosis* and actively pursued the amendment of the Constitution and the related Treaties to facilitate this ultimate objective' (Republic of Turkey, 1998, p.5). According to Clerides, the signature of the agreements had been a 'tactical retreat' (Clerides, 1989a, p.328). *Enosis* would be achieved more easily through Cypriot independence than as a British colony. After three years of 'retreat', the Archbishop was ready to make the next move in pursuit of his unchanged objectives.

The next move implied the creation of a unitary and centralized state with minority rights for the Turkish Cypriots. Hence, the thirteen-point proposal that would be implemented with or without Turkish Cypriot approval. Indeed, the predictable constitutional crisis, resulting from the Turkish Cypriot rejection of the proposals and the ensuing departure of all Turkish Cypriot officials from public institutions, cleared the way for a centralized state in which Greek Cypriots governed alone.

The 'Akritas Plan' is also worth mentioning. The Plan was formulated in 1963 and first revealed in 1966 in the Greek newspaper *Patris*. Its aim was to attain *enosis* either through constitutional means as an independent state or through unilateral action accompanied by the forceful suppression of Turkish Cypriot resistance if necessary. The government never officially adopted the Plan. However the Plan was known to the Archbishop. Moreover, the head of the operation was Minister of the Interior Polycarpos Georgadis.

With the constitutional crisis, fighting broke out on 21 December 1963 and Greek Cypriot fighters attacked the Omorphita suburb of Nicosia. Finally, Makarios allowed Major General Young to supervise a cease-fire and create a British patrolled buffer zone through Nicosia, which became known as the 'green line' dividing the city. Violence burst out again with the Greek Cypriot attacks in Limassol and Ktima in early 1964. By June 1964, the Greek government sent troops to the island and Grivas returned to organize and lead the Greek Cypriot National Guard. Its operations began with the task of eliminating the Turkish Cypriot enclaves of Kokkina and Mansoura. The operations against Turkish Cypriot villages and enclaves continued throughout that period. In 1967 Grivas launched attacks against the Turkish Cypriots in the villages of Kophinou and Ayios Theodoros.

With the outbreak of violence in late 1963, most Turkish Cypriots gathered into enclaves, which the government blockaded in the summer of 1964. The leadership regarded the Turkish Cypriot flight to enclaves both as a tactic to gather forces and retaliate, and as a means to create a 'state within the state' (Polyviou, 1976, p.242). Hence, the blockade of strategic military material and the limited delivery of mail and food. Their inhabitants received no salaries or state revenues and were excluded from public employment. The strict implementation of the blockade lasted during the summer of 1964, but the blockade policy persisted thereafter. Hence, as of 1964, apart from a few exceptions, bi-communal contact ceased to exist.

By the time of the first set of negotiations in 1964-68, the Greek Cypriot leadership had hardened its position. The thirteen amendments were no longer sufficient. Archbishop Makarios sought to establish a Republic built on new foundations. The RoC was to be a truly independent, unitary and centralized state. In 1964 Makarios unilaterally revoked the Treaties of Guarantee and Alliance. During negotiations the Greek Cypriots pushed for a unitary state, with Turkish Cypriot minority rights in matters of culture, education, religion and personal status. They rejected the concept of power-sharing and called for a single electoral list in legislative elections, an executive headed by a single President and a unified judiciary. Internally the Greek Cypriot government passed important constitutional amendments and invited Turkish Cypriot officials to return within the Republic's institutional fold provided they accepted the amended constitution.

The Greek Cypriot position marginally softened during the 1968-71 and 1972-74 negotiations. Although remaining firmly committed to a unitary and centralized state, Makarios accepted the concept of local government. In 1964-68 the Greek Cypriots only accepted a conventional form of local government based on administrative or economic criteria. In 1968-71 they accepted an ethnic basis for the sub-division of districts; and by 1973 they had accepted two central organs for the administration of local competences. However, they remained firmly opposed to a bi-communal state and to any form of federalism.

The role and position of Greece in 1960-74 was also critical. When in 1963 Makarios decided to present the thirteen amendments, the Karamanlis government strongly advised the President not to proceed. The Greek government endorsed the content of the proposals, but objected to the timing of the initiative. Given Greece's acute domestic economic problems and its dependence on the US, Karamanlis deliberately kept a low profile on Cyprus.

The situation changed with the advent of military dictatorship in Greece. After 1967, relations between Makarios and the Greek regime began to sour. Following a narrow escape from war with Turkey in 1967, the Greek junta was adamant to avert military confrontation and was willing to resolve the question bilaterally within the NATO framework. In order to enact this solution, Athens needed to ensure Greek Cypriot compliance and curb Makarios' power. It thus sponsored an anti-Makarios campaign in Cyprus. Yet, contrary to the junta's alleged aims, opposition to Makarios was transformed into a revitalized violent movement for *enosis* by 1971, with the formation of EOKA-B led by General Grivas.

The situation worsened in November 1973 when General Papadopoulos was ousted by Brigadier Ioannides. This second junta embraced openly the goal of *enosis* and more overtly supported EOKA-B. It opposed vehemently Makarios' strategy of gradual constitutional change and preferred the route of overt military struggle. By 1973, with the change in the Greek regime and the intensification of the EOKA-B struggle, the ongoing inter-communal talks, that had come close to an agreement on local government, were stalled.

This intra- and inter-state conflict culminated with the Greek coup in Cyprus on 15 July 1974. The coup was carried out under the leadership of Brigadier Ioannides, and former EOKA fighter Nicos Sampson. The trigger for the intervention was Makarios' letter to Greek President Phaedon Gizikis demanding greater distance between the regime and the internal affairs of the island. At this point Greece intervened, ousting Makarios. It extended its dictatorship to Cyprus by sending around 200 Greek civilians and soldiers to the island. In four days the regime had killed over 2,000 supporters of the Archbishop. The junta was on its way to consolidating what had been the long-sought dream of *enosis*.

*The Turkish Cypriot and Turkish Reactions*

In 1959-60 the Turkish Cypriots and Turkey did not view the agreements as temporary arrangements. The Turkish Cypriots rejected the idea of a Cypriot nation and believed that the island was composed of two equal communities whose separate rights had to be safeguarded. They considered the constitutional arrangements and treaties as adequate satisfiers (Küçük, 1963, p.16-17). This position lasted until the constitutional crisis and outbreak of violence in 1963-64.

In 1963 Ankara, followed by Vice-President Küçük, immediately rejected Makarios' constitutional package. The proposals drastically altered the essence of the partnership, that very essence that had determined Turkish and Turkish Cypriot consent three years earlier. The amendments would have created a Greek Cypriot state, freer to proceed to *enosis*. With the rejection of the proposals, tensions rose within state institutions, until the Turkish Cypriots left all public positions.

With the departure of the Turkish Cypriots, both sides accelerated paramilitary preparations. Particularly after the failure to agree on the structure of the Cypriot army, the Turkish Cypriots, supported by Turkey, had begun military preparations. However, they remained relatively unprepared compared to the Greek Cypriots. Hence, with the outbreak of violence, the rehabilitated TMT could not prevent the forced exodus of over 30,000 Turkish Cypriots from 103 mixed villages to enclaves. The enclaves were concentrated in the triangular area north of Nicosia's green line to the Hillarion path outside Kyrenia and to Famagusta, and amounted to less than three percent of the total area of the island. By the late 1960s approximately 60,000 Turkish Cypriots had left their homes and moved into enclaves (Kyriakides, 1968, p.112).

Although the Turkish Cypriots and Turkey had regarded the 1959-60 settlement as an acceptable permanent solution, following the events of 1963-64 their position changed. So by the time of the 1964-68 inter-communal talks, Turkish and Turkish Cypriot positions were also far from the 1959-60 understandings. The collapse of the constitutional RoC proved to the Turkish Cypriots the inadequacy of the 1959-60 accords. According to the Turkish Cypriot leadership, given the persisting Greek Cypriot aim of *enosis,* territorial separation was necessary to safeguard Turkish Cypriot security. The Turkish Cypriots demanded the establishment of a federation. This entailed the creation of two cantons and the accompanying exchange of populations. They also pushed for stronger external security guarantees.

In return for gains at the local level, the Turkish Cypriots were ready to make concessions in terms of bi-communality at the centre. During the 1968-71 negotiations, they conceded on many of the points in the thirteen amendments including the abolition of the presidential vetoes and separate majorities, the reduction of Turkish quotas in the civil service, and the unification of the judiciary and of the police forces. However, they insisted on the establishment of local government and local police forces based on the ethnic make-up of villages. This, in their view, would have ensured Turkish Cypriot communal survival through positive local autonomy rather than negative veto power at the centre. Indeed, in parallel to these negotiations, the Turkish Cypriots established *de facto* ethnic-based local governments. By 1967, they set up the Provisional Turkish Cypriot Administration, governing the enclaved community.

Turkey supported the Turkish Cypriots from 1963 to 1974. With the outbreak of violence, Turkey twice planned military intervention to rescue the Turkish

Cypriots. Twice it was deterred by American and British diplomacy. Turkey first planned to invade in 1964 with the first outbreak of inter-communal clashes. Britain immediately responded by appealing to the UN, which in turn passed Security Council Resolution 186 deploying 7,000 peacekeepers on the island (UNFICYP). The US directly stepped in to prevent a Turkish military intervention. The second threat of war, again deterred by the US, was in November 1967, following the Greek coup and the renewed round of Greek Cypriot attacks on Turkish Cypriot enclaves.

However, following the 15 July 1974 coup, Turkey intervened. It first attempted consultations with London, but Foreign Secretary Callaghan refused to discuss the issue. Hence, on the basis of Article 4 of the Treaty of Guarantee, 40,000 Turkish troops landed near Kyrenia on 20 July 1974. The army initially took control of a narrow ten-mile strip of coastline around Kyrenia, which was then joined to the triangular enclaved land under Turkish Cypriot control. After the first attack, the parties met in Geneva in August. They agreed on an exchange of prisoners and UN protection of the Turkish Cypriot enclaves.

Under the given circumstances, the first military intervention was probably justified under the Treaty of Guarantee (Council of Europe, 1974). But by the mid-1960s Turkey and the Turkish Cypriots were no longer content with the 1959-60 agreements and demanded the maximum physical separation of the two communities. In Geneva, they were in no mood for compromise. Turkish Foreign Minister Güneş proposed a cantonal federal system and Turkish Cypriot representative Rauf Denktaş suggested a bi-zonal federal system as take-it-or-leave-it offers. Under both proposals, the Turkish Cypriot areas would amount to 34 percent of the island. When acting President Glafcos Clerides asked for an adjournment of 36-48 hours for consultations, Turkey attacked a second time and occupied 37 percent of the island's territory.

## The Position of the United States and the European Community

From the early years of the Republic, the US had mixed feelings about Cypriot independence. The Americans were deeply concerned with Archbishop Makarios' flirtations with the Soviet Union, as well as with the relative strength of the Greek Cypriot communist party AKEL. Hence, with the abrogation of the treaties and the outbreak of inter-communal violence, the US stepped in, proposing its own version of a solution. In the summer of 1964, Secretary of State Dean Acheson proposed an effective double *enosis*. Most of Cyprus would be Greek Cypriot and could ultimately unite with Greece. In exchange Turkey would be allowed several military bases in the north as well as a number of autonomous Turkish enclaves including one in Nicosia. In addition Turkey would gain the island of Castellorizon (Meis), parts of Western Thrace and receive compensation for the Turkish Cypriots that would emigrate to the mainland. The double *enosis* solution was in line with the conceptualization of the problem as a 'double minority' one, a view that up until today is shared by many in Cyprus, Turkey and Greece. Internally, in view of their relative size, the Turkish Cypriots were the smaller and weaker party. This was counterbalanced externally given Turkey's greater size and military might compared to Greece. Given the volatile situation on the island, the implications for NATO's cohesion and the possibility of 'losing' Cyprus to the Soviet Union, the US was cautious in its support for an independent RoC. In American eyes, the region would be considerably safer if Cyprus became a province of ally Greece together with adequate compensation for ally Turkey.

Between 1963 and 1967, the US did little to re-establish the 1960 arrangements and only intervened to prevent war between the two NATO members. The US intervened twice to deter a Turkish military intervention. In 1964 Turkey's invasion was deterred by President Johnson's letter to Ankara warning that in the event of a Turkish attack and a Soviet response in defence of the Greek Cypriots, the US would not support Turkey. In November 1967, Turkey's intervention was deterred by the shuttle diplomacy of Deputy Defense Secretary Cyrus Vance, who persuaded Greece to scale down its military presence and ensure Grivas' departure from the island. Both in 1964 and in 1967 the US successfully prevented war between its NATO allies. However, other than the 1964 Acheson initiative, neither did the US actively seek solution, nor did it work towards the re-establishment of the constitutional RoC.

Perhaps the most evident manifestation of lack of US engagement with Cyprus was in 1974. Evidence suggests that the US both accepted the 15 July coup and, preoccupied by Watergate domestically and China and Vietnam externally, tolerated the ensuing Turkish military intervention. Relations between the right-wing military establishment in Greece and the US were warming with the home porting of the American sixth fleet in Greece. At the same time, the Americans refrained from sending negative signals to Turkey concerning its planned attack. Kissinger's apparent indifference was read by Turkey as a tacit green light for intervention (Hitchens, 1997). US passivity towards Turkey's intentions also contributed to the failure of the Geneva talks, the second Turkish attack and the ensuing partition of the island. In the summer of 1974, American Ambassador Davies was assassinated in Nicosia by Greek Cypriot activists in protest at the perceived American betrayal.

Turning to the EC, between 1972 and 1988 Cyprus and the EC conducted their relations exclusively through an Association Agreement (Council of Ministers, 1973). In 1962, following the UK's first EEC membership application, Cyprus, heavily dependent on its exports to the UK, also applied for full membership. With de Gaulle's rejection of the British application, Cypriot interest in the Community evaporated and only re-emerged with the third British attempt to accede in the early 1970s. By then the Community had already signed Association Agreements with Greece in 1961 and Turkey in 1963. Finally, in December 1972 the RoC signed an Association Agreement that envisaged two stages, culminating in a full customs union. Unlike the agreements with Greece and Turkey, the Cyprus agreement did not foresee the option of future full membership.

Despite the existence of an Association Agreement, the Community deliberately kept out of the internal affairs of the island and never actively encouraged an agreement. In 1972 the Community did not question the legitimacy of the wholly Greek Cypriot government to sign an EC agreement but simply followed the UN approach of recognizing the Greek Cypriot Republic as the only legitimate government of the island. In a similar fashion, in March 1986, the Commission (spurred by Greece) insisted on opening negotiations with the RoC for the second stage of the Association Agreement arguing that there were no sound economic reasons to justify its persistent postponement.

In 1974, the member states through European Political Cooperation (EPC) played a more active role. During and immediately after the first Turkish military intervention, the French Presidency convened a meeting of member state ambassadors, which led to EPC démarches in Athens and Ankara calling for cease-fire and supporting the British initiatives for negotiations in Geneva. Internal European divisions, however, blocked EPC during and after the second invasion. Between the first and the second Turkish attacks, the Greek junta collapsed and the new premier Constantine Karamanlis immediately voiced the intention to apply for EC membership. The pro-European regime in Athens and the Turkish occupation of over one third of the island made member states such as France more supportive of the Greek Cypriot side. Other member states like Germany and the UK preferred to retain a neutral approach towards Greece and Turkey, and supported American and UN mediation. As a result, since 1974 the EC has refrained from active collective involvement in conflict resolution efforts.

**The Years of Partition and Failed Negotiations: 1974-88**

Following military intervention, the Turkish troops remained in Cyprus and the 1960 constitutional order was not restored as provided for under the 1959 Treaty of Guarantee. A radically different order emerged instead. The Turkish invasion resulted in the occupation of 37 percent of the island including 57 percent of the coastline (Borowiec, 2000, p.97). The occupied territory included 70 percent of the island's economic potential with over 50 percent of the industrial enterprises, 60 percent of natural resources, 65 percent of the total cultivated land and 73 percent of the tourist infrastructure. The intervention and the ensuing Vienna Accords on the exchange of populations in April/May 1975 created 140-160,000 Greek Cypriot displaced persons from the north and 60,000 Turkish Cypriot displaced persons from the south. Both areas were almost ethnically-cleansed. Only in the northern Karpass peninsula did 13,000 Greek Cypriots remain. In addition, since partition Turkey encouraged mainland immigration to northern Cyprus. Today the number of Turkish settlers ranges between 40,000 and 80,000.[2] Property formerly belonging to Greek Cypriots was nationalized and distributed to Turkish Cypriots through certificates of usufruct on the basis of lost property in the south.

Since 1974 Cyprus has been divided into two distinct zones (see Map 1 in Annex). In the north the Turkish Cypriot community first declared the Turkish Federated State of Cyprus in 1975 and in 1983 unilaterally declared the Turkish Republic of Northern Cyprus (TRNC). The international community, excluding

---

[2] Figures on the numbers of Turkish immigrants vary enormously, with Greek Cypriot figures citing around 110,000 Turkish settlers and Turkish Cypriot figures arguing that not more than 40-60,000 of the population was born in Turkey.

Turkey, condemned the unilateral declaration of independence (UDI) as a secessionist act against the spirit of conflict resolution (UN Security Council Resolutions 541 [1983] and 550 [1984]); and Council of Europe Recommendation 1056 [1987]). In the south, the Greek Cypriots retained the title of the RoC, and despite the absence of Turkish Cypriots, the international community continued to view the RoC as the only legitimate authority on the island.

Ensuing rounds of inter-communal negotiations under UN auspices amounted to little more than a few superficial and inconsequential successes and a myriad of failures (Mirbagheri, 1998). The chances for a settlement were considerably higher in 1974 than they were in 1988. The only steps forward were made shortly after partition. The 1975 UNSC Resolution 367 proposed a solution based on an independent, sovereign, bi-communal and bi-zonal federation. A federation would take into account the post-1974 realities, while respecting the single sovereignty of Cyprus advocated in UNSC resolutions.

Resolution 367 prepared the ground for the high-level agreements of 1977 between Rauf Denktaş and Archbishop Makarios and of 1979 between Denktaş and Spyros Kyprianou. The 1977 agreement established four guidelines for a settlement: it would be based on an independent, bi-communal and non-aligned federation. Territorial readjustments would take into account the economic viability of the two entities and communal land ownership. Provisions on the 'three freedoms' of movement, settlement and property would be included in the agreement. And the federal government would ensure the unity of the country. The 1979 agreement stipulated ten further points: a settlement would be reached via inter-communal talks and would address human rights and freedoms on the island. It would also provide for the resettlement of 35,000 Greek Cypriot refugees in a demilitarized Varosha, the now uninhabited and formerly developed tourist resort area bordering the town of Famagusta. No action would be taken which could jeopardize the peace process.

The international community continues to uphold the high-level agreements. However, their substance was so general that almost any negotiating position could be considered as compatible with them. Hence, since the late 1970s when the community leaderships began discussing the finer details of a settlement, the peace process has been through an unending series of setbacks and failures.

Between 1980 and 1983 UN Special Representative Hugo Gobbi attempted mediation in Cyprus. Negotiations ultimately broke down when in May 1983 the RoC, supported by Greece (led by Andreas Papandreou) brought its case to the UN General Assembly securing Resolution 37/253 in favour of the immediate withdrawal of Turkish forces. Frustrated by the Greek Cypriot advantages of recognized statehood, the Turkish Cypriots responded with the UDI in November. In response to the UDI, the Greek Cypriot team left the negotiations and rejected the UN Interim Agreement.

Talks resumed in Vienna in August 1984. The UN drafted three agreements under Secretary General Javier Pérez de Cuéllar in 1984-86 (the 1984 Working Points, the 1985 Integrated Documents and the 1986 Draft Framework Agreement). The proposals suggested that a federation would consist of two provinces and the Turkish Cypriot province would amount to 23-30 percent of the island. The legislative would have two houses. The lower house would be governed either by proportional representation or by a 70:30 ratio. The executive would be a presidential system, which would either follow the 1960 Constitution (with a Greek Cypriot President and a Turkish Cypriot Vice-President) and a 60:40 ratio in the Cabinet, or would include a rotating presidency and a 70:30 ratio in the Cabinet. The federal level would be responsible for foreign and security policies, federal finance, monetary policy, utility networks, infrastructure and social policy. The two provinces would have the residual competences. Talks also covered the 'three freedoms', the withdrawal of Turkish troops, the resettlement of Varosha and the reopening of the Nicosia airport. The Turkish Cypriot side accepted the first and third draft agreements for a federal settlement. However, both Papandreou and Kyprianou rejected them. With the referendum on the TRNC's constitution, the talks were postponed. When they recommenced in 1987-88 (with the UN 1987 Procedural Formula and the 1988 Overall Agreement), agreement again failed to materialize.

*Greek Cypriot and Turkish Cypriot Positions on State and Sovereignty*

Both communities and the three guarantors accepted the concept of a bi-communal and bi-zonal federation. But their understanding of this vaguely defined solution was substantially different. In order to legitimize their inflexibility, the parties relied on legalistic formulations grounded on the notion of monolithic sovereignty, that were inherently inimical to any shift towards compromise. In the words of current UNSG Kofi Annan: 'in the decades during which it has resisted efforts at settlement, the Cyprus problem has become overlain with legalistic abstractions and artificial labels, which are more and more difficult to disentangle and which appear increasingly removed from the actual needs of both communities' (UN Secretary General, 1999, point 7).

Absolutist views of statehood and sovereignty led to contrasting positions over constitutional issues. The Turkish Cypriot vision of communal security and justice led to an emphasis on separate sovereignty. This entailed that a federal state would emerge from the aggregation of the Greek Cypriot and Turkish Cypriot sovereign federated states. Hence, the 1975 declaration of the Turkish Federated State of Cyprus and the 1983 UDI. The sovereign and largely self-governing cantons would then delegate limited powers to a subordinate centre, governed by maximum equality in communal representation and unanimity in decision-making. The Greek Cypriot leadership also accepted the concept of a bi-communal and bi-zonal federation, but emphasized the single and indivisible sovereignty of the Republic of Cyprus, which would disaggregate through constitutional change (Chrysostomides, 2000, p.357).

Both the Greek Cypriot and Turkish Cypriot positions were motivated by historical and political arguments. In Turkish Cypriot eyes, recognizing the RoC as the basis of a future settlement entailed a dismissal of the atrocities of 1963-74. The creation of a federation by disaggregation would imply the recognition of the RoC's legitimacy as the sole representative of the island. To the Turkish Cypriots, the legal RoC had ceased to exist in 1963 when the Turkish Cypriots had departed.

A federation by disaggregation would also allow for renewed Greek Cypriot domination in the event of a constitutional breakdown. A solution would thus require the creation of a new state. To the Greek Cypriots on the other hand, accepting the prior existence of two sovereign states would imply a recognition of the legitimacy of the 1974 military intervention and partition, and thus the ultimate victory of the historical Turkish cause of *taksim*. It would also create the basis for a future dissolution of the state and Turkish Cypriot secession.

Interpretations of political equality also differed considerably. The Turkish Cypriots held as sacrosanct the principle of political equality. The creation of a federation from the disaggregation of the Greek Cypriot RoC could not provide the adequate basis for equality in so far as Turkish Cypriot inclusion in the Greek Cypriot Republic would leave the latter in a position of inferiority. It would suggest that Cyprus was Greek and that Turks could be accommodated within its structures. In terms of the federal structure, the Turkish Cypriot leadership insisted that political equality should be reflected in all governing arrangements. This would entail equality between the two federated states, equality between the federated states and the federal level, and equality of the two communities within the federal level.

To the Greek Cypriots, the principle of political equality predominantly entailed equality between the two federated states. The 1989 proposals essentially rejected the equality of the federated states vis-à-vis the centre (Republic of Cyprus, 1989). It stated that the provinces would 'coordinate' with the central level, but in practice the text provided for a system of subordination. It only mentioned a limited set of regional competences and provided for extensive concurrent powers. Equality would not be guaranteed within the centre, as proportionality and majority rule would be the guiding principles for federal representation and decision-making. Bi-communal representation was accepted but within the limits of efficiency, fairness and workability of the central institutions. As put by then opposition DIKO leader and current President Tassos Papadopoulos: 'political equality can only be achieved within the confines of one state, one sovereignty and one citizenship'.[3]

The prism of absolute sovereignty also led to contrasting positions over territory, Turkish immigrants and the three freedoms. The Turkish Cypriot leadership demanded sufficient territory to be economically self-sufficient and thus sustain Turkish Cypriot sovereignty. This concept was rejected by the Greek Cypriot side, to whom territorial boundaries would not divide two sovereign entities but would trace an invisible line within the sovereign federation. That boundary should account for the demographic balance on the island. Effectively following the same demographic logic, the Turkish Cypriot leadership objected to the Greek Cypriot demand for the repatriation of Turkish settlers. Finally, to the Greek Cypriots, the three freedoms should be liberalized because the Cypriots, as the ultimate repositories of the single sovereignty of the state, should enjoy equal rights throughout the island. The Turkish Cypriots rejected this position, insisting

---

[3] Debate between Nicos Anastasiades, Demetris Christofias and Tassos Papadopoulos, in Cyprus College, Nicosia, 11 March 2002.

on their separate sovereign self-rule. Cyprus, in their view, was composed of two, not one, sovereign peoples.

Differing perceptions of security threats articulated within the prism of state sovereignty also led to contrasting positions over external guarantees. To the Turkish Cypriots, within a system of two sovereign entities, Turkey alone could protect the security of the smaller Turkish Cypriot state. However, Turkey's self-interested strategic interests were precisely the reason for Greek Cypriot resistance against Turkey's interference in the affairs of the single state of Cyprus.

So long as the parties espoused absolute views of statehood and sovereignty, their positions could not converge. Paradoxically their positions were based on a similar understanding of the options available to them. Either there would be one state with single sovereignty in which all individuals would enjoy the same rights throughout the island and no external power would interfere in the internal affairs of the island. Or there would be two states with separate sovereignty and external protection, in which individuals would enjoy equal rights within their states and the two communities would be equal to one another. Given this conceptual paradigm, the Greek Cypriots naturally opted for the first variant, while the Turkish Cypriots for the second.

*Greek Cypriot and Turkish Cypriot Reluctance to Settle*

Compounded to these polarized positions was the reluctance of the two leaderships to move from the status quo. In the language of negotiation theory, the community leaderships (and the respective 'motherlands') were perceived to have high BATNAs, and as such the bargaining range was extremely narrow.

Since 1963 and more visibly since 1974, the Greek Cypriot authorities have enjoyed greater political and economic strength compared to their Turkish Cypriot counterparts. Beginning in 1964 with UNSC Resolution 186, the international community, while acknowledging the anomalies in the structure of the state, recognized the Greek Cypriot government as the RoC. Political expediency (i.e., the need for UN peacekeeping) led the UN to neglect the unconstitutional nature of the state and to deal with the RoC as the only legitimate authority on the island.

This fundamental Greek Cypriot political advantage rose after 1974. The international community viewed Turkey's military intervention, particularly after its second attack, and its ensuing occupation, as a gross violation of international law. In November 1974 the UN General Assembly voted unanimously for Resolution 3212 calling for 'the speedy withdrawal of all foreign armed forces' and for negotiations under the good offices of the UN. The fact that the Turkish intervention had resulted in the displacement of around 40 percent of the total population of the island further enhanced the Greek Cypriot moral high-ground. The result was a condemnation of Turkey's actions (even the US suspended its military aid to Turkey until 1978) and secessionist Turkish Cypriot moves. The by-product was the confirmed recognition of the RoC's legitimate authority over the whole island. This position was reinforced following the 1983 UDI of the TRNC, condemned by the international community. The longer the Turkish occupation persisted, the less international support it garnered. Particularly since the 1980s, the

Greek Cypriots have used their direct access to international forums to win further support and legitimacy.

The Greek Cypriot political advantage was reinforced by Greece, particularly after the rise to power of Andreas Papandreou in 1981. The Greek socialist government, less wary of antagonizing Europeans and Americans, began pursuing a consistent policy of internationalization of the Cyprus question, presenting internationally the Greek Cypriot moral, political and legal case. This further reduced the Greek Cypriot willingness to compromise in negotiations. Perception of political, moral and legal superiority induced the Greek Cypriot leadership and public to assume that concessions should come predominantly from the other side.

Superior political standing was also linked to the superior economic performance of southern Cyprus compared to the north. Since 1974, while the Greek Cypriot economy experienced significant economic prosperity, the Turkish Cypriot economy remained stagnant and undeveloped. The Greek Cypriot economic success was facilitated by the RoC's status as the only internationally recognized state on the island. Southern Cyprus hugely benefited from international trade and investment. Trade enabled the Greek Cypriots to develop two major comparative advantages, the light manufacturing industry and tourism. The RoC also successfully developed a lucrative offshore financial services sector.

**Table 3.1      Comparison between the Economies of Southern and Northern Cyprus: 2000**

|                              | South  | North |
|------------------------------|--------|-------|
| GNP growth, %                | 5.1    | -0.6  |
| GNP per capita, $            | 13,272 | 4,978 |
| Exports, $ million           | 843    | 50    |
| Imports, $ million           | 3,564  | 425   |
| Tourist revenue, $ million   | 1,880  | 198   |
| Inflation, %                 | 4.1    | 53.1  |

*Sources*: RoC, 2000b; TRNC, 2002b

Northern Cyprus presented a starkly opposite picture (Dodd, 1993) (see Table 3.1). Economic stagnation was fuelled to a large extent by international non-recognition and dependence on Turkey. International isolation induced the under-exploitation of the country's economic potential. International trade was restricted. In particular since 1974 the RoC and Greece have imposed economic embargoes on the north, and since 1994 EU markets have refused Cypriot exports not bearing RoC certification. Investment was deterred by inflation and the unrecognized status of the state. Tourism was minimal, given the absence of international air-links from destinations other than Turkey, the restricted access from the south to the north, the inability to travel to the RoC after having visited northern Cyprus via Turkey and the penalties imposed on foreign ships calling at Turkish Cypriot ports. Northern Cyprus also developed a large and inefficient public sector and became increasingly dependent on Turkey. Other than relying on Turkish trade and financial transfers, the TRNC recognized the Turkish lira as its legal tender and thus imported Turkey's fiscal and monetary instability. Standing in sharp contrast to southern Cyprus, in the north inflation fluctuated around 60 percent and public deficits relied completely on Turkish transfers for rectification.

The Greek Cypriots would only accept a settlement which led to an improvement of the status quo. They were reluctant to give up their political status and only showed readiness to accommodate Turkish Cypriots into governing arrangements by federalizing the existing RoC and retaining effective control within it. In return they demanded a redefinition of territorial boundaries, the withdrawal of most Turkish troops, the return of Greek Cypriot refugees to the north, the liberalization of the 'three freedoms' and some emigration of Anatolian settlers. Given the economic disparity between the two sides, reunification would also entail a significant economic cost to the Greek Cypriots, reducing further pressures for a federal solution (Theophanous, 1996). Aware of its political and economic strength, the Greek Cypriot side pursued a policy of 'wait and see', expecting and acting to induce a Turkish Cypriot cave-in. The Greek Cypriot negotiators attended meetings and accepted settlement principles. But in practice they felt no need to settle on terms other than their own.

The Turkish Cypriot authorities were also relatively content with their *de facto* situation post-1974. Despite international non-recognition, the Turkish Cypriot authorities have governed northern Cyprus since 1974, being recognized as the legitimate government by the population of the north. The TRNC equipped itself with all government institutions and was secured by Turkish troops in addition to the 4,500 Turkish Cypriot soldiers. Northern Cyprus suffered greatly from non-recognition, particularly in economic terms. However, by constantly articulating the primary importance of physical security and identity over material well-being, the authorities prevented (up until 2002) mass pressure for change. They were thus unwilling to settle for a federation in which their *de facto* achievements would be negated through unequal power-sharing arrangements with the larger and wealthier Greek Cypriot community. Turkish Cypriot relative reluctance to settle also had an important time dimension to it. The leadership hoped and assumed that with the passing of time there would be a *de jure* recognition of the *de facto* realities.

Turkey supported the Turkish Cypriots diplomatically, economically and militarily. Turkey was the only country which officially recognized the TRNC and used its own status to articulate the Turkish Cypriot cause in international forums. Economically, Turkey supported the TRNC, with most of the Turkish Cypriot deficit being financed by Turkey through loans or grants. Turkey also supported northern Cyprus militarily through the presence of 35-45,000 mainland troops in an area inhabited by approximately 200,000 citizens.

This historical review has sought to highlight the underlying absence of sufficient political commitment of all the parties to an independent Cyprus based upon a shared understanding of the relationship between its communities. Over the decades, lack of commitment expressed itself in different ways by different actors.

The conflict emerged in the 1930s-1950s when the Greek Cypriot community supported by Greece articulated its struggle for self-determination in terms of *enosis*. Unlike other former Ottoman possessions in the Eastern Mediterranean swept by the tide of ethnic nationalism and reciprocal ethnic-cleansing, the Greeks of Cyprus were faced with the additional obstacle of British colonial rule, adamantly opposed to *enosis*. Thereafter, the Turkish Cypriot community and Turkey mounted a reactive counter-*enosis* campaign, which by the late 1950s found form in the diametrically opposed position of *taksim*. In 1960 a compromise was found. Cyprus would become an independent bi-communal republic. Yet, the Greek Cypriot leadership remained implicitly devoted to *enosis* and by 1963 the bi-communal republic had collapsed. With its breakdown, both the Greek Cypriot and the Turkish Cypriot leaderships lost their already limited commitment to the 1959-60 agreements. Other European governments neglected the problem, while the Americans became increasingly uncomfortable with an independent Cyprus led by Archbishop Makarios, also known as the 'red monk'. Little international effort was exerted to stop the 1974 Greek coup and the ensuing Turkish military intervention. With the 1974 partition, Greek Cypriot and Turkish Cypriot positions moved further apart and showed little signs of compromise.

The decades that followed witnessed a series of failed negotiations and rejected proposals. Neither the Greek Cypriot nor the Turkish Cypriot leaders supported by Greece and Turkey respectively were ready to abandon the status quo for the re-establishment of a unified state where both communities would coexist on the basis of a shared understanding of their political equality. The Greek Cypriot leadership was relatively content with the political and economic supremacy of the RoC, while the Turkish Cypriot leadership was unwilling to renounce its *de facto* independence. Both parties articulated their claims in the mutually exclusive language of absolute statehood and sovereignty. No third party, other than the UN, actively attempted to alter these perceptions. However, as the following chapters argue, while the Community remained passive, its effective role in the dynamics of the conflict changed by the late 1980s, following Turkey's application to join the EC in 1987 and the beginning of the political dialogue between the RoC and the Community in 1988.

## References

Attalides, M.A. (1979), *Cyprus Nationalism and International Politics*, Q Press, Edinburgh.
Borowiec, A. (2000), *Cyprus: A Troubled Island*, Praeger Publishers, Westport.
British Colonial Office (1961), *Cyprus Report for the Year 1958*, Her Majesty's Stationery Office, London.
Chrysostomides, K. (2000), *The Republic of Cyprus: A Study in International Law*, M. Nijhoff Publishers, The Hague, London.
Clerides, G. (1989a), *Cyprus: My Deposition*, Volume 1, Alithia Publishers, Nicosia.
Clerides, G. (1989b), *Cyprus: My Deposition*, Volume 2, Alithia Publishers, Nicosia.
Council of Europe (1974), Recommendation 573 of the Assembly of the Council of Europe, Strasbourg.

Council of Europe (1987), Recommendation 1056 of the Assembly of the Council of Europe, Strasbourg.

Council of Ministers of the European Community (1973), Council Regulation (EEC) No. 1246/73, 'Agreement Establishing an Association between the European Economic Community and the Republic of Cyprus', *Official Journal*, L133, 21 May 1973, Brussels.

Dodd, C. (ed.) (1993), *The Political, Social and Economic Development of Northern Cyprus*, Eothen, Huntingdon.

Durrell, L. (1958), *Bitter Lemons*, Marlowe & Co., New York.

Ertekün, N.M. (1981), *In Search of a Negotiated Cyprus Settlement*, Ülüs Matbağacılık, Nicosia.

Faulds, A. (1988), *Excerpta Cypria for Today: A Source Book on the Cyprus Problem*, K. Rustem and Brother, Lefkoşa, London.

Hitchens, C. (1997), *Hostage to History: Cyprus from the Ottomans to Kissinger*, Verso, London.

Küçük, F. (1963), *Turkish Reply to Archbishop Makarios' Proposals*, Nicosia, n.d.

Kyriakides, S. (1968), *Cyprus Constitutionalism and Crisis Government*, University of Pennsylvania Press, Philadelphia.

Mirbagheri, F. (1998), *Cyprus and International Peacemaking*, Hurst & Co., London.

Polyviou, P.G. (1976), *Cyprus in Search of a Constitution*, Chr Nicolaou & Sons Ltd, Nicosia.

Reddaway, J. (1986), *Burdened with Cyprus - The British Connection*, Rustem & Bro. and Weidenfeld & Nicolson, Ltd., London, Nicosia, Istanbul.

Republic of Cyprus (1989), 'Outline Proposals for the Establishment of a Federal Republic and for the Resolution of the Cyprus Problem', Submitted on 30 January 1989, Appendix 20 in *The Cyprus Problem, Historical Review and the Latest Developments*, April 1999, Information Office, Republic of Cyprus, Nicosia.

Republic of Cyprus (2000b), Department of Statistics, *Economic and Social Indicators*, Nicosia.

Republic of Turkey (1998), *Background of the Cyprus Problem*, Directorate General of Press and Information, Ministry of Foreign Affairs, Ankara.

Richmond, O. (1998), *Mediating in Cyprus*, Frank Cass, London.

Stefanidis, I.D. (1999), *Isle of Discord: Nationalism, Imperialism and the Making of the Cyprus Problem*, Hurst & Company, London.

Theophanous, A. (1996), *The Political Economy of a Federal Cyprus*, Intercollege, Nicosia.

Turkish Republic of Northern Cyprus (2002b), State Planning Organization, *Economic and Social Indicators*, Nicosia.

United Nations General Assembly (1974), Resolution 3212 (XXIX) of 1 November 1974.

United Nations General Assembly (1983), Resolution 37/253 of 13 May 1983.

United Nations Security Council (1964), Resolution 186 of 4 March 1964.

United Nations Security Council (1975), Resolution 367 of 12 March 1975.

United Nations Security Council (1983), Resolution 541 of 18 November 1983.

United Nations Security Council (1984), Resolution 550 of 11 May 1984.

United Nations Secretary General (1999), *Report of the Secretary General on his Mission of Good Offices in Cyprus*, 22 June 1999, S/1999/707, New York.

Chapter 4

# Cyprus' EU Accession Process
# and the Evolution of the Conflict

*'There is a very strange situation...the side that said "yes" will not participate
in the EU. The side that said "no" will participate'*
(Abdullah Gül, quoted in *Turkish Daily News*, 2004b)

On 1 May 2004, over a decade after the Commission and the member states had
expressed the belief that Cyprus' accession process would catalyse a settlement on
the island, the Greek Cypriot Republic of Cyprus entered the European Union,
leaving the Turkish Cypriots on the other side of the 'green line'. The introduction
of the EU variable acted as an important external determinant of the internal
dynamics of the conflict, both between the two communities, between Greece and
Turkey, as well as between the communities and their respective 'motherlands'.
The impact of the EU is analysed by pointing out the major turning points in the
accession process and the parallel policy developments in Cyprus, Greece and
Turkey.

## The Introduction of the EU Variable in the Cyprus Conflict: 1988-93

Until the late 1980s, despite the existence of an Association Agreement with
Cyprus, neither the European Commission nor the Council of Ministers had played
a significant role in the evolution of the conflict. The conflict had been affected
primarily by the two communities, Greece, Turkey, the UN Secretariat, the UK
and, to a lesser extent and on particular occasions, the US. However, since the
launch of a political dialogue between the RoC and the EC in 1988, the EU, as a
collective actor, gradually became an integral element of the dynamics of the
conflict.

On 18 July 1988 the General Affairs Council (GAC) of the EC formally
invited Cyprus to initiate a political dialogue with EC member states. The initiative
came from Andreas Papandreou's government in Greece, at the time holding the
rotating EC Presidency, which spurred RoC President George Vassiliou to apply
for full membership. At the time Vassiliou rejected the suggestion, but initiated a
political dialogue with the Community, which in turn triggered a public debate on
the option of accession.

During the same period, Turkey, under the leadership of Turgut Özal, applied
for EC membership. Having overcome a period of military rule in 1980-83 and

embarked upon unprecedented economic liberalization in the mid-1980s, Prime Minister Özal took the bold step of applying for EC membership on 12 April 1987. However, in the case of Turkey, the Commission was not forthcoming. While accepting Turkey's eligibility for membership, the Commission refused to recognize Turkey as a candidate for accession. The economic and political system in Turkey was considered too different from that of the EC member states for a fruitful accession process to begin. The 1989 Opinion also mentioned the 'negative effects of the disputes between Turkey and an EC member state including the situation in Cyprus' (Commission, 1989).

The late 1980s and early 1990s also witnessed the most active UN effort to reach a settlement in Cyprus since the 1974 partition. Following the failure of the 'Draft Framework Agreement' talks in 1986 between Kyprianou and Denktaş, UN-sponsored talks resumed in August 1988 between Denktaş and the newly elected Greek Cypriot President Vassiliou. The talks continued during the autumn of 1988 and the early months of 1989. In July 1989 Secretary General Pérez de Cuellar presented his ideas for a settlement. The ideas provided for a new 'common home' for the two communities, with a new Constitution that would establish a single bi-zonal and bi-communal federal Cyprus. The federation would have a single international personality and citizenship. But it would embody the political equality of the two communities. The single sovereignty of the federation would in fact 'emanate equally' from the two communities. Negotiations culminated in a summit on 2 March 1990. The summit failed when Denktaş demanded the right of separate Turkish Cypriot self-determination and was turned down by Vassiliou. Nevertheless, UN Security Council (UNSC) Resolution 649 called for an agreement negotiated on an equal footing by the two parties and based on the Secretary General's ideas. It also called on the parties to 'refrain from any action that could aggravate the situation' (UNSC, 1990, Article 5).

Notwithstanding the Security Council's appeal, the RoC applied for EC membership on 4 July 1990. The application triggered a strong Turkish Cypriot reaction. On 12 July 1990 the Turkish Cypriot government closed the crossing point on the green line and sent a memorandum to Italian Prime Minister Gianni de Michelis holding the EC Presidency, strongly condemning the application on behalf of the whole island. The Turkish Cypriot leadership argued that the application was illegitimate because it was made by the Greek Cypriot government claiming to represent the Turkish Cypriots as well. It stated that the application was illegal because it violated both the 1960 Constitution (Article 50) and the Treaty of Guarantee (Articles 1a, 1b and 170) (Mendelson, 2001). It also stated that the application ran contrary to the 1977 and 1979 high-level agreements, as well as to the request of the UNSC to refrain from unilateral actions that could hamper negotiations. Notwithstanding, in September 1990 the EC Council called the Commission to express its Opinion on the application.

Despite the RoC's application, the 1990-93 period witnessed persisting and intense UN mediation efforts. UN ideas on the principles of a solution became increasingly clear. UNSC Resolution 716 reaffirmed the principle of a single state of Cyprus based on the political equality of the two sides (UNSC, 1991, paragraphs 4-6). Political equality would be reflected in the process of negotiations and in the framework of a future solution. In December 1991, the UN Secretary General (UNSG) stated that: 'sovereignty will be equally shared but indivisible' and that the solution would be based on a 'new constitutional arrangement' which would be negotiated on an 'equal footing' and approved through 'separate referenda' (UNSG, 1991, paragraph 6).

In early 1992, the new UNSG Boutros Boutros Ghali immediately picked up the Cyprus dossier from where his predecessor had left it. Vassiliou and Denktaş repeatedly met in January-February 1992 and the process culminated with a full-fledged UN proposal for a settlement, known as the 'Set of Ideas' (UNSG, 1992a). The 'Set of Ideas' fleshed out in greater detail previous UN ideas and proposals for a loose bi-zonal and bi-communal federation. The substance of the document is reviewed in Chapter 7. The UNSC endorsed the document in Resolution 750 and the Secretary General actively mediated negotiations. In June-August and October-November 1992, the parties negotiated on the basis of the 'Set of Ideas'. While remaining far from an agreement, significant steps forward were made. The Greek Cypriot team accepted the document as a basis for negotiation, while the Turkish Cypriot side endorsed 91 out of the 100 points of the document. Ultimately the talks ended in November 1992 with the Secretary General concluding that negotiations suffered from a deep crisis of confidence between the parties (Bölükbaşı, 1995).

The crisis of confidence induced the UN Secretary General to focus on confidence building measures (CBM). The proposed CBM package foresaw the Greek Cypriot re-settlement in the ghost town of Varosha under a UN administration and the establishment of an inter-communal tax-free trade area there, together with the re-opening of the Nicosia international airport. Discussions over the package took place in May-June 1993. Negotiations ultimately failed. Both sides had deep reservations about the package, which was finally rejected by the TRNC Assembly.

In the backdrop of these events, an EC consensus concerning Cyprus' application emerged over the course of 1992, and was then formalized in the Commission Opinion published on 30 June 1993 (Commission, 1993). The EC accepted the RoC application on behalf of 'Cyprus', while assuming that accession negotiations and ultimate membership would occur after a settlement. In other words, the accession process would begin but with a strong form of conditionality on both sides.

The Opinion was clear in its acceptance of Cyprus' European credentials, and thus the country's eligibility for membership (Commission, 1993, paragraph 44). Furthermore, the Commission stated that it did not envisage major economic obstacles to the accession of the island, despite the socio-economic disparities between north and south. However, the June 1992 European Council in Lisbon was explicit about its position on a settlement, concluding that 'in the case of Cyprus, there is inevitably a link between the question of accession and the problem which results from the *de facto* separation of the island into two entities...' (European Council, 1992, paragraph 30). Following this line, the Commission Opinion stated that while 'the Community considers Cyprus as eligible for membership', accession negotiations would only begin 'as soon as the prospect of settlement is surer' (Commission, 1993, paragraph 48). The Commission also stated that 'Cyprus' integration with the community *implies* a peaceful, balanced and lasting settlement of the Cyprus question' (Commission, 1993, paragraph 47, my italics). Given that accession negotiations would begin when the prospect of a settlement was 'surer', the fact that Cyprus' integration 'implied' a settlement, suggested that membership would occur after a solution.

The motivating factor for this explicit form of conditionality was the *acquis communautaire*. A settlement was a *sine qua non* in order for Cyprus to 'participate normally in the decision-making process of the EC...' and ensure '...the correct application of Community law throughout the island' (Commission, 1993, paragraph 47). The *acquis* was presented as the apolitical explanation for this fundamental precondition. It was the technical shield behind which hid the underlying political reservations of several member states about the accession of a divided island.

However, the Opinion's articulation of conditionality retained a balance. Conditionality on the Greek Cypriots was designed not to induce greater Turkish Cypriot intransigence. The Commission feared that unqualified conditionality on the Greek Cypriot side would reduce Turkish Cypriot incentives to compromise. The Opinion therefore stated that 'should this (a failure of negotiations) eventuality arise, the Commission feels that the situation should be reassessed in view of the positions adopted by each party in the talks and that the question of Cyprus' accession to the Community should be reconsidered in January 1995' (Commission, 1993, paragraph 51). In other words, if the Greek Cypriots demonstrated goodwill and the ultimate failure to reach an agreement was due to Turkish Cypriot intransigence, accession negotiations without a settlement could be possible. Turkish Cypriot intransigence could open the way for the accession process of a divided Cyprus. Already in 1993, this prospect was not excluded.

**The Turning Point in Cyprus' Accession Process : 1994-96**

Up until and including the 1993 Opinion, the EC role in the Cyprus conflict was marginal. By mid-1994 this situation had transformed; EU decisions, and particularly those taken in June 1994 and March 1995 became major external determinants of the evolution of the conflict. Under the Greek Presidency, the Corfu European Council on 24 June 1994 decided to include Cyprus (and Malta) in the next round of enlargement (European Council, 1994). While the formal condition of conflict settlement was not formally revised, in practice the clarity of conditionality as put in 1993 started to erode. The case of East Germany gradually became part of the political discourse both in official and academic circles as a model for the *de facto* sequential accession of the two sides of Cyprus with a single set of negotiations (Bahceli, 1999, p.112). This would entail the accession of a divided Cyprus, whereby the *acquis* would be implemented immediately in the RoC, and extended to the rest of the island following a settlement.

The second critical decision was taken on 6 March 1995, when the General Affairs Council under the French Presidency brokered what was to become the first 'historic compromise' in the EU-Cyprus-Turkey triangle (Council of Ministers, 1995). The Council agreed to begin accession negotiations with Cyprus six months after the 1996 Intergovernmental Conference (IGC). In return, Greece removed its veto on the pending Turkey-EU customs union, cast in December 1994. Turkey would also have received the long-awaited accumulated funds from the fourth Financial Protocol, which amounted to $1.2 billion in aid and European Investment Bank loans.

With the concrete prospect of accession negotiations with a divided Cyprus, what in 1993 had been presented as a hypothetical possibility, became an increasingly likely scenario by mid-1995. This in turn triggered negative Turkish and Turkish Cypriot reactions, which hampered the peace process. In addition, EU actors did little to make the accession process conditional on internal developments in south Cyprus. What by 1994 had consolidated into a strong Greek Cypriot desire to join the Union began to hinge less on progress in conflict settlement.

*Greek and Greek Cypriot Assertive Nationalism*

The period just before and immediately after the Commission Opinion was marked by greater assertive nationalism in the policies of the RoC and Greece, triggered by domestic changes in Nicosia and Athens. In Nicosia, Glafcos Clerides from the centre-right party DISY won over incumbent George Vassiliou in February 1993. Clerides had run his presidential campaign on the basis of a nationalist agenda, i.e., that of 'purging' the Set of Ideas of their negative elements and upgrading Greek Cypriot defence policy. The ideas for thin central government, extensive power-sharing and strong bi-zonality in the Set of Ideas were anathema to Greek Cypriot nationalists. While Clerides himself was not considered an uncompromising nationalist, his hardline stance was taken in the context of the 1993 election campaign, won with the support of Spyros Kyprianou's nationalist centre-right DIKO and Vassos Lyssarides' nationalist socialist EDEK.

True to his electoral pledges, President Clerides moved away from the Ghali Ideas and negotiations did not resume. Following the failure of the inter-communal talks, discussions on the CBMs were on the verge of resuming in October 1994, but were ultimately stalled by Clerides. This position persisted when in January 1995 Clerides rejected Denktaş's fourteen-point peace initiative foreseeing EU membership for a federal Cyprus along the lines of the 'Set of Ideas' and proposing to discuss the CBM package without preconditions. The RoC also upgraded significantly its defence capability. Immediately after the elections, Clerides announced an increase in defence spending to $1 million per day, i.e., seven percent of the RoC's GNP.

Internal political changes in Nicosia dovetailed those in Athens. In October 1993, Andreas Papandreou's PASOK returned to power in Athens, taking over from the conservative Constantine Mitsokakis (New Democracy), known to be a moderate on the Cyprus conflict. Papandreou immediately strengthened Greece's ties with the RoC, most notably in the field of defence policy. This move was also strongly advanced by then Defence Minister Yerasimos Arsenis, who in view of

Papandreou's illness at the time, aimed at the leadership of PASOK by advocating assertive nationalist defence policies.

More specifically, in December 1993 the Greek and Greek Cypriot government signed a 'Joint Defence Doctrine', which placed the RoC under Greece's military umbrella (Demetriou, 1998). Greece and the RoC would coordinate military strategies and the acquisition of military assets, and their military forces would engage in joint exercises once a year. Plans were made for the construction of a new air base in Paphos intended to accommodate Greek F-16 planes. Greece also committed itself to intervene militarily in the event of a Turkish attack on Cyprus. The declared aims of the upgraded defence capability were to deter a Turkish aggression, to redirect international attention towards Cyprus, and to induce Turkey to review its foreign policies.

Finally, the Greek Cypriot and Greek governments began to exert greater pressure in European legal forums for a condemnation of Turkish and Turkish Cypriot actions. The resulting court cases had a profound negative impact on the conflict and future peace efforts. The first critical case was that of Titina Loizidou, a Greek Cypriot who in March 1989 attempted to cross the 'green line' in order to reach her property in Kyrenia and was stopped by Turkish forces. In July 1989 Ms Loizidou independently filed a complaint to the Commission of the European Court of Human Rights (ECHR, 1989). Initially (July 1993) the ECHR Commission dismissed the case as unfounded. But in November 1993 the Loizidou case was reintroduced in the ECHR, with the full backing of the RoC government. On 18 December 1996, the Court found Turkey guilty of violating the European Convention for Human Rights guaranteeing Ms Loizidou's peaceful enjoyment of her possessions. On 28 July 1998, the ECHR requested a compensation of €800,000 from Turkey to Ms Loizidou for denying the enjoyment of her property in Kyrenia.

The aims of the Loizidou case were both to discredit further the TRNC and to increase pressure on Turkey. The case gave international support to the view that the conflict was driven by Turkey and that the TRNC was a mere puppet in Ankara's hands. The ECHR ruling indeed described the TRNC as the subordinate local authority under Turkey's control, exacerbating the legal and political hierarchy between the Greek Cypriot and Turkish Cypriot authorities. The case also highlighted the human rights violations committed by Turkey in northern Cyprus. Most critically, the Loizidou case was intended to strengthen the Greek Cypriot negotiating position by altering the basis for future negotiations on the right of refugee return. Not only did international law provide unreserved support for the Greek Cypriot position; the Loizidou precedent also made the acceptance of Turkish Cypriot proposals less feasible. Even if the two communities were to agree to property exchange and ethnic quotas in the two federated states, could the issue be considered settled if any Greek Cypriot individual deprived of his/her property could challenge the agreement by appealing to the ECHR? By 2002 there were over one hundred Greek Cypriot cases filed against Turkey in the ECHR.

The Loizidou case had a negative impact on the peace process, not necessarily because of the actual ruling of the Court, but because it represented an attempt to settle one of the key issues of the conflict through arbitration rather than negotiation. As such it exacerbated Turkish Cypriot resentment of the way Greek Cypriots exploited their international recognition to strengthen their bargaining position. Perhaps most crucially it complicated future talks on the other items on the conflict settlement agenda. This was because of the inextricable link between all of these items and their possible resolution only through a comprehensive agreement.

The second court case was the Anastasiou case in the European Court of Justice (ECJ, 1994). Up until 1994, the EC traded with northern Cyprus despite the international non-recognition of the TRNC. In particular the UK and Ireland imported Turkish Cypriot goods under preferential treatment by appealing to Article 5 of the 1972 EC-Cyprus Association Agreement, which stated that the Community would not discriminate between the nationals or companies of Cyprus (Brewin, 2000, pp.196-199). Given that the Agreement had been signed almost a decade after the 1963 constitutional breakdown, Article 5 had been inserted to ensure the Community's even-handedness towards the two communities. However, with the 1994 Anastasiou case, the effective embargo of Greece and the RoC on northern Cyprus was extended to the rest of the EU. On 5 July 1994 the ECJ ruled in favour of Anastasiou Ltd (a Greek company which filed the case with the support of the Greek government) banning Cypriot exports that did not bear RoC documentation. At the time of the ECJ judgement, 74 percent of Turkish Cypriot exports were directed to the EU and only 14 percent went to Turkey. In 1996 Turkish Cypriot exports to the EU fell to 35 percent, while exports to Turkey rose to 48 percent (Brewin, 2000, p.198). The ECJ ruling thus significantly raised the TRNC's isolation and dependence on Turkey. Consequently, it reduced dramatically Turkish Cypriot living standards, raising the costs of the status quo (and reducing the Turkish Cypriot BATNA).

*Turkish Cypriot and Turkish Antagonizing Reactions*

EU decisions directly triggered negative Turkish and Turkish Cypriot reactions. Immediately following the Anastasiou ruling, Rauf Denktaş argued that economic needs would now necessitate the full integration between the TRNC and Turkey. Indeed in September 1994, Turkey and the TRNC signed the thirteenth joint economic protocol foreseeing a set of harmonization measures and the use of the Turkish lira as the sole currency in northern Cyprus. In August 1994, the same ECJ case was presented as the motivating factor behind the TRNC Assembly's revocation of past commitments to a federal settlement made in the context of the 1984-85 UN-sponsored negotiations.[1] In October 1994 following the Corfu European Council, Denktaş declared that he would reject all Greek Cypriot offers of a federation if the RoC began accession negotiations.

The 1994 ECJ judgement and the Corfu Council's decision were followed by harsher Turkish Cypriot reactions than the arguably more significant 1995 GAC decision, which essentially gave Cyprus a date to begin accession negotiations. The

---

[1] Interviews with Turkish Cypriot officials and opposition leaders, Lefkoşa, February 2002.

difference was that the 1995 decision was brokered as a package deal that included a Cyprus *and* a Turkey component. While all parties adamantly denied the linkage, the package partially soothed Turkey, which in turn understated its opposition to the EU's Cyprus policy.

The customs union deal was widely criticized in Turkey and northern Cyprus on the basis that it entailed Turkey's recognition of the RoC (Bıçak, 1997). Nevertheless, neither did the 1995 decision trigger an immediate Turkish reaction, nor was the customs union agreement revoked by successive Turkish governments. Unlike the ECJ case and the Corfu decision that triggered visible reactions, the 1995 package deal led neither to a softening nor to a meaningful hardening in Turkish and Turkish Cypriot positions.

## The Progressive Deterioration of the Conflict: 1996-99

Immediately following the March 1995 decision, EU institutions took the necessary steps to prepare for accession negotiations with the RoC. The 16th EU-Cyprus Association Council meeting in June 1995 decided to launch a structured dialogue for Cyprus' familiarization with the *acquis*. The dialogue also envisaged Cyprus' participation in several Community programmes and the disbursement of €136 million in pre-accession aid. During the period of structured dialogue, EU institutions made no statements concerning conditionality on Cyprus. On the contrary, the possibility of membership prior to a solution was no longer excluded. In March 1996, Commissioner Hans Van der Broek declared that EU membership of a divided Cyprus was 'possible although not preferable' (*Agence Europe*, No.6681, 06 March 1996).

In 1997, two critical EU decisions were taken. In July 1997 the Commission published its 'Agenda 2000', which stated that 'if progress towards a settlement is not made before the negotiations are due to begin, they should be opened with the government of the Republic of Cyprus, as the only authority recognized by international law' (Commission, 1997b). Appealing to the review clause in the 1993 Opinion (Commission, 1993, paragraph 51), a settlement, while preferable, would not be a prerequisite for accession negotiations.

The second significant decision was taken at the Luxembourg European Council in December 1997 (European Council, 1997). In the light of the conclusion of the IGC, the European Council decided to open accession negotiations with the first wave of candidate countries (including Cyprus) in March 1998 (actual negotiations were launched in November 1998 after an eight-month 'screening' process). As far as Cyprus was concerned, the Presidency conclusions did not state that membership could occur before reunification. However, if no agreement was reached, accession negotiations could not be upheld indefinitely. The Luxembourg Council not only set a date for negotiations with Cyprus. It also denied Turkey 'EU candidate status'. Unlike the 1995 'historic compromise', which retained an element of balance in the EU's approach towards Turkey and Cyprus, the Luxembourg Council took a momentous step in Cyprus-EU relations without an equivalent step in Turkey-EU relations. Rather than candidacy, the

European Council offered Turkey a 'European Strategy' of unclear content. The content of the Strategy was partially substantiated in June 1998 at the Cardiff European Council under the British Presidency.

Precisely because of these key EU decisions, 1996-97 was rife with British, American and UN diplomatic initiatives to settle the conflict so as to enable accession negotiations to be launched with a reunified Cyprus. In May 1996, the UK appointed David Hannay as the British Special Representative to Cyprus. In June 1996, the US launched a new initiative led by Richard Beattie. In June 1997, the Clinton administration stepped up its involvement with the appointment of the Dayton Treaty architect, Richard Holbrooke, to work on the Cyprus impasse. The UN Secretary General also deployed its resources to re-launch a dialogue, stalled since October 1994. Under UN Special Assistant Diego Cordovez, direct talks were held on 9-13 July in Troutbeck, New York. In Troutbeck, the UN tabled a proposal similar to the 1992 'Set of Ideas'. At the Troutbeck meeting, Clerides rejected the formulation of sovereignty 'emanating equally' from both communities. The talks were reconvened on 11-15 August 1997 in Glion, Switzerland. They failed, this time due to the Turkish Cypriot position. The very progress in Cyprus' accession path proved critically detrimental to all peace efforts. In view of the approaching EU deadline for accession negotiations, all peace initiatives in 1996-97 ended in failure.

*Turkish and Turkish Cypriot Antagonizing Reactions*

Unlike the 1993-95 period, the Turkish Cypriots were held predominantly responsible for the failure of these peace initiatives. Turkey and the TRNC openly admitted the direct effect of EU decisions on their positions and the evolution of the conflict. Naturally they did not accept any blame for the failure of peace initiatives, but portrayed their policies as unavoidable reactions to one-sided EU decisions. Nonetheless, these very reactions (unavoidable or not) admittedly added new and critical obstacles to the peace process.

Between late 1995 and 1999, what had previously been vaguely articulated threats of integration between Turkey and the TRNC acquired more tangible significance. In December 1995, Turkey and the TRNC published a Joint Declaration of intention to work towards the integration of the two entities. The Declaration was explicitly described as a reaction to EU decisions (the initiation of the structured dialogue between the EU and the RoC in November 1995) as well as to the ongoing Greek Cypriot rearmament policy. In January 1997, Presidents Demirel and Denktaş signed the Joint Declaration, which stated that Turkey and the TRNC would emulate every integration step taken by the EU and the RoC. In other words, Turkey and northern Cyprus deliberately spelt out the parallelism between Turkey-TRNC integration (and its evident repercussions on the conflict) and Greek Cypriot-EU initiatives.

The substance of Turkish and Turkish Cypriot integration was then elaborated. In July 1997, four days following the publication of 'Agenda 2000', Bülent Ecevit and Rauf Denktaş agreed on partial integration talks in the fields of economy, finance, foreign affairs, security and defence. In August 1997, Turkey and the

TRNC signed an Association Agreement. The Agreement provided the framework for the implementation of several measures. From January 1998, Turkish Cypriot officials were included in Turkish Embassies and Delegations. Following the EU Association model, Turkey and the TRNC established a joint Association Council, whose first meeting ostentatiously took place in April 1998, only a few days following the formal launch of the accession negotiations. In March 1998, Turkey and the TRNC established a joint economic zone. This allowed northern Cyprus to receive Turkish agricultural bank credits on the same terms as Turkish applicants. In July 1998, Turkey and the TRNC declared their plans to transport water from Turkey to northern Cyprus via a balloon system. In the course of 1998, northern Cyprus received TL 41,800 million from Turkey, i.e., almost half the TRNC's total budget of TL 93,600 million.

Moves towards integration between Turkey and northern Cyprus were discarded by European officials as irrelevant, in so far as they were considered legally void, as well as practically meaningless given the high degree of *de facto* integration between Turkey and northern Cyprus already in place.[2] Nonetheless, the political significance of these developments was noteworthy. Turkish-Turkish Cypriot integration illustrated Ankara and Lefkoşa's antagonizing attitudes towards the EU as well as their reduced readiness to settle the conflict. The more Turkey and the TRNC proceeded along the path of integration, the more distant became the prospect of a settlement based on the reunification of the island within the EU.

Turkish Cypriot reactions also contributed directly to the failure of the peace efforts. In August 1997, shortly after the publication of 'Agenda 2000', the two community leaders participated in a second round of talks in Glion. The talks failed and UN officials blamed the Turkish Cypriot side. Denktaş rejected the UN's principles for a settlement on the grounds that these entailed a shift towards the Greek Cypriots. However he also demanded an immediate freeze in the procedures to launch accession negotiations with the RoC (as well as the annulment of the Greek Cypriot order of S-300 missiles) as a precondition for future talks. On his departure, Denktaş declared that he would not meet Clerides again until the EU clarified its position on Cyprus' future accession. Hence, regardless of the UN's positions, the ensuing Turkish Cypriot demands suggested that Denktaş's main source of suspicion in Glion were the decisions disclosed in 'Agenda 2000'.

Matters deteriorated to their lowest point following the 1997 Luxembourg European Council. Turkey perceived the European Council's decisions as evidence of clear EU discrimination and viewed itself as being unjustly de-coupled from the enlargement process, which included countries with significantly less developed economies and ties with the Union. It therefore froze its political dialogue with the Union, both by refusing to attend the European Conferences that would take place alongside European Council meetings and by suspending the Turkey-EU Association Council. Frozen relations set the scene for harder Turkish Cypriot reactions. In December 1997, Denktaş announced the end of all EU information

---

[2] Interview with British Foreign Office official, London, July 2001.

campaigns in northern Cyprus and ended all informal contacts between TRNC and Commission officials. He also banned bi-communal activities.

With the opening of accession negotiations with the RoC in March 1998, the Turkish and Turkish Cypriot authorities hardened their position further. In April 1998, the Turkish and Turkish Cypriot governments jointly declared:

> the EU has disregarded international law and the 1959-60 agreements on Cyprus by deciding to open accession negotiations with the Greek Cypriot administration and has dealt a blow to the efforts for a solution. Currently any negotiating process aimed at finding a solution to the Cyprus question can have a chance of success only if it is conducted between two sovereign equals (*Anadolu Agency*, 24 April 1998).

The initiation of accession negotiations thus induced the TRNC and Turkey to add a further precondition: the acceptance that negotiations would be carried out between two sovereign states rather than between two communities.

Following this line, in August 1998 Denktaş tabled a new proposal. Having rejected the concept of federation as a basis of an agreement in 1994, the Turkish Cypriot leader now proclaimed that a future settlement should be based on a confederation between two sovereign states. The confederation proposal was a logical consequence of the previous request to conduct negotiations on a state-to-state basis. Some analysts argued that the change in the Turkish Cypriot negotiating position was cosmetic and not substantive (Dodd, 1999a). Long before the official confederation position was adopted, Denktaş had been calling for the creation of a federation 'by aggregation', which implied the prior existence of two states that pooled their sovereignties into one internationally recognized state. A confederation thus could be viewed as the first step in the creation of a federation. Yet the change in the Turkish Cypriot position signalled the leadership's reduced readiness to negotiate and settle. The confederation proposal increased the gap between the two parties' formal positions and their legal implications. Precisely because the proposal did not entail a substantive change in Turkish Cypriot demands, it could be viewed within the logic of reduced Turkish Cypriot willingness to seek an early solution within the Union.

Finally, it is interesting to note the more muted Turkish and Turkish Cypriot attitudes in November 1998, when the actual accession negotiations with Cyprus began. Increased EU attention to Turkey at the Cardiff European Council was insufficient to alter Turkey's attitude towards the Union. Ankara still refused to re-launch its political dialogue. Nonetheless, in the light of the European Council's opening in Cardiff, the beginning of substantive accession negotiations with Cyprus did not cause more than verbal Turkish and Turkish Cypriot accusations. The argument could be made that following the pattern of March 1995, and, as we shall see below, December 1999 and December 2002, the Cardiff opening towards Turkey contributed to a more silent Turkish reaction to the opening of accession negotiations with Cyprus.

*Greek Cypriot Defence Policies*

The 1995-99 period saw an exacerbation of nationalistic Greek Cypriot defence policies. Within the framework of the upgraded Greek Cypriot defence policy and the Joint Defence Doctrine, in January 1997 Clerides, largely supported by public opinion and political parties, announced the forthcoming acquisition of S-300 missiles from Russia. The announcement immediately raised tensions in the Eastern Mediterranean. Turkey declared that the deployment of the missiles would be considered a *casus belli*.

In December 1998, the Greek and Greek Cypriot governments agreed to deploy the missiles in Crete rather than Cyprus. In the light of increased tensions in the region and in Cyprus, considerable British, French and German pressure, in addition to American influence, proved instrumental in deterring the Greek Cypriots. The role of the Greek government led by Costas Simitis was also important in persuading the RoC not to accept the missiles. At the time Greece was struggling to enter the eurozone and the deployment of the S-300s complicated Greece's attempts to concomitantly push for eurozone entry and Cyprus' accession negotiations. The Simitis government thus persuaded the Greek Cypriots that their membership bid would suffer as a consequence of the deployment. The high priority goal of EU membership triggered the Greek Cypriot retreat, despite the outcry this caused in southern Cyprus, including the resignation of two ministers. The role of the EU in this decision was explicitly recognized by the Greek Cypriot government. As put by then Foreign Minister Cassoulides: 'without the prospect of Cyprus' entry to the Union, the missiles would be on the island' (*Agence Europe*, No.7397, 4 February 1998).

However, although the S-300 time-bomb was ultimately diffused, it contributed to two years (January 1997-December 1998) of increased tensions, suspicions and Turkish and Turkish Cypriot counter-reactions, which severely harmed all peace efforts. Throughout this period, EU actors did little to dissuade Greek Cypriot decision-makers from their plans. And yet, as the events of late 1998 and 1999 demonstrated, EU actors had the necessary leverage to influence Greek Cypriot decision-making. Precisely because European pressure had sufficient clout to prevent the Greek Cypriot deployment of the missiles, why was it not exerted before?

*Greek-Turkish Brinkmanship*

Incidents in bilateral Greek-Turkish and inter-communal relations also contributed to rising tensions and the failure of peace efforts in 1996-98. Most importantly, in January 1996 tensions between Greece and Turkey rose due to disagreements over the sovereignty of the tiny uninhabited islets of Imia/Kardak . The crisis was ultimately diffused through the mediation of US envoy Richard Holbrooke. As Holbrooke himself put it, Europe was 'asleep' while the US intervened to prevent a possible war between Greece and Turkey (Theophanous, 2001, p.240). In response to Turkey's moves over the islets on 29 January 1996, the Greek government recast its veto in the Council of Ministers over the €375 million due to Turkey as part of the customs union agreement. Brinkmanship between Greece and Turkey rose again in the summer of 1998, when in mid-June four Greek F-16 planes landed in the newly constructed air base in Paphos, provoking Turkey to send six fighter jets to northern Cyprus. Within Cyprus tensions rose in the summer of 1996, when clashes along the green line provoked the death of two Greek Cypriots.

Incidents in Greek-Turkish and inter-communal relations were profoundly linked to the wider context of EU-Turkey and EU-Cyprus relations (Kramer, 1997). In 1996-98 Greek-Turkish tensions rose to their highest levels since 1974. This reduced Greek willingness within EU institutions to agree to forthcoming steps towards Turkey (for example at the 1997 Luxembourg and 1998 Cardiff European Council meetings). It also encouraged the Greek government to push ahead both with the Cyprus dossier within the EU and with its cooperative defence policies with the RoC. Yet EU decisions concerning Cyprus and Turkey in 1996-98 raised the climate of distrust between the conflict parties, which fuelled the hardening Turkish and Turkish Cypriot positions. Closing the circle, these Turkish/Turkish Cypriot reactions raised Greek Cypriot support for the deployment of the missiles. In short, the complex interactions in the EU-Greece-Turkey-Cyprus quadrangle interlocked in a vicious circle of escalation, antagonism and intransigence in 1996-98. Against all hopes and expectations that 1997 would be 'the year of Cyprus' (Commission, 1997a), the 1996-98 period witnessed the lowest level of confidence and reconciliation between the two communities since the 1974 partition.

### The Short-lived Thaw: 1999-2001

In the light of progress in Cyprus' accession path, by mid-1999 the US and the UK in particular felt that a new initiative was necessary to re-launch the Cyprus talks, deadlocked since August 1997. Their first move was made at the G-8 meeting in Cologne in June 1999. The G-8 invited the parties to resume negotiations without preconditions. This initiative was immediately followed up by the UN Security Council in Resolution 1250 (UNSC, 1999). Immediately, the UNSG Kofi Annan invited the parties to re-launch the talks on the basis of Resolution 1250. The obstacle that needed to be circumvented was the question of recognition, given Denktaş's demand for negotiations on a state-to-state basis. The etiquette row was resolved in November 1999 by opting for proximity rather than direct talks between the parties.

The re-launch of proximity talks occurred in the context of an important shift in EU positions towards Turkey. Building on the tentative opening of the 1998 Cardiff European Council, the EU's Turkey policy began to change by mid-1999. This culminated in the decision of extending EU candidacy to Turkey at the Helsinki European Council in December 1999. The Helsinki Council abandoned the 1997 Luxembourg position. Turkey was not only 'eligible' to EU candidacy, but was recognized as a candidate state 'destined to join the Union on the basis of the same criteria as applied to other candidate states' (European Council, 1999, paragraph 12). Turkey's formal inclusion in the enlargement process entailed benefiting from a single framework for financial assistance and an Accession Partnership, as well as from inclusion in Community programmes and agencies. In addition, the Helsinki decision foresaw an extension of the customs union to services and public procurement and the receipt of financial transfers due to Turkey under the customs union agreement (€177 million per year). Indeed in 2000 Turkey received €209 million in financial transfers as well as €30 million in emergency assistance and €575 million in EIB projects.

However, the Helsinki decision retained a gap between Turkey and the other candidates, including Cyprus. As well as granting Turkey candidacy, the Helsinki Council also removed the distinction between the 'screening' and 'negotiation' stages in the enlargement process. Hence, with the exception of Turkey, the other twelve candidates were formally put in the same category, i.e., they were all included in the 'negotiation' stage. EU decisions on each of the twelve would be made on the grounds of their individual progress in the adoption of the *acquis*. Turkey instead was left in a formal category of its own. On the basis that Turkey did not comply with the Copenhagen political criteria, accession negotiations were not opened.

The Helsinki European Council also took a crucial decision concerning Cyprus. The Presidency conclusions stated that 'if no settlement has been reached by the completion of the accession negotiations, the Council's decision on accession will be made without the above being a precondition. In this the Council will take into account all relevant factors' (European Council, 1999, paragraph 9b). In other words, while the 1994-98 period was characterized by the lifting of conditionality for the initiation of accession negotiations, the Helsinki Council lifted conditionality for the eventual membership of Cyprus. However, the European Council was adamant not to give the impression that the lifting of conditionality entailed Cyprus' automatic accession. '(A)ll relevant factors' could have meant that accession could have been stalled if the absence of a solution was due to an intransigent Greek Cypriot attitude. Yet neither was this interpretation spelt out, nor did the European Council call for any change in Greek Cypriot positions.

Since the Helsinki European Council, EU actors have taken several key decisions concerning Turkey. The Helsinki decision initiated Turkey's long path towards full membership. In July 2000, the Commission proposed a single financial framework for the Accession Partnership with Turkey (amounting to €177 million in 2000). Although aid to Turkey was still not comparable to that received per capita by other candidates, it represented a significant rise from the 1996-99 period where the annual average EU aid to Turkey had been €90 million. In March 2001 the Council agreed on an Accession Partnership with Turkey (Council of Ministers, 2001). The purpose of the document was to set out the reform priorities necessary for Turkey's fulfilment of the Copenhagen criteria, and the conditional financial means to assist these reforms.

Nevertheless, the Helsinki euphoria in EU-Turkey relations was short-lived, as new problems surfaced on the political agenda. First was the reference to the Armenian genocide in a European Parliament Report on Turkey in October 2000, followed by the recognition of the genocide in the French Parliament in January

2001. Tensions rose further with the Commission's first publication of the Accession Partnership document in November 2000, which included a reference to Cyprus under the list of short-term political conditions. Even more acute was the dispute over Turkey's role in European Security and Defence Policy (ESDP), which lasted until December 2002 (Tocci and Houben, 2001).

With regards to Cyprus, over the course of 2000-01 EU statements made it increasingly clear that the Helsinki decision almost assured Cyprus' membership in 2004. In the light of the continuing stalemate on the island, the fast progress in accession negotiations with Cyprus, and Greece's threat not to ratify an enlargement which excluded Cyprus, by late 2001 EU leaders recurrently mentioned the 'inevitability' of Cyprus' accession in 2004. In October 2001, Enlargement Commissioner Gunter Verheugen declared that enlargement was 'not conceivable' without Cyprus (*Kathimerini*, 2001). Shortly afterwards Commission President Romano Prodi declared that 'Cyprus will join the EU and will be among the first candidate countries to do so' (*Cyprus Weekly*, 2001a). By mid-2001 the formal abandonment of conditionality as put in Helsinki had become a substantive accepted reality in Brussels.

The Helsinki Council was the second 'historic compromise' in EU policies towards Cyprus and Turkey. While the most important obstacle to Cyprus' membership was explicitly removed, Turkey was given the important, albeit still uncertain, prospect of membership. In the course of 2000-01, the effect of the Helsinki double deal was diluted, as new problems re-emerged in Turkey-EU relations, and the lifting of conditionality on the Greek Cypriot side became increasingly accepted within the Union. The short-lived Helsinki honeymoon had critical effects on the development of the conflict.

Between December 1999 and November 2000 the UN held five rounds of proximity talks. But round after round, the talks appeared to make negligible progress towards opening direct talks, let alone towards a settlement. Indeed the Secretary General later defined the process as one of 'procedural wrangling', 'verbal gymnastics' and 'shadow boxing' (UNSG, 2003, paragraph 23). The UNSG Special Representative Alvaro de Soto engaged in shuttle diplomacy between the sides and worked on a set of bridging proposals. The substance of these proposals was disclosed in the form of 'oral remarks' during the fifth round of proximity talks in November 2000. In December 2000 the Turkish Cypriot side declared its unilateral withdrawal from the talks. The peace process was once again plunged into deadlock.

Particularly during the summer of 2001, UN, US, European Commission and UK officials exerted considerable pressure on Turkey and the Turkish Cypriots to return to proximity talks. Yet despite the meetings in August 2001 between Denktaş and both Commissioner Verheugen and UNSG Annan, the Turkish Cypriot leader rejected a return to the talks on the grounds of insufficient 'common ground' between the parties (TRNC, 2001a).

The positions and attitudes of the principal parties were responsible for the outcome of the talks. But to what extent did EU decisions concerning both Turkey and Cyprus impinge on the parties' positions and attitudes? Evidence suggests that the decisions taken in Helsinki and thereafter were major determinants of Greek

Cypriot and Turkish Cypriot positions, which led both to the initiation of the proximity talks and to their ultimate failure.

*Turkish and Turkish Cypriot Positions*

Domestic changes in Turkey set the stage for the Turkish Cypriot re-engagement in the peace process. The Turkish governing coalition in power since April 1999, comprising the centre-left Democratic Left Party (DSP), the liberal Motherland Party (ANAP) and the right-wing National Action Party (MHP), was keen to portray itself as a reformist and pro-European administration. The new government, and in particular Foreign Minister Ismail Cem, was also willing to succeed in its rapprochement with Greece, initiated in August-September 1999. There were also moderate, pro-settlement forces in the Turkish Cypriot government, represented by the centre-left TKP as the junior coalition partner of the nationalist UBP since the 1998 elections.

Domestic changes and the nascent Greek-Turkish rapprochement contributed to greater optimism in Turkey-EU relations and a positive build-up to the Helsinki European Council. This was a key determinant of the Turkish Cypriot acceptance to participate in proximity talks. Following UNSC Resolution 1250, the Turkish Cypriots were faced with a choice. They either refused the UN's invitation, in which case EU resistance to membership of a divided Cyprus would reduce; or they accepted it, in which case European support for Turkey's EU candidacy would rise. From a Turkish Cypriot standpoint, accepting participation in the proximity talks also entailed low costs. The talks implied that the parties would not be forced into substantive negotiations immediately. In addition, the wording of Resolution 1250 concerning previous UN resolutions was looser than in the past: all issues were on the table and a settlement only had to 'take into account' (rather than be 'based on') past UN resolutions in favour of the single sovereignty and international personality of Cyprus (UNSC, 1999). Hence, even if the Turkish Cypriot side was unwilling to shift its positions, participating in the talks entailed low costs and added momentum in favour of a positive EU decision towards Turkey.

The Helsinki decision to extend candidacy to Turkey was well-received by the Turkish government. This had a positive effect on Turkish and Turkish Cypriot positions in the conflict. Despite the fact that the European Council had taken an important decision against Turkish Cypriot interests (i.e., concerning Cyprus' unconditional EU accession), Denktaş's tone post-Helsinki was conciliatory. In December 1999 (one week after the European Council), he declared that together with a Turkish guarantee on the state and territory, there could be a reunification on the island within the EU: 'call it a federation or a confederation...the name is not important' (*TDN*, 1999).

However, during the proximity talks, Turkish and Turkish Cypriot authorities showed minimal signs of moderation. The Turkish Cypriot leadership's repression of the anti-establishment, pro-European and pro-settlement forces intensified. The opposition newspaper *Avrupa* (Europe) came under increasing harassment throughout 2000 and 2001. In June 2000, the Turkish Cypriot government imposed restrictions on the movement of UNFICYP in northern Cyprus. In July 2000, the UNFICYP reported the movement of Turkish troops 300 metres into the demilitarized buffer zone of Strovilia. Finally in the summer of 2001, the UBP-TKP governing coalition fell with the open clash between the TKP and the Turkish military due to the former's call for greater independence from Turkey and a return to negotiations.

The Turkish Cypriot withdrawal from the talks also cast doubt on their readiness to reach an early settlement. The official reason for the withdrawal was the content of the November 2000 UN 'oral remarks', that allegedly diluted past references to the political equality of the Turkish Cypriots. Following a meeting with the Turkish National Security Council, the TRNC Assembly voted to withdraw from the proximity talks in December. Denktaş in turn moved back to his pre-Helsinki position stating that Cyprus' EU membership would only be possible following Turkey's entry.

However, it is debatable whether the substance of the oral remarks was the cause of the Turkish Cypriot withdrawal from the talks. Neither did the oral remarks mark a significant shift in the UN's positions, nor were they full-fledged proposals requiring a response. Had the substance of the remarks been the main source of Turkish Cypriot discontent, the leadership could have objected to them while persisting in proximity talks. The withdrawal from the talks suggested a far more deep-rooted reluctance to reach an early settlement within the EU.

The reluctance to conclude an early settlement was also highlighted by the renewed Turkish-Turkish Cypriot integration efforts. In January 2001 the Turkey-TRNC Association Council signed two cooperation agreements. The Economic and Financial Cooperation Protocol envisaged a financial transfer package of $350 million to be disbursed over the course of three years. In the second agreement the parties agreed to simplify bureaucratic procedures, subsidize private investment in northern Cyprus, harmonize trade laws, develop energy cables, include northern Cyprus in Turkey's 'tourist regions', facilitate the conversion of Turkish Cypriot into Turkish citizenship and allow reciprocal rights of property acquisition.

Finally, over the summer/autumn of 2001, Turkish and Turkish Cypriot threats became more frequent. In May 2001 Prime Minister Ecevit proposed a velvet divorce à la Czechoslovakia for Cyprus (Pope, 2001).[3] In November Turkish Foreign Minister Cem declared that 'definite decisions' and 'drastic measures' would have to be taken by Turkey in the event of Cyprus' entry into the EU (Kanli, 2001). Asked to clarify Cem's statement, Ecevit stated that Turkey could annex the TRNC following Cyprus' EU membership (*Cyprus News*, 2001). Denktaş went further, arguing that the EU's admission of a divided Cyprus could trigger a Greek-Turkish war (*Cyprus Weekly*, 2001b).

The questionable depth of the pro-reform nature of the Turkish government and of the Greek-Turkish rapprochement, within the wider context of problematic EU-Turkey relations in the post-Helsinki period, had a negative impact on the proximity talks. An underlying Turkish/Turkish Cypriot reluctance to reach a

---

[3] Ecevit, who had been Prime Minister at the time of the 1974 military intervention, was a long time supporter of full partition.

settlement in the EU may have been present back in December 1999, when the proximity talks were launched. However in late 1999 the optimism in Turkey-EU relations set the scene for the re-launch of the peace process. After five rounds of UN shuttle diplomacy the context had altered. On the one hand, the passing of time raised the potential costs of engaging in the process. Proximity talks were no longer sufficient and third parties expected progress towards a settlement. On the other hand, the euphoria in Turkey-EU relations subsided by the autumn of 2000 as new disputes emerged between the two. A change in context from the autumn of 1999 to that of 2000 thus led the Turkish Cypriot and Turkish sides to reveal their reluctance to allow the parallel reunification and EU accession of the island. As in the case of the 1995 'historic compromise', the Helsinki *de facto* package was insufficient to create genuine and long-lasting Turkish and Turkish Cypriot readiness to seek a settlement within the EU. With the parallel developments in Cyprus-EU relations, Turkish and Turkish Cypriot decision-makers dug in their heels and opted for brinkmanship.

*Greek Cypriot Positions*

In 1999-2001, the Greek Cypriot position was not overtly uncompromising. However neither did the RoC display genuine willingness to reach an early settlement on the island prior to EU membership. The most evident illustration of this was the Greek Cypriot reaction to the UNSG's opening statement of the fourth round of proximity talks. In September 2000, Kofi Annan referred to the 'political equality' of the two communities, to the principle that 'each leadership could only represent its own community' and to the aim of establishing a 'new partnership' on the island (UNSG, 2000). The concept of political equality was not new and had been endorsed and defined by the UN since the late 1980s. Yet the Greek Cypriot leadership reacted strongly to the statement. Clerides postponed the talks for two days awaiting clarification. The UN did not alter its wording, and in October 2000 the RoC House of Representatives defined the statement 'outside the letter and the spirit of the framework of the talks and the basis of a solution of the Cyprus problem as determined by UN principles, decisions and resolutions'. It claimed that the RoC 'will neither accept nor discuss a framework for the solution of the Cyprus problem containing confederal elements'(RoC, 2000a).

    But unlike the Turkish Cypriot side, Greek Cypriot officials did not withdraw from the peace process. In fact, the blunt Turkish Cypriot withdrawal aided Greek Cypriot efforts to appear moderate. The spotlight was on the other side. The Greek Cypriots could not be held responsible for the failure of the talks. In addition, the absence of inter-communal negotiations allowed the Greek Cypriot authorities to present moderate positions to international audiences. As put by Foreign Minister Cassoulides in November 2001: 'neither the UNSG nor others who support his efforts are asking anything of us, either to make any moves or concessions to entice Denktaş to return to the talks ...the ball is not in our court' (Christou, 2001).

**The Approaching Deadline of Accession and the Re-launch of Talks: 2002-04**

With the complete stalemate in negotiations in 2001, the international community increasingly condemned Turkey for the Cyprus impasse. The approaching deadline of EU accession was finally raising concerns both in the EU and in the US about the implications of the accession of a divided Cyprus.

In response, in November 2001 Rauf Denktaş invited Glafcos Clerides for a 'heart-to-heart' talk in northern Nicosia. Reciprocal dinner invitations set the stage for a restart of direct talks, stalled since 1997. Talks, in the presence of UN Special Assistant de Soto, began in January 2002. They were intended to reach an agreement by June, so as to allow the December 2002 European Council to invite the whole island to join the Union.

During the conduct of the direct talks, the role of the UN Secretary General and in particular of the small team under de Soto was critical. The UN team worked in close contact with the British Foreign Office representative Lord Hannay and to a lesser extent the American equivalent Tom Weston. The Commission and the member states continued to play a passive role in the peace process. However, Commission officials intensified their communication with the UN mediators, informing the UN team about the ways in which the terms of a settlement could be accommodated within the EU. In turn the UN persuaded the Commission and the member states to be more forthcoming in their statements concerning the accommodation of the terms of an agreement.[4]

The most critical contribution of the UN team was the publication of a comprehensive settlement proposal in November 2002 (a second version was published later the same month). The Annan Plan was published as the deadline for an agreement in June 2002 was missed and it became evident that the principal parties would not reach an agreement alone. The proposed Plan, including a Foundation Agreement and all accompanying laws and treaties, represented the most detailed and only comprehensive attempt by the international community to advance a settlement since inter-communal fighting erupted in 1963. The aim was to reach an agreement by or at the Copenhagen European Council on 12-13 December 2002.

The Copenhagen European Council took key decisions affecting Turkey and Cyprus. It concluded that if the December 2004 European Council deemed that Turkey fulfilled the Copenhagen criteria, accession negotiations with Turkey 'will start' 'without delay' (European Council, 2002b). The European Council also invited 'Cyprus' (not the 'Republic of Cyprus') to join the Union. The Presidency conclusions called for a continuation of negotiations until 28 February 2003. This would have been the last attempt to secure the accession of a reunified island prior to the signature of the Treaty of Accession.

The direct talks under UN auspices resumed in January but again failed to deliver a settlement by February 2003, despite the publication of a third version of

---

[4] On 14 May 2001, at an EU Foreign Ministers meeting in Brussels, UNSG Kofi Annan urged the member states and the Commission to account for the critical need to accept special arrangements in the case of Cyprus.

the Annan Plan. This was followed by another failure to reach an agreement on 10 March 2003 in The Hague. In The Hague, the UN Secretary General expected a response to his request to submit the third Plan to referendum, despite a lack of agreement between the leaders. The Turkish Cypriot side rejected the request. The UNSG was clear in his prerequisites for a restart of UN-mediated talks. Either the parties mutually reached an agreement on the basis of the Annan Plan or they accepted to refer the Plan, as it stood, to separate popular referenda. After The Hague meeting, the peace process plunged into deadlock.

In the meantime, under the Greek Presidency, the 'Republic of Cyprus' (rather than 'Cyprus') and nine other candidate states signed the Accession Treaty in Athens in April 2003. Protocol No.10 of the Treaty provided for a suspension of the application of the *acquis* in northern Cyprus.

In the months following the signature of the Treaty of Accession, the Commission half-heartedly attempted to entice the Turkish Cypriots through an aid and trade package. The Commission offered €12 million in aid and stated that it would accept Turkish Cypriot exports documented by the Turkish Cypriot Chamber of Commerce, provided the goods were inspected (and certified in the case of agricultural products) by the 'appropriate authorities'. With the outright Greek Cypriot rejection of exports through the Turkish Cypriot port of Famagusta and their insistence that the RoC represented the only 'appropriate authority', the Commission trade offer was left pending.

The window of opportunity during the year of ratification of the Accession Treaty by national parliaments was missed. But the process was re-launched in 2004. On 10 February 2004, the UNSG invited the parties to New York to respond to his unchanged request: either the parties resumed negotiations aiming to reach an agreement on the basis of the Annan Plan and/or they agreed that the Plan, finalized by the Secretary General, would be put to separate referenda. An agreement was reached in New York and it envisaged three phases (UNSG, 2004a). In the first stage direct talks between the leaderships would resume in Nicosia in the presence of Alvaro de Soto. If the talks failed to reach an agreement by 22 March 2004, the community leaderships would be joined by the leaders of Greece and Turkey to bridge the remaining gaps. In the case of persisting deadlock by 29 March, the Annan Plan, finalized by the Secretary General, would be submitted to separate referenda before the accession of Cyprus on 1 May 2004.

The first phase began in February and failed to seal an agreement. The parties exchanged mutually exclusive position papers on their proposed changes to the Annan Plan. On 24 March the two community leaderships were joined by representatives of Greece and Turkey in the Swiss resort of Burgenstock. In Switzerland almost equal emphasis was put on the question of accommodating the terms of a settlement within the EU *acquis* and on the actual substance of the UN Plan. The former question was the concern that the Plan, with all of its deviations from the EU *acquis,* would be undermined by individual cases brought forward (by Greek Cypriots) to the European Court of Justice.

Substantive four-party talks again failed to deliver a deal and on 29 March the UNSG presented the fourth version of the Plan, to be followed by a fifth version on 31 March. The separate referendum took place on the 24 April on the basis of the fifth Plan. 64.9 percent of the Turkish Cypriots voted in favour of the Plan. 76.8 percent of the Greek Cypriots rejected it.

## Turkish Cypriot Positions and the Role of Turkey

The direct talks in 2002 were re-launched following a turnaround in the Turkish Cypriot position, supported by the Turkish establishment. Apart from the re-launch of the peace process, there was a new tone of moderation in Turkish Cypriot statements. Denktaş's November 2001 letter to the UNSG made no reference to the establishment of a confederation. Denktaş advocated two politically equal partner states that would form a new partnership with single international personality. Most critically, Denktaş accepted that the partnership would join the EU as a single fully functioning member state before Turkey (TRNC, 2001b, paragraph 11).

During negotiations there were further signs of moderation in the Turkish Cypriot positions, as shown by the April 2002 proposals and subsequent speeches (TRNC, 2002a; Olgun, 2002b). The Turkish Cypriots warmed to the concept of a Basic Law rather than a Treaty between the partner states, as would normally be the case in a confederation. They endorsed the concept of a five-year constitutional review mechanism that would allow for greater levels of integration. They foresaw a common state equipped with legislative, executive and judicial organs dealing with a limited set of functions. By September 2002 the Turkish Cypriot team had accepted ten central ministries including a finance ministry responsible for federal finance. In June-July 2002, the Turkish Cypriots were keen to discuss aspects of the Belgian federal model. A September 2002 paper endorsed the concept of 'triple sovereignty': 'while the co-founder states will retain a layer of sovereignty in the form of residual powers, one layer of sovereignty will be assigned to the Partnership state and another layer transferred to Brussels as a result of accession to the EU' (Olgun, 2002c).

But in the summer of 2002, Turkish politics went through a major upheaval. With Prime Minister Ecevit's illness in May-June 2002, internal tensions mounted and culminated with the departure of 63 parliamentarians from the ruling DSP. With an effective minority government, the country moved towards early elections scheduled for November 2002. The political crisis in Turkey had critical effects both on the Cyprus negotiations and on EU-Turkey relations. The political crisis led to the replacement of Foreign Minister Cem by hawkish Sına Şükrü Gürel and created the necessary political vacuum which favoured a retention of the status quo in Cyprus. In parallel, the June target for a settlement was rejected by Denktaş. On several constitutional questions, the Turkish Cypriot side refused to make concessions. Perhaps most problematic of all was its refusal to discuss territorial adjustments before securing the 'sovereign equality' of northern Cyprus. Contrary to the letter and spirit of the Union, the Turkish Cypriot side proposed border points between the two partner states.

By late August 2002, Denktaş publicly announced the possibility of a failure of negotiations: 'if talks do not work by the end of the year, and if the EU makes the mistake of saying they will accept Cyprus now as it is, then we have to look for new alternatives for our future' (Tezgor, 2002). Indeed Ankara and Lefkoşa discussed a protocol merging foreign affairs, defence and monetary policies. In September 2002 Turkey and the TRNC signed three cooperation agreements. Denktaş also delayed by three months the work of technical committees on the drafting of federal laws and treaties.

There appeared to be new hope for a breakthrough following the 3 November 2002 general elections in Turkey, which brought to power the Justice and Development Party (AKP), the progressive offshoot of the banned Virtue Party led by former Istanbul mayor Tayyıp Erdoğan. The AKP won a landslide victory gaining 363 seats in the 550-seat Assembly. The only other party to pass the ten percent threshold and enter parliament was the centre-left Republican People's Party (CHP). The elections led to the first single-party government in fifteen years. With the AKP's victory and the publication of the UN Plan, pressure on Denktaş from both Turkish Cypriots and from Ankara mounted. The declared aim was to reach a settlement at the European Council in Copenhagen.

The political crisis in Turkey and the ensuing elections also affected critically EU-Turkey relations. Despite the political turmoil, on 3 August 2002 the Turkish Assembly succeeded in passing an extensive EU harmonization package to improve Turkey's human rights and democracy standards. With the passing of the reforms, Turkish pressure on EU capitals for a 'date' to begin accession negotiations mounted. However, the style and substance of Turkish demands changed after the general elections. The former DSP-MHP-ANAP government had raised expectations too high, arguing that either 'the EU sets a date for accession talks or it declines to do so. There is no third way. The EU setting forth any other conditions to begin accession negotiations is unacceptable' (Şükrü Gürel, 2002). The AKP government, while disappointed at not having obtained a firm date to start accession negotiations, reacted positively to the conclusions of the Copenhagen Council. As put by Erdoğan: 'EU-Turkey relations have become clearer and on the right track … the reason why the decision did not fully satisfy our expectation is that we raised the bar too high' (*TDN*, 2002).

Yet while the Turkish government reacted positively to the Copenhagen Council's decision, it refused both to sign the Annan Plan and to allow it to be referred to referendum. Following the failure of talks in The Hague, the Turkish Cypriot leadership proposed a set of confidence building measures in late March 2003 that included the opening of the border between north and south. Neither the Greek Cypriot side nor the international community responded. The Turkish Cypriot leadership thus proceeded with a spectacular unilateral confidence building measure. On 23 April 2003 it opened the border closed since 1974. The measure led to a huge flux of Cypriots crossing the green line. The decision was taken in circumstances of growing domestic pressure and international condemnation. The growing popular criticism and international condemnation of the Turkish Cypriot leadership induced Denktaş to act. However, the action did not compromise Turkish Cypriot bargaining positions. On the contrary, the unilateral measure served both to improve the economic situation in the north and to highlight the existence of two separate states.

Regardless of the commotion generated by the opening of the green line, all attention focused on the TRNC legislative elections scheduled for December 2003.

The Turkish Cypriot President and the Turkish Cypriot government composed of the nationalist UBP-DP coalition had ruled out a solution based on the Annan Plan. However, the TRNC establishment had come under mounting pressure from the opposition and civil society, which successfully mobilized large sections of the population in favour of the Plan and EU membership in a series of demonstrations in December 2003 and January 2004.

However, the parliamentary elections of 14 December 2003 did not result in a clear victory for the centre-left parties. The two parties on the nationalist side, the UBP led by Derviş Eroğlu and the DP led by Serdar Denktaş gained an equal number of seats as the two centre-left parties, the CTP led by Mehmet Ali Talat and the BDH led by Mustafa Akıncı. In January 2004 a new government was formed between the centre-left (and pro-Annan Plan) CTP and the centre-right (and sceptical of the Annan Plan) DP.

Thereafter at a meeting on 23 January 2004, the Turkish National Security Council declared itself in favour of a resumption of negotiations taking the Annan Plan as a 'reference point' (and not as a 'basis for an agreement'). The Turkish position shifted further two days later when at the World Economic Summit in Davos, Prime Minister Erdoğan conveyed to the UNSG his readiness to allow the Secretary General to 'fill the blanks' in the event that mutually agreed changes to the Plan could not be reached.

Yet the most spectacular move from the Turkish side occurred on 11 February during the meeting at the UN headquarters. In New York, the Turkish side tabled a proposal for a three-stage peace process. The proposal was elaborated and adopted by the parties. Key to the proposal was the acceptance of the two key principles demanded by the Secretary General. The Turkish and Turkish Cypriot sides accepted both that the UNSG could 'fill the blanks' in the final version of the Annan Plan, and that the Plan would be put to referendum before 1 May 2004, despite the absence of an agreement between the parties.

In the resumed direct talks in Nicosia, the Turkish Cypriot side was represented by Chief Negotiator Rauf Denktaş, and by the two principal exponents of the newly formed government: namely, Prime Minister Mehmet Ali Talat (CTP) and Deputy Prime Minister Serdar Denktaş (DP). Rauf Denktaş, as well as his son, Serdar, were highly sceptical of the Plan. Indeed Rauf Denktaş had accepted the Turkish proposal in New York only under heavy pressure by the Turkish government.

Despite internal differences, the newly formed team agreed to work together seeking what in their view constituted an improvement of the Plan. In the course of the talks, the Turkish Cypriot side presented its proposed modifications to the Plan. Some of the major demands concerned voting rights within the Senate (based on community affiliation rather than residency), a reduction in the share of Greek Cypriots allowed to settle and own property in the north and specified support for the rehabilitation of those Turkish Cypriots affected by the territorial readjustments. The Turkish Cypriot side also demanded that adequate legal assurances were provided by the EU to assure that the terms of an agreement were incorporated into EU primary law.

As the first stage of the talks moved into the second, the Turkish Cypriot leader Denktaş abandoned the process. In view of the (expected) rejection of the Turkish Cypriot proposals by the Greek Cypriot side and the general trends in the UN-mediated talks, Denktaş manifested his rejection of the process and of the Plan by declaring that he would not attend the second stage in Switzerland. Nevertheless, the Turkish and Turkish Cypriot governments did not pull out of the process. They attended the talks in Burgenstock and supported the final version of the Annan Plan.

As the parties returned from Switzerland, the different actors in northern Cyprus and Turkey began positioning themselves in the referendum campaign. Rauf Denktaş had already declared his intention to campaign for the 'no' vote, declaring that the Plan and EU membership would mark the end of the Turkish Cypriots and of Turkey. He was joined by the nationalist UBP. Senior coalition party CTP as well as opposition parties BDH, ÇABP and several civil society movements campaigned for the 'yes' vote. Junior coalition party DP was internally split and refrained from taking a position on the Plan. In Turkey, the government signed their approval to submit the Plan to referendum. It was generally understood that the AKP government supported a settlement based on the Annan Plan V, while the opposition CHP rejected it. Interestingly, the Turkish Armed Forces refrained from passing judgement on the referendum question. Chief of General Staff Hilmi Özkök simply stated that the Turkish Parliament and the Turkish Cypriot people had the final say on the matter and 'we wholeheartedly believe they will make the right decision' (*TDN*, 2004a). In the referendum while 35 percent of the Turkish Cypriots rejected the Plan, an overwhelming 65 percent accepted it.

*Greek Cypriot Positions and the Role of Greece*

The Greek Cypriot leadership immediately accepted the Turkish Cypriot proposal for a resumption of direct talks in December 2001. However the Greek Cypriot team was also reluctant to engage in a serious give-and-take process. While their own proposals differed marginally from those of the past, their replies to Turkish Cypriot proposals were dismissed as simple rehashes of old two-state ideas (RoC, 2002). The Greek Cypriots initially displayed little flexibility on the questions of sovereignty and state succession. On sovereignty, the Greek Cypriot side categorically rejected the concept of shared sovereignty. It also dismissed the idea of the establishment of a new state. Perhaps most problematic of all, the Greek Cypriot leadership did little to prepare the population for the compromises entailed in a settlement. As such, the public was deluded into thinking that a settlement would lead to a reinstatement of the status quo ante. Hence, the wide public opposition to the Annan Plan upon publication in the winter of 2002.[5]

However, as negotiations proceeded, the Greek Cypriot team led by Clerides appeared to engage more genuinely in the process. Marking a clear shift from earlier positions, it accepted a continuing, albeit significantly reduced, presence of

---

[5] In late November 2002 opposition to the Plan in south Cyprus stood at 64 percent. The results were quoted in *Cyprus Weekly*, 2002.

Turkish forces, a retention of the Treaties of Guarantee and Alliance and some degree of property exchange. It was open to discuss the extension of citizenship and residence of some Turkish immigrants. Ultimately it also displayed flexibility on the thorny question of state succession. When the UN Plan was presented, both the Greek government and Clerides' team accepted to negotiate on the basis of the Plan. Following the Copenhagen Council, Clerides indicated to Denktaş that if they were unable to reach an agreement by the end of February, he was ready to accept the Plan as it stood (UNSG, 2003). Eighty-three-year-old Clerides' last-minute decision in early January 2003 to stand for re-election in February 2003 with a fourteen-month mandate to conclude negotiations also indicated his willingness to seal a deal.

Yet Clerides lost the elections in the first round to Tassos Papadopoulos in February 2003. Papadopoulos was known for his nationalist positions. Indeed on his electoral victory night he stated that he would 'fight for the right of all displaced persons to return in conditions of safety' (Christou, 2003a). Prior to the publication of the Annan Plan III, Papadopoulos called for radical changes, including the full liberalization of the three freedoms (Hadjipapas, 2003). In The Hague in March 2003, given the Turkish Cypriot rejection, it is difficult to assess the implications of Papadopoulos' conditional acceptance of the Secretary General's request. Yet most indicative of a more hardline attitude have been Papadopoulos' statements and positions following the signature of the Accession Treaty in April 2003. In late 2003, Papadopoulos openly declared that he would not have signed the Plan in The Hague without appropriate account being taken of his concerns (Christou, 2003b).

When the Turkish side proposed the three-stage peace process in February 2004, the Greek Cypriot team reluctantly accepted. With the re-launch of the direct talks in Nicosia, the Greek Cypriot side also tabled its proposals for changes in the Plan (CEPS, 2004). These included the full compliance of the Plan with the EU *acquis* and the finalization of all federal laws and parliament ratifications before the referenda. The Greek Cypriot side also called for increases in the members of the Presidential Council (from six to nine), in the Presidency term, in territorial readjustments and in the number of Turkish settlers and troops that would return to Turkey.

When the negotiations moved to the second stage in Switzerland, the Greek Cypriot team was joined by Greek representatives. Yet since the 7 March 2004 parliamentary elections, Greece was no longer represented by the Simitis PASOK government. The elections had brought to power New Democracy under the leadership of Costas Karamanlis, ending the almost uninterrupted PASOK rule since 1981. On the whole the new Greek government, while not acting as proactively in favour of a solution, did not shift significantly from PASOK's positions on the conflict. But neither did it attempt to deter the Greek Cypriot leader from rejecting the Plan.

In fact upon his return to Cyprus, Papadopoulos flatly rejected the Plan. In April 2004 Papadopoulos declared to the Greek Cypriot public: 'I call on you to reject the Annan Plan. I call on you to say a strong "no", I am asking you to defend what is right, your dignity and history' (Christou, 2004). His party DIKO also rejected the Plan, together with the socialist EDEK. To the disappointment of many moderates, leftist AKEL initially called for the improbable delay of a referendum and ultimately rejected the Plan two days before the referendum. Opposition party DISY backed the Plan and most notably former President Clerides declared his strong support for the 'yes' campaign. Former President and former EU Chief Negotiator Vassiliou (EDI) also backed the Plan. In Greece, while the Karamanlis ND government refrained from taking a clear stance on the referendum question, former Foreign Minister and PASOK leader George Papandreou openly supported the 'yes' campaign.

Unfortunately the positions of the current leadership in south Cyprus reflected widespread popular opinion. While a mere 24 percent of the Greek Cypriots voted in favour of the Plan, an overwhelming 76 percent majority rejected it.

This chapter has sought to outline the major developments between 1988 and May 2004 in EU-Cyprus and EU-Turkey relations on the one hand and the evolution of the conflict on the other. Over the course of the 1990s, the EU factor in the context of accession became the major external determinant of the evolution of the conflict. Up until November 2001, EU policies towards Cyprus and Turkey developed in parallel with the negative evolution of the conflict. Tracing back the major developments in the EU-Cyprus-Greece-Turkey quadrangle between 1988 and late 2001, what emerges is that EU decisions triggered a hardening of the Turkish and Turkish Cypriot positions, while not deterring antagonizing Greek Cypriot policies. The policies of the principal parties were intricately related to developments in both the domestic and international realms. However, accounting for these developments does not detract from the conclusion that the EU represented the major external structural determinant of the conflict and its deterioration over the course of the decade.

The 2002-04 negotiations appeared to mark a change in the negative dynamics of earlier years. The approaching deadline of Cyprus' accession seemed to create a window of opportunity for a settlement prior to EU membership. However, the intense efforts between January 2002 and May 2004 failed to deliver an agreement. On 1 May 2004 the Republic of Cyprus entered the EU, leaving behind the Turkish Cypriots on the other side of the green line.

One may legitimately ask what would have happened in Cyprus had the EU factor not come into play. While no conclusive answer can be provided, what may be tentatively concluded is that, excluding the EU factor, there is no evidence to suggest that other structural determinants both within the island, the region or the international system significantly exacerbated the conflict. At most, in the absence of the EU factor, the stalemate on the island would have persisted. But as this chapter has shown, developments between the late 1980s and 1993 suggested that some progress was being made in the context of the UN to find a settlement to the drawn-out conflict on the island. This progress was overturned by 1994 in the context of the EU's entry onto the scene. The next serious attempts at reunification were not made until January 2002, and even then, they failed to secure an agreement prior to EU accession. Reading in between the lines of this account it is possible to detect why EU decisions (unwittingly) triggered the deterioration of the conflict. The next chapter will delve deeper into this question, attempting to uncover the reasons why EU policies in the framework of accession failed to catalyse a settlement in Cyprus.

# References

Bahceli, T. (1999), 'Turkish Cypriots, the EU Option and Resolving Ethnic Conflict in Cyprus', in A. Theophanous, N. Peristianis and A. Ioannou (eds.), *Cyprus and the EU*, Intercollege, Nicosia. pp.107-124.

Bıçak, H.A. (1997), 'Recent Developments in Cyprus-EU relations', in E. Doğramaci et al. (eds.), *Proceedings of the First International Conference on Cypriot Studies*, Eastern Mediterranean University, Famagusta.

Bölükbaşı, S. (1995), 'Boutros-Ghali's Cyprus Initiative in 1992: Why did it Fail?', *Middle Eastern Studies*, Vol.31, No.3, pp.460-482.

Brewin, C. (2000), *The European Union and Cyprus*, Eothen, Huntingdon.

CEPS (2004), *Turkey in Europe Monitor*, Issue 3, March 2004, CEPS, Brussels.

Christou, J. (2001), 'Cassoulides Warns Window of Opportunity will Close Soon', *Cyprus Mail*, 14 November 2001.

Christou, J. (2003a), 'What chance of a solution now?', *Cyprus Mail*, 18 February 2003.

Christou, J. (2003b), 'Would he have Signed? Papadopoulos Reopens Doubts over Annan Plan', *Cyprus Mail*, 26 November 2003.

Christou, J. (2004), 'Papadopoulos trashes Plan', *Cyprus Mail*, 8 April 2004.

Commission of the EC (1989), *Opinion on Turkey's Request for Accession to the Community*, SEC(89) 2290 final, 18 December 1989, Brussels.

Commission of the EC (1993), *Opinion on the Application for Membership from Cyprus*, COM(93) 313, EC Bulletin 6-1993, Brussels.

Commission of the EC (1997a), *Press Release*, Speech 97/45, Hans Van der Broek Speech at the North Cyprus Young Businessmen Association, Reuter Briefing, 27 February 1997, Brussels.

Commission of the EC (1997b), *Agenda 2000*, 15 July 1997, Extracts available on www.cyprus-eu.org.cy/eng/07_documents/documents003.htm

Council of Ministers of the European Union (1995), General Affairs Council Decision on Cyprus' Accession, 06/03/95C, Presidency Proposal, on www.cyprus-eu.org.cy

Council of Ministers of the European Union (2001), General Affairs Council Decision on the Principles, Priorities, Intermediate Objectives and Conditions in the Accession Partnership with the Republic of Turkey, 24/03/2001, 2001/235/EC, *Official Journal*, L85, 24 March 2001, Brussels.

*Cyprus News* (2001), 'Turkey Threatens to Annex Northern Cyprus', 7 November 2001.

*Cyprus Weekly* (2001a),'Cyprus Will Join', 30 October 2001.

*Cyprus Weekly* (2001b),'Turks Threaten War', 16 November 2001.

*Cyprus Weekly* (2002), 'Greek Cypriot Opposition to UN Plan Grows', 29 November 2002.

Demetriou, M. (1998), 'On the Long Road to Europe and the Short Path to War: Issue-Linkage Politics and the Arms Build-up on Cyprus', *Mediterranean Politics*, Vol.3, No.3, pp.38-51.

Dodd, C. (1999a), 'Confederation, Federation and Sovereignty', *Perceptions - Journal of International Affairs*, Vol.4, No.3, September-November 1999, on www.mfa.gov.tr

European Council (1992), Meeting on 26-27 June 1992 in Lisbon, *Presidency Conclusions.*

European Council (1994), Meeting on 24-25 June 1994 in Corfu, *Presidency Conclusions*, extracts available on www.cyprus-eu.org.cy/eng/07-documents/document004.htm

European Council (1997), Meeting on 12-13 December 1997 in Luxembourg, *Presidency Conclusions*, extracts available on www.cyprus-eu.org.cy/eng/07-documents/document004.htm

European Council (1999), Meeting on 12-13 December 1999 in Helsinki, *Presidency Conclusions*, SN300/99.

European Council (2002b), Meeting on 12-13 December 2002 in Copenhagen, *Presidency Conclusions*, SN 400/02.

European Court of Human Rights (1989), Court Case No.15318/89, Strasbourg.

European Court of Justice (1994), *S.P. Anastasiou Ltd. Versus the UK*, Case C-432/92, ECR3087, Luxembourg.

Hadjipapas, A. (2003), 'Greek Cypriots call for Radical Changes to Annan Plan on Rights and Freedoms', *Cyprus Weekly*, 11 February 2003.

Kanli, Y. (2001), 'Moment of Truth Draws Closer for Cyprus', *Turkish Daily News*, 6 November 2001.

*Kathimerini* (2001), 'EU enlargement with Cyprus or not at all', 25 October 2001.

Kramer, H. (1997), 'The Cyprus Problem and European Security', *Survival*, Vol.39, No.3, pp.16-32.

Mendelson, M. (2001), *Why Cyprus Entry into the EU would be Illegal*, Embassy of the Republic of Turkey, London.

Olgun, E. (2002a), 'Cyprus: Settlement and Membership', Conference Paper presented at the European Parliament on 3 June 2002, Brussels.

Olgun, E. (2002b), 'Some Characteristics of the Belgian State that may Apply to the New Partnership State of Cyprus', Non-paper dated 26 June 2002, Brussels.

Olgun, E. (2002c), 'Significant Openings made by the Turkish Cypriot Side for a Resolution of the Cyprus Issue', Non-paper dated 11 September 2002, Nicosia.

Pope, N. (2001), 'Le Durcissement Turc sur la Question Chypriote Risque de Devenir un Casse-Tête pour les Quinze', *Le Monde*, 31 May 2001.

Psyllides, G. (2002), 'Crunch time in Copenhagen', *Cyprus Mail*, 12 December 2002.

Republic of Cyprus (2000a), *House of Representatives Resolution*, 11 October 2000, Nicosia, www.pio.gov.cy/news/special_issues/special_issue034.htm

Republic of Cyprus (2002), 'Observations of Mr Clerides to the Document of Mr Denktaş, 29/04/2002', Non-paper dated 1 May 2002, Nicosia.

Şükrü Gürel, S. (2002), enews@anatolia.com, 25 October 2002.

Tezgor, G. (2002), 'Denktaş Warns of Deeper Integration if Divided Cyprus Joins EU', *Cyprus Mail*, 28 August 2002.

Theophanous, A. (2001), 'Cyprus, Greece, Turkey and the EU', in F. Attina and S. Stavridis (eds.), *The Barcelona Process and Euro-Mediterranean Issues from Stuttgart to Marseilles*, Università di Catania, Catania, pp.227-247.

Tocci, N. and Houben, M. (2001), 'Accommodating Turkey in ESDP', *Policy Brief No.5*, CEPS, Brussels.

*Turkish Daily News* (1999), 'Denktaş suggests a Cyprus Settlement in the EU', 18 December 1999.

*Turkish Daily News* (2002),'Turkey Happy with Bright Side of the EU Decision', 16 December 2002.

*Turkish Daily News* (2004a), 'Özkök: Final say rests with Parliament, Turkish Cypriots', 14 April 2004.

*Turkish Daily News* (2004b), 'Greek Cypriots face rancour for "no"', 26 April 2004.

Turkish Republic of Northern Cyprus (2001a), 'Objectives and Basic Elements of a Cyprus Settlement', Letter by Rauf Denktaş to the UN Secretary General, Non-paper dated 29 August 2001, Nicosia.

Turkish Republic of Northern Cyprus (2001b), 'Rauf Denktaş's Letter to the UN Secretary General', Non-paper dated 10 November 2001, Nicosia.

Turkish Republic of Northern Cyprus (2002a), 'General Remarks on Draft Outline', President's Office, Non-paper dated 29 April 2002, Nicosia.

United Nations Security Council (1990), Resolution 649 of 12 March 1990.

United Nations Security Council (1991), Resolution 716 of 11 October 1991.

United Nations Security Council (1992), Resolution 750 of 10 April 1992.

United Nations Security Council (1999), Resolution 1250 of 26 June 1999.

United Nations Secretary General (1991), *Report of the Secretary General to the UN Security Council*, S/23300, 19 December 1991, New York.

United Nations Secretary General (1992a), *Set of Ideas for the Reunification of Cyprus*, S/24472 English, New York.

United Nations Secretary General (2000), 'Secretary General Stresses Equal Status of the Parties in Cyprus Proximity Talks', *Press Release*, SG/SM/7546, 12 September 2000, New York.

United Nations Secretary General (2003), *Report of the Secretary General on his Mission of Good Offices in Cyprus*, 7 April 2003, New York.

United Nations Secretary General (2004a), 'Transcript of the Press Conference by Secretary General Kofi Annan at the UN Headquarters', *Press Release*, SG/SM/9159, 13 February 2004, New York.

Chapter 5

# Incentives and Disincentives in the EU 'Catalytic Effect'

*'I feel cheated by the Greek Cypriot government ... Under no circumstances was a resolution to the conflict to fail as a result of opposition by the Greek Cypriot authorities.'*

(Gunter Verheugen, quoted in Christou, 2004)

Why did the accession process proceed in parallel with the deterioration of the conflict between 1994-95 and late 2001? What explains the return to negotiations in 2002 and their ultimate failure? Implicit in Commissioner Verheugen's statement quoted above is the presumed rationale of the EU 'catalytic effect', as well as the explicit admission of its flaws. This chapter explores how EU decisions affected the underlying incentive structure of the conflict by interlocking with the principal parties' interests and perceptions.

**The EU's Expected 'Catalytic Effect'**

Since 1993, EU actors have agreed in assuming that the process of accession would catalyse a settlement of the decades-old conflict on the island. In doing so they shared a similar reading of the conflict and its resolution as the Greek and Greek Cypriot sides. EU institutions and member states did not expect to bring about an agreement through active mediation, replacing the role of the UN. The Commission would only advise the parties on the compatibility of proposed arrangements with the *acquis* (Commission, 1997b).

Having embarked on a specific policy course, EU actors found a rationale to justify their decisions. This rationale was not the strategic basis for the policy adopted. The policy was driven by other predominantly intra-EU factors, analysed in detail in Chapter 6. The 'catalyst' logic was mentioned to justify the adopted policy. Accepting the Greek and Greek Cypriot narrative, the Commission and the member states expected the accession process to trigger a settlement by altering the incentives of the principal parties. Although neither the Commission nor the Council ever spelt out an official argument, an implicit reasoning underpinned these expectations. Turkish Cypriot intransigence, fuelled by Ankara, was held responsible for the persisting stalemate. The accession process would raise the incentives of these two actors to reach an agreement, because it entailed appetizing carrots that were made conditional on conflict settlement. In addition, by lifting conditionality on the Greek Cypriot side, the EU both created a deadline for an agreement and presented Turkey with a conditional cost (i.e., the accession of a divided Cyprus). The deadline and the stick would further encourage Turkey and the Turkish Cypriot leadership to reach an early settlement.

The 'catalyst' rationale rested on a realist logic of conflict settlement. The Turkish and Turkish Cypriot desire to reap the conditional benefits of membership, and the high costs entailed in the absence of a solution before accession, would create the 'ripe' conditions for a settlement by generating Turkish incentives to change their positions. In other words, a conditional stick both to Turkey and the TRNC would raise the costs of the status quo (and thus reduce their BATNA). In addition, an EU carrot would encourage the parties to support reunification within the EU (Emiliou, 1997, p.131).

## Conditional Carrots to the Turkish Cypriots

The 'catalyst' logic rested on the assumption that conditional gains to the Turkish Cypriots would induce a shift in the leadership's position. This would occur either directly (i.e., the prospect of gains would alter the government's position) or indirectly through the pressure generated within the community. Indeed, on several occasions EU decisions focused on the need to articulate the gains from membership to the Turkish Cypriots. The 6 March 1995 GAC decision stated that 'this (Turkish Cypriot) community must perceive the advantages of EU membership more clearly and its concerns at the prospect must be allayed' (Council of Ministers, 1995). In Agenda 2000, the Commission observed that the absence of a solution was due to '(in)sufficient incentives for the two communities to reach an agreement' (Commission, 1997b). It focused on the need to increase Turkish Cypriot incentives through intensified EU efforts to inform this community about the gains of membership. Thereafter, the Commission sponsored an EU information centre in the Turkish Cypriot Chamber of Commerce.

For the Turkish Cypriots, the carrot of EU membership was automatically conditional on a settlement. No member state recognized the TRNC. Given that only states can enter the EU, northern Cyprus could only benefit from accession following some form of reunification. Such a settlement would entail Cyprus' single membership of the Union. In principle, single EU membership could be compatible with a wide range of solutions including both federal and confederal variants (Neuwahl, 2000). However, it would not be compatible either with the separate EU membership of the TRNC, or with the TRNC's entry together with Turkey (European Parliament, 2001, point 3).

What were the gains being offered to the Turkish Cypriots? At times the Commission and the member states referred to the protection of Turkish Cypriot human rights and democracy within the Union, the participation of Turkish Cypriots in EU institutions or the benefits of EU citizenship. However, the conditional gains offered to the Turkish Cypriots were predominantly economic (Commission, 1997a, 2001a; Council of Ministers, 1995; RoC, 1998a). The EU could offer important economic benefits to a small, poverty-stricken and potentially trade-dependent area like northern Cyprus. Economic gains would include an end of thirty years of economic isolation. Northern Cyprus would be included in the EU customs union with Turkey as well as in the EU single market. Tourism and investment would boom and, with this, infrastructure and services would also improve greatly. With the adoption of the euro, Turkish Cypriots would no longer suffer from monetary instability, linked to the use of the Turkish lira. Turkish Cypriot citizens would also be able to freely access the education opportunities and labour markets in other EU states.

Finally, EU membership would include a considerable transfer of EU funds to the undeveloped northern economy. Northern Cyprus would gain access to EIB facilities and loans at the lowest interest rates. Moreover, the region would benefit from considerable EU financial assistance in the form of structural funds, given that only northern Cyprus would be classified as an 'objective 1' area under the structural fund classification. The EU could also offer special funds to northern Cyprus to encourage its development in the context of an agreement. In the case of Northern Ireland, the EU provided €100 million to accompany the peace process. Indeed on 30 January 2002, the Commission published its proposals for the financing of enlargement. A special section devoted to Cyprus stated that the north could receive a three-year €206 million package under a reunification scenario (Commission, 2002a).

*Conditional Sticks and Carrots to Turkey*

The consensus within the EU viewed Ankara at the very least as providing the indispensable support for Denktaş's positions, if not being the motor behind Turkish Cypriot polices. A policy change in Ankara was thus seen as critical to a settlement. The Commission and the member states believed that Cyprus' accession process would catalyse such a change. This was due to Turkey's own aspirations to join the Union; aspirations that were made official in its 1987 application for membership. In Brussels it was widely believed that Ankara valued far more its ties to the EU than to Cyprus. In the words of Eberhard Rhein, a former Commission official: 'Turkey will not want to sacrifice its perspective for membership for the sake of maintaining a puppet regime in northern Cyprus. It will therefore prevail on the Turkish Cypriot leader Rauf Denktaş to accept a deal for the whole island to join the EU by 2004' (Rhein, 2002).

On the one hand, European and American officials thought that Turkish strategic military interests in Cyprus had decreased. The relative size of the Turkish army and the significant development of military technology since the 1970s drastically reduced the likelihood of a Greek attack on the Turkish mainland. On the other hand, EU policy-makers believed that the value attached by Turkey to its EU membership ambitions was extremely high. Since the foundation of the Kemalist Republic, Turkey has sought to associate itself with the West and with Europe in particular (Robins, 1998). Since 1987, Turkey's EU membership application has been at the heart of this policy.

Following the December 1999 Helsinki European Council, Turkey's long-cherished goal of EU membership appeared more achievable. Although the prospect of full membership remained distant, the December 1999 decision formally placed Turkey on the future EU map. This strengthened the expectation in Brussels that Ankara would pursue its EU goals more actively and concretely. This also entailed actively encouraging a settlement in Cyprus. As put by Enlargement Commissioner Gunter Verheugen: 'in Helsinki we made a tremendous offer to Turkey, when we granted her the candidacy status ... this is the best means we have for actively and positively finding a solution to the Cyprus question' (*Kathimerini*, 2001).

Although a settlement in Cyprus was never presented as an explicit condition for Turkey's EU entry, all EU institutions made frequent references to the conflict. In 1987 the European Parliament called on Turkey to encourage a rectification of the 'situation in Cyprus' in view of its objectives to join the Community (European Parliament, 1987). In 1989 the Commission mentioned the 'negative effects' of the Cyprus conflict and of bilateral Greek-Turkish disputes on EC-Turkey relations (Commission, 1989). In 1990 the Dublin European Council concluded that the conflict inevitably affected Turkey-EU relations (Stivachtis, 2002, p.51). Since 1990, most European Parliament resolutions on Turkey have called on Ankara to show the necessary will to settle the conflict (e.g., European Parliament, 1990, 1991 and 1993). Since 1998, all Commission Progress Reports on Turkey have referred to the importance of a Cyprus settlement (Commission, 1999b, p.15; 2000b, p.20; 2001b, p.14-15; 2002c, p.44, p.138). Turkey's 2001 Accession Partnership stated that Turkey should '...strongly support the UN Secretary General's efforts to bring to a successful conclusion the process of finding a comprehensive settlement of the Cyprus problem...' (Council of Ministers, 2001, p.13).

But the most important reason why Commission and member state officials expected Ankara to work towards a settlement was because of the accession of Cyprus. While the 1993 Opinion only allowed for the hypothetical possibility of accession negotiations with Cyprus prior to a settlement, between 1994 and 1998 this became increasingly likely, until it materialized in March 1998. Between 1994 and 1999, the EU was deliberately ambiguous on whether a settlement was a condition for the ultimate membership of the island. Finally, the 1999 Helsinki Council eliminated this precondition for the accession of Cyprus. Although a narrow margin for manoeuvre was retained in the Helsinki formulation (i.e., taking into account 'all relevant factors'), conditionality with respect to a settlement had been removed. By December 2002, when the European Council invited the divided Cyprus to join the Union, 'all relevant factors' were no longer applicable.

Moreover, Greece's threat to veto the entire fifth enlargement unless Cyprus was included in it also raised the likelihood of Cyprus' accession irrespective of a settlement. In November 1996, then Greek Foreign Minister Theodoros Pangalos declared that 'if Cyprus is not admitted, then there will be no enlargement of the Community, and if there is no enlargement there will be no end to the negotiations now going on for the revision of the Treaties, and the Community will thus enter into an unprecedented crisis' (*Cyprus News*, 1996). On 13 November 2001, then Foreign Minister George Papandreou delivered the same message in a different form, when he asserted that the Greek Parliament would not ratify the forthcoming enlargement without Cyprus (*Cyprus Mail*, 2001). Given the historic importance of the fifth enlargement, it was highly unlikely that any member state would veto the accession of a divided Cyprus, despite its potentially negative consequences. As put by Commission President Prodi, Cyprus would join the Union because 'there can be no question of delaying an historic process in which the security, stability and well-being of Europe as a whole is involved' (*Cyprus Weekly*, 2001).

If a divided Cyprus entered the EU, Turkey's interests would be severely harmed. The Greek-Turkish conflict over Cyprus would become an EU-Turkish conflict. As such it would severely hamper Turkey's ambitions to join the Union. With the entry of a divided Cyprus, Turkey, an EU candidate, would be viewed as an illegal occupier of EU territory. The problems this would pose were made painfully explicit by the Commission in 2003, that stated bluntly that the conflict posed a 'serious obstacle' to Turkey's accession path (Commission, 2003, p.16). As later clarified by Prodi, the need for a solution, while not being a 'precondition', simply reflected a 'political reality' (CEPS, 2004). This was not least because of the likelihood of Greece and the RoC demanding a settlement before consenting to Turkey's accession. As put by Greek Prime Minister Simitis in January 2004: 'Turkey's accession course would be inconceivable without a solution of the Cyprus problem' (*Cyprus Mail*, 2004).

Finally, EU actors believed that the accession of a reunited Cyprus would be beneficial to Turkey. EU member Cyprus would support Turkey's own entry and Turkish would become an official EU language. The Annan Plan indeed stipulated that the United Cyprus Republic would be committed to Turkey's accession course (UNSG, 2004b, Main Articles, point viii). A settlement would also allow for a phasing out of Turkish financial transfers to northern Cyprus, and thus eliminate a considerable economic burden on the Turkish economy. Turkish transfers to northern Cyprus amounted to approximately $150-200 million per year, not a negligible sum for a country with chronic deficit problems.

## The Flaws in the EU 'Catalytic Effect'

Having observed in Chapter 4 the entrenchment of the conflict, let us analyse why EU policies failed in their declared intent (Tocci, 2002 and 2003). Why did EU policies fail to catalyse a solution prior to accession and on the contrary triggered (or failed to deter) the deterioration of the conflict until late 2001? What explains the re-engagement in peace efforts in 2002 and their failure prior to the EU accession of the island?

### Greek Cypriot Interests and EU Policies

Since 1964 the Greek Cypriot side accepted the UN's involvement in the conflict given its recognition of the RoC as the only legitimate government on the island. The UN was viewed as the shield protecting the Greek Cypriots against Turkish Cypriot secession. The UN provided the RoC with a forum to present its case to the international community, a strategy that traditionally lay at the heart of the Greek Cypriot approach towards the conflict.

Yet between the mid 1980s and early 1990s, Greek Cypriot governments became progressively more disenchanted with the UN's approach to the conflict. In particular, as the UN progressed in fleshing out proposals in 1985-86 and then culminating in the 1992 'Set of Ideas', the Greek Cypriot side became uncomfortable with several UN ideas. On some occasions these were rejected (as in the case of the first and third Draft Framework Agreements in January 1985 and March 1986). On other occasions, the proposals received general support on paper, yet in practice the leadership adopted a 'wait-and-see' approach (as in the case of the 1992 'Set of Ideas'). In particular the Greek Cypriot side objected to the UN's definition of political equality (in UNSC Resolution 689), to its vagueness on the issue of state succession (i.e., whether a solution would entail a new state or a continuation of the RoC), to the retention of Turkish troops and settlers, and to the restrictions on the three freedoms.

It is in this context that that 1990 application for membership was made. Frustration with the UN's approach by the late 1980s and its perceived shift towards the Turkish Cypriots induced the Greek Cypriot government to turn to the EU. The UN, by simply representing the international system, was unable to induce Turkey and the Turkish Cypriots to do what they were unwilling to do alone. The EU instead was considered as having sufficient leverage on Turkey to induce a policy shift. This logic was presented by then President Vassiliou at the margins of the 1988 Rhodes European Council, when he stated that if the negotiations under the UN failed to yield a settlement, the RoC would apply for EC membership (*Financial Times*, 1988). Moreover, Greek Cypriot leaders believed that EU membership would provide the ideal framework for what they viewed as a desirable settlement, automatically purging the undesirable elements in the UN's ideas. Hence, the statement by then Foreign Minister Michaelides: 'The main axis of our foreign policy is what we call our European orientation. By this we (also) mean the activation of the European factor in the efforts to find a solution to the Cyprus problem' (Tasrdanidis and Nicolau, 1999, p.173).

But why exactly did Greek Cypriot governments believe that accession favoured a settlement in line with their interests? First, enhanced relations with the EU bolstered the RoC's status as the only legitimate government on the island, discredited further the TRNC and provided the RoC with an additional forum in which to present its case. The RoC applied for EU membership on behalf of the whole island and EU institutions conducted the accession process on these premises. In addition, exclusive relations with the Greek Cypriots exposed EU officials predominantly to the Greek Cypriot narrative, inevitably making them more sympathetic towards it. If the divided island joined the Union these gains would rise further.

Second, Cyprus' accession process increased Greek Cypriot leverage on Turkey and thereby redressed the balance in the 'double minority' situation characterizing the conflict. Following a realist approach to the conflict and its settlement, the principal parties viewed the stalemate on the island as a product of its 'double minority' nature, in which the weaker internal Turkish element in Cyprus was counterbalanced by a weaker external Greek element. The introduction of the EU variable shifted the Greek-Greek Cypriot vs. Turkish-Turkish Cypriot context into a wider EU framework. As such it altered the balance of power, unlocking the situation in favour of Greek Cypriot interests. As the Union became progressively more involved in the conflict in the context of enlargement, it was expected to exert greater pressure on Turkey to reunify the island. Furthermore, Greek Cypriot leverage on Ankara would rise with the RoC's acquired veto rights, as an EU member state, over Turkey's future accession.

Third, EU membership entailed critical security gains for the Greek Cypriot community. Since the emergence of the conflict, Turkey embodied the primary security threat to the Greek Cypriots. EU membership alleviated considerably this perceived threat, given the unlikelihood of a Turkish attack on an EU member state. Particularly in view of its own EU objectives, any Turkish military initiatives in Cyprus entailed extremely high political costs to Turkey. As such, even without a solution, EU membership increased Greek Cypriot security. EU membership encouraged also a security agreement that was more favourable to the Greek Cypriot side. The retention of a high number of Turkish troops in northern Cyprus and the continuation of an operational Article 4 of the Treaty of Guarantee allowing for unilateral rights of intervention by the guarantors was less likely. Hence, Clerides' remarks: 'if Turkey has any expansionist visions on Cyprus, and it has, it will be forced to abandon them from the moment we will be part of Europe' (Clerides, 1994).

Finally, Cyprus' membership would create a framework for the liberalization of the freedoms of movement, settlement and property with the implementation of the *acquis communautaire*. In principle the *acquis* liberalizes the movement of goods, services, persons and capital. These freedoms also comprise the freedoms of movement, settlement and property called for by the Greek Cypriots, adamant to settle (and re-settle) and acquire property (and reclaim property) in northern Cyprus. Therefore shifting the conflict into an EU framework would contribute to the Greek Cypriot cause. The Greek Cypriot side could appeal to the *acquis* when rejecting restrictions to the three freedoms, either proposed by the Turkish Cypriot side or by the UN. In 1992, one of Clerides' oft repeated reasons for opposing the 'Set of Ideas' during his presidential election campaign, was on the grounds that these would 'block Cyprus' path to Europe' given its provisions limiting the three freedoms. In October 2000, the RoC House of Representatives rejected UNSG Annan's opening statement in September 2000 also on the grounds that 'it is a basic and fundamental principle of the talks that any proposals or ideas should be fully in line with the *acquis communautaire*' (RoC, 2000a). With the publication of the Annan Plan, the proposed limitations to the three freedoms were criticized because they entailed derogations to the EU *acquis* (Friends of Cyprus, 2003, p.4). Indeed when negotiations resumed in 2004, the Greek Cypriot side demanded modifications to the Plan in accordance with the *acquis*.

The choice of applying for EU membership was also based on other factors. Globalization and EU enlargement raised the opportunity cost of exclusion, particularly for small and peripheral states such as Cyprus. However, EU membership would also entail economic costs to southern Cyprus with the abolition of all trade and non-trade barriers, and the reform of banking legislation that would inhibit the growth of the island's offshore financial services. As Table

5.1 shows, throughout the 1990s the southern economy performed remarkably well, primarily because of the share and growth of the services sector (i.e., tourism and offshore financial services). Indeed back in 1988, President Vassiliou was sceptical of EU accession, partly due to the possible economic costs it entailed. At the time Vassiliou was attracted by the prospect of transforming Cyprus into the 'Singapore of the Mediterranean'. Yet unlike in the case of the 1972 Association Agreement, economic rationale was secondary to the application.

**Table 5.1      Performance of the Southern Cyprus Economy**

|  | 1994 | 1995 | 1996 | 1997 | 1998 | 1999 | 2000 | 2001 |
|---|---|---|---|---|---|---|---|---|
| GDP per capita € (thousand) | 9.9 | 10.5 | 10.8 | 11.5 | 12.3 | 13 | 14.3 | 15.1 |
| Agriculture as % of Total Gross Value Added | 5.2 | 5.3 | 4.8 | 4.3 | 4.4 | 4.2 | 3.7 | 3.9 |
| Services as % of Total Gross Value Added | 69.8 | 70.7 | 71.6 | 73.1 | 73.8 | 74.9 | 76.1 | 76.6 |
| Inflation CPI % | 4.6 | 2.6 | 3 | 3.3 | 2.3 | 1.1 | 4.9 | 2 |
| Unemployment rate % | 2.7 | 2.6 | 3.1 | 3.4 | 3.4 | 5.9 | 4.9 | 4.0 |

*Source:* Commission, 1999a; 2000a; 2001a; 2002b; Statistical Annexes

By the early 1990s, a near consensus across the Greek Cypriot political spectrum and public opinion had emerged concerning the desirability of Cyprus' accession. EU membership received full support from all parties, including the leftist AKEL. Despite being considered a moderate party, AKEL was historically a strong supporter of maximum intermixing between the communities. The EU with its *acquis* and the leverage it could bring to bear upon Turkey contributed to the fulfilment of this aim.

But the important political gains of accession not only led to overwhelming support for the EU in southern Cyprus. The increasingly unconditional EU-related gains interlocked with the rising trend of Greek Cypriot nationalism in the mid-1990s, reducing the incentives of the least compromising forces in southern Cyprus to make early compromises. The accession process both encouraged the hardening of positions on the Greek Cypriot side, and was drawn into the Cyprus equation as a consequence of the rise of Greek and Greek Cypriot nationalism.

Between the mid-1980s and the late 1990s, southern Cyprus witnessed a re-emergence of a redefined form of Greek Cypriot nationalism, which while no longer advocating *enosis*, emphasized the 'Greekness' of Cyprus and called for strong relations with motherland Greece. This was encouraged by the election of Andreas Papandreou in Greece in November 1981 and his historic visit to southern

Cyprus in 1982, in which the conflict was re-defined as a Greek national cause. Greek Cypriot nationalism gained new strength after 1993, with the return to power of Papandreou in Greece and the election of Glafcos Clerides in Cyprus.

EU policies failed to discourage the surge in Greek Cypriot nationalism in the 1990s. This was because of the gains accruing to the Greek Cypriot side from EU membership, together with the fact that by the mid/late 1990s these gains were increasingly disassociated from the need for a solution. Some Greek Cypriots viewed EU membership and the ensuing adoption of the *acquis* as a critical supplement to the general principles advanced by the UN to ensure a more favourable agreement. To others, unconditional EU accession was a means to improve the status quo and thus raise the Greek Cypriot BATNA. A higher BATNA meant greater Greek Cypriot bargaining strength post-membership. It implied also that more people viewed accession as an alternative to a settlement. In the words of a Greek Cypriot interlocutor 'it is better to be in the EU without a settlement than to accept a bad settlement'.[1] According to Theophanous, most Greek Cypriots felt that 'if talks do not produce a genuine federation, the Greek Cypriots should concentrate on other objectives such as EU membership, economic growth and relations with other regions' (Theophanous, 2000, p.221).

The significance of this result hinged on what a 'genuine federation' entailed. To the extent that Greek Cypriots considered that a 'genuine federation' excluded a highly decentralized system of governance, EU membership was viewed as an alternative to a 'bad' solution. In 1993, Clerides, supported by the majority of the public, clearly did not consider that the 'Set of Ideas' provided for a 'genuine federation', and so concentrated on EU accession instead.

Hence, one narrative could be that since 1993, a more nationalist Greek Cypriot leadership engaged tactically in inter-communal talks without real willingness to compromise, because it assessed that if it could secure EU membership, it could then negotiate a more favourable agreement. This did not entail a refusal to participate in the talks. On the one hand, engagement in the peace process had low political costs. The Commission, the Council and European Parliament's recurrent references to a settlement in line with the *acquis* supported the Greek Cypriot position. The Commission also warned against an excessively loose constitutional system. On the other hand, refusal to participate in negotiations was too costly. In this context it is interesting to note that prior to the July 1997 Troutbeck negotiations, Clerides declared that he would attend the talks as 'a cosmetic move in order not to appear as the negative side and so harm the Republic's prospect of accession to the EU' (Stivachtis, 2000, p.21).

Since the 1999 Helsinki European Council, although a settlement was no longer considered a condition of membership, the Greek Cypriot government has not perceived accession as automatic (at least at the level of public discourse). Prior to the re-launch of the talks in January 2002, Clerides stated: 'the behaviour of the Greek Cypriot side will have to be such as to actually prove that we

---

[1] Interview with Greek Cypriot journalist, Nicosia, March 2002. The same argument was made by several other interlocutors, including politicians, academics and civil servants in south Cyprus.

fervently desire the finding of a solution' (Christou, 2002). As late as November 2002, DISY leader Nicos Anastassiades reiterated: 'whether we like it or not the island's accession is linked to the settlement of the Cyprus problem' (*Cyprus Weekly*, 2002a).

The relative balance between purely tactical considerations and more genuine willingness to seek a solution prior to accession appeared to change with the turn of the century. By the end of the 2002-03 negotiations, the Greek Cypriot team appeared to engage more genuinely in the peace process. In assessing why this change may have happened, it is important to bear in mind the change in Clerides' leadership over the decade of his two presidencies (1993-2003). Three key reasons appear to lie behind this change.

First is the contrast between the 1993 and the 1998 presidential elections. In 1993, Clerides (DISY) ran his election campaign on a hard-line nationalist agenda, supported by nationalist DIKO, against moderate incumbent Vassiliou (EDI) supported by moderate AKEL. In 1998, the situation was far more blurred, as Clerides, with the support of moderate EDI and nationalist EDEK, won the elections against George Iacovou, backed by AKEL and DIKO.

Second, the immediate prospect of EU membership imbued the Greek Cypriot political elites with an increased sense of security. A rise in perceived security raised the readiness of the moderate forces to make new concessions (such as accepting Turkey's role in Cyprus' security arrangements for example). In this respect lifting conditionality on the Greek Cypriot side in 1999, and thus guaranteeing Cyprus' EU membership, may have had some positive influence on the positions of the former Greek Cypriot leader.

A third crucial factor was the changing role of Greece. Being a Greek Cypriot nationalist in 2003 had a profoundly different meaning from what it did in 1993. And this was due to the transformation of Greece over the course of the decade. In particular, the Simitis government marked a historic turn in official Greek attitudes towards Turkey, advocating a policy of European inclusion rather than exclusion. Given the government's commitment to rapprochement with Turkey and closer EU-Turkey relations, it genuinely pushed for an early settlement in 2002-03. A settlement would have eliminated all chances of a serious rift in EU-Turkey relations, and most important it would have consolidated the nascent Greek-Turkish rapprochement. Hence, PASOK's relative support for the Annan Plan in 2002-03. This in turn constrained the level of criticism of the Plan by the Greek Cypriot opposition in 2002.[2]

To the extent that by 2002, the Greek Cypriot government was genuinely willing to reach a settlement, the accession deadline may have raised their incentives for an early deal (Wallace, 2002). While Greek Cypriot officials gave little importance to Turkish threats of annexation, they appreciated that the international and domestic momentum generated in 2002 would have evaporated post-accession. As such, despite the greater Greek Cypriot bargaining strength

---

[2] At the 2002 Copenhagen European Council, then Greek Cypriot opposition parties AKEL and DIKO moderated their criticism of the negotiating team of wanting to 'sell off Cyprus' after the support expressed of the team's approach by the Greek government.

post-membership, this strength could remain latent given the absence of inter-communal talks (at least until Turkey's uncertain accession prospects became clearer). Furthermore, time could work against the Greek Cypriots, given the trends of Turkish Cypriot emigration from and Turkish immigration to the island. The EU 'deadline' thus may have raised Clerides' genuine intentions to settle the conflict.

Yet the same cannot be said of the ensuing Papadopoulos administration. The presidential victory of Tassos Papadopoulos led to a resurfacing of Greek Cypriot nationalism. Although the President's party (DIKO) was in government with the historically moderate AKEL, the latter's rhetoric on the conflict since the turn of the century had hardened. Having secured EU membership and aided by the non-committal stance of the New Democracy government in Athens, Papadopoulos felt unconstrained in his flat rejection of the Annan Plan in April 2004. The President was well aware of the stronger Greek Cypriot bargaining position post-accession. In his rejection of the Plan, Papadopoulos evidently felt that he would be able to use his increased bargaining strength post-membership to secure a more favourable agreement. Not only would member state Cyprus be able to exert pressure on Turkey by hindering its EU accession course, but it would also be in a stronger position to reject any provisions that contravened the EU *acquis*. Furthermore, Greek Cypriot cases in the ECHR would persist in calling on Turkey to pay compensation for Greek Cypriot lost properties in the north.

The effects of domestic developments in southern Cyprus and Greece in 2003-04 came to the fore during the referendum campaign in April 2004. While actors from former governments in both southern Cyprus and Greece backed the UN Plan (i.e., Clerides and Vassiliou in Cyprus and Papandreou in Greece), the new leaderships in both Athens and Nicosia either rejected the Plan or remained ambiguously silent about it.

*Turkish Cypriot Interests and EU Policies*

The Commission attempted to lure the Turkish Cypriots into an agreement mainly by offering conditional economic carrots (Bahceli, 2001). Yet the prospect of economic gains was an insufficiently strong incentive to shift the Turkish Cypriot negotiating positions. This was particularly true until the late 1990s, when living standards in the north were rising, particularly if the revenues from the large black economy were taken into account. Decades of economic isolation and subsidization by Turkey had passed without mass pressure to reunite with the south, despite the considerably higher living standards there. Additional economic carrots alone were unlikely to fundamentally alter the Turkish Cypriot position. The Turkish Cypriot leadership preferred the options of international recognition followed by EU membership or of economic integration with Turkey, to EU membership with the Greek Cypriots as a subordinate community in a unified state.

Moreover, economic carrots in a context of international isolation stemming from trade embargoes had perverse effects. The lure of economic incentives was branded as a 'bribe' and an 'insult' by many Turkish Cypriot and Turkish officials.[3] They argued that the total aid on offer only approximated the annual transfers from Turkey (around $160-200 per year). They also argued that if Europeans had been genuinely concerned about the welfare of the Turkish Cypriots they would not have restricted trade since 1994. The 1994 ECJ ruling was interpreted in northern Cyprus as a deliberate and unethical attempt by the EU to strangle the northern economy and bend the Turkish Cypriots into compliance with Greek Cypriot demands. The EU traded with Taiwan despite its non-recognition of Taiwan's independence. Why, other than the sheer attempt to exert pressure on the Turkish Cypriot side, did the EU impose an embargo on the Turkish Cypriots?

The Turkish Cypriot leadership also did not view human and minority rights protection within the EU as a sufficiently attractive prospect. First and foremost, the consensus in the north was that the Turkish Cypriots were not a political minority in Cyprus, and had to be treated as an equal community to the Greek Cypriots. Second, the Turkish Cypriots were sceptical of the EU's willingness to prevent Greek Cypriot discrimination and prevarication against them, given their perception of the Union's structural bias against Turks. They frequently cited the example of discrimination against the Turks of Western Thrace, notwithstanding their EU citizenship.

Moreover, given the depth of mistrust between the two communities, the Turkish Cypriot leadership was automatically suspicious of anything that Greek Cypriots sought. The perceived zero-sum nature of Greek Cypriot gains from EU membership automatically made the Turkish Cypriot side view EU accession as a threat. Enhancement of the RoC's status, increased leverage on Turkey, the adoption of the *acquis* and the reduced ability of Turkey to intervene in Cyprus' security affairs were viewed as heavy costs. As such, the accession process reduced the leadership's incentives to reach a settlement.

In particular, the Turkish Cypriot leadership believed that Cyprus' EU membership with Turkey being left outside for an indeterminate future entailed a considerable security risk. Following the same realist 'double minority' characterization of the conflict, the TRNC establishment felt that Cyprus' accession prior to Turkey's would disrupt unfavourably the balance of power in the region. More specifically, the leadership argued that in the event of a new constitutional breakdown and inter-ethnic violence, unless Turkey was an EU member together with Cyprus, Turkish Cypriot security would be at risk. This would be so even with a continuation of the Treaty of Guarantee, given that in practice Turkey would be impotent vis-à-vis internal Cypriot affairs, while the Union could choose to step aside. As argued by Denktaş: 'Turkish Cypriots want Turkish and not EU security guarantees because they alone are willing to die for the Turkish Cypriots ...' (*Le Monde*, 1996).

The Turkish Cypriot side also felt threatened by the liberalization of the three freedoms within the EU internal market, that would erode bi-zonality on the island. Turkish Cypriots feared that within the EU and under the jurisdiction of the ECJ,

---

[3] Interviews with Turkish and Turkish Cypriot officials in Ankara and Nicosia, February and May 2002.

any agreement concerning the retention of a predominantly Turkish Cypriot population in the north could be challenged and become obsolete in practice. Bi-zonality in Cyprus could be eroded not only by the inter-mixing of Greek Cypriots and Turkish Cypriots. It could occur also with the extension of the EU four freedoms to Greek citizens. Cyprus' EU membership prior to Turkey's would entail that Greek EU citizens would enjoy the full rights and freedoms in Cyprus, but Turkish citizens, outside the Union, would not. The hardening of the leadership's position in mid-1998, when a federal solution was discarded in favour of a confederal one, was explicitly presented as a reaction to the opening of accession negotiations between Cyprus and the EU. The leadership, misinterpreting the implications of EC law, claimed that Cyprus would remain bi-zonal only through a confederation. The accession process also generated mistrust of Greek Cypriot overtures to a bi-zonal settlement, such as Clerides' acceptance of the 'Set of Ideas' principles in 1997. The Turkish Cypriot leadership feared that these gestures were made only because the *acquis* would have eliminated all safeguards for the Turkish Cypriots.[4]

EU decisions also led to a hardening of Turkish Cypriot positions by raising the perceived importance of statehood and sovereignty as a means to ensure political equality. As such, the Turkish Cypriot leadership felt legitimized to explicitly demand recognition. This was primarily due to the non-involvement of EU institutions in mediation efforts. While the UN also recognized the sole legitimacy of the RoC, it historically attempted to downplay the inevitable hierarchy between the two sides by addressing the conflict through inter-communal negotiations, i.e., by stressing the equality between the two communities. In negotiations, the RoC leadership spoke for the Greek Cypriot community and not for the entire island. Other state actors like the UK and the US also enjoyed direct relations with Turkish Cypriot officials in the context of their mediation activities. However, given the non-involvement of EU institutions in mediation and their exclusive relations with the RoC in the context of enlargement, the EU was unable and unwilling to adopt the UN's approach. Yet by conducting its relations with Cyprus on this basis, the EU further enhanced the perceived importance of statehood in Turkish Cypriot eyes. Paradoxically, the theoretically post-nation-state EU enhanced the importance of being a fully-fledged state in Cyprus. The UN instead, symbol of the international state system, attempted to mitigate the importance of independent separate statehood.

The ways in which EU actions and attitudes enhanced the importance of statehood in Cyprus can be illustrated by two concrete examples. First, the 1994 ECJ ruling effectively banning Turkish Cypriot exports demonstrated in a very tangible way the critical importance of recognized statehood for the development of the Turkish Cypriot economy. It was no coincidence that in August that same year, the Turkish Cypriot Assembly withdrew its commitments to a federal

---

[4] Turkish Cypriot suspicions of Greek Cypriot overtures in the context of the accession process were also fuelled by the memory of Greek Cypriot rejection or reservations towards UN proposals in 1984-86 and in 1992. Interview with Turkish Cypriot negotiator, Nicosia, February 2002.

settlement as agreed to in the 1985-86 negotiations. In Turkish Cypriot eyes, the ECJ case reconfirmed the importance of separate recognized sovereignty to the economic survival of the north. Second, given the non-recognition of the TRNC, relations between the EU and Turkish Cypriot officials were conducted 'through' the RoC, raising the perceived hierarchy between the two communities. This confirmed to the Turkish Cypriots that political equality hinged on the prior recognition of the TRNC. So for example in the March 1995 Council decision, the EU emphasized the need to present the gains from EU membership to the Turkish Cypriot community and as such establish contact with them. Yet it stated that contacts would be established 'in consultation with the government of Cyprus' (Council of Ministers, 1995). Perceived hierarchy between the parties was reinforced when in 1998 the European Council, keen to include the Turkish Cypriots in accession negotiations, pressurized the Greek Cypriot government to extend an invitation to the Turkish Cypriot authorities. However, further specifications called for Turkish Cypriot participation in negotiations '*under* the government of the Republic of Cyprus' (EU-Cyprus Joint Parliamentary Committee, 2000; Republic of Cyprus, 1998b) (my italics).

Due to these concerns, throughout the 1990s, Turkish Cypriots and the TRNC establishment only supported EU membership after a settlement and/or after Turkey's accession. Membership after a settlement would mitigate the threats from EU accession, while membership together with Turkey would provide additional guarantees. The accession process therefore reduced the incentives to reach an early agreement for those who supported EU membership only after Turkey's entry. To the most nationalist forces in northern Cyprus, the accession of a divided island was seen as potentially beneficial. They perceived a higher BATNA following the membership of a divided Cyprus, and as such they were less willing to seek an early agreement. Several high-ranking officials argued that the accession of a divided Cyprus could settle the conflict on the basis of partition. As put by Denktaş: 'EU membership of the South will only underline the separate existence of the Northern Republic', thus allowing the conflict to be solved on the basis of two separate states (*Kibris*, 2001). Short of recognized independence, some were content with the progressive integration with Turkey, facilitated by a cooling down of EU-Turkey relations following the accession of a divided Cyprus. They viewed accession as an externally-given opportunity to pursue integration with Turkey.

The situation in northern Cyprus changed in 2002-03. The momentum for change emerged from the public, in the form of civil society initiatives in cooperation with the centre-left parties. Following the July 2000 bankruptcies and the public's concerns about the increasing subordination of the TRNC to the Turkish military, 41 NGOs organized themselves and demonstrated under the banner 'this country is ours'. At the 30 June 2002 municipal elections, the moderate CTP gained a significant share of the vote, winning the three largest cities of Lefkoşa, Famagusta and Girne. With the publication of the UN Plan, opposition to Denktaş's stance in negotiations rose to unprecedented levels, resulting in a series of demonstrations in December 2002 and January 2003 that mobilized between 45,000-70,000 Turkish Cypriots in favour of the Annan Plan and EU membership. The December 2003 parliamentary elections, when the centre-left CTP (pro-Annan Plan and pro-EU membership) for the first time won the highest share of the vote, also highlighted the changes in popular political sentiment prevalent in the north. The referendum results, where 65 percent of the Turkish Cypriots voted in favour of the Annan Plan and EU accession, was the most powerful sign of political change within the community.

These political shifts in northern Cyprus suggested that EU economic carrots did generate key incentives amongst the Turkish Cypriot public. While the government continued to snub economic incentives as a cheap bribe to turn the people against their government, the lure of EU membership appeared to have increasing hold over the public. This was because since the late 1990s, the economy in the north steadily deteriorated. The 1999-2000 IMF disinflation programme in Turkey also hit the northern Cypriot economy. Real output growth fell from 7.4 percent in 1999 to –0.6 percent in 2000 (see Table 5.2). The situation worsened further following the Turkish economic crisis in February 2001, which led to a serious devaluation of the Turkish lira and a subsequent rise in inflation and unemployment. In 2000-01, 76 companies in northern Cyprus went bankrupt. Dependence on financial transfers from Turkey increased further (see Table 5.3).

**Table 5.2        Northern Cyprus Budget, % GDP**

|  | 1990-94 | 1995-99 | 2000 |
|---|---|---|---|
| Total Revenues | 24.6 | 26.5 | 28.0 |
| Total Expenditures | 36.2 | 47.2 | 51.0 |
| Budget Deficit | 11.3 | 16.0 | 23.0 |
| Financed by Turkish Aid | 4.0 | 10.3 | 16.4 |
| Loans | 7.5 | 5.7 | 6.6 |

*Source:* TRNC (2002b)

**Table 5.3        Sectoral Composition of Growth of Northern Cyprus**

| % Growth |  |  |  | % share GDP |
|---|---|---|---|---|
|  | 1990-99 | 2000 | 2001 | 2000 |
| Agriculture | 3.4 | -13.2 | - | 7.9 |
| Industry | 1.9 | 4.0 | - | 12.2 |
| Construction | 5.9 | 18.7 | - | 9.3 |
| Transport | 6.4 | 6.7 | - | 12.3 |
| Trade-tourism | 4.9 | -5.4 | - | 16.4 |
| Financial services | 7.1 | -6.8 | - | 5.9 |
| Rents | 2.0 | 2.2 | - | 5.1 |
| Business | 16.2 | -10.7 | - | 7.8 |
| Public Services | 2.0 | 3.1 | - | 16.4 |
| Total | 3.5 | -0.6 | -3.6 | 100 |

*Source:* TRNC (2002b)

However, what appeared to lie at the heart of the public's concern was not simply the fear of poverty accentuated by the allure of EU-prosperity. It was rather the fear that economic ills and isolation would lead to their disappearance through emigration as a self-governing and well-defined community in northern Cyprus.[5] Another consequence of isolation was the rising dependence on Turkey. This led to a growing sense amongst the public that in fact the Turkish Cypriots were not governing themselves, but were being controlled by Ankara. The public increasingly understood poverty and isolation not simply as 'economic' factors but also as security/identity related factors. Their struggle for self-determination and communal security was increasingly viewed as dependent on a solution and EU membership. Their position was further bolstered by the publication of the Annan Plan, which showed in detail how a solution and EU membership could satisfy Turkish Cypriot basic needs.

*Turkish Interests and EU Policies*

Another important element of the EU's expected 'catalytic effect' concerned Turkey. Turkey's EU accession aspirations, the problems posed by the membership of a divided Cyprus, and the opportunities created by the entry of a united island, led the member states and the Commission to believe that Ankara would encourage an early settlement. However, 'there are many Ankaras', and the incentives to reach a settlement for one face of the establishment acted as disincentives to the other. The expected 'catalytic effect' failed to materialize until late 2002 because EU policies failed to present the relevant incentives to the relevant actors. Since then, domestic political changes in Turkey have led EU policies to have their desired effects.

Commission and member state officials appeared oblivious to Turkish state attitudes towards Cyprus. External observers rightly pointed out that Turkish strategic military interests in Cyprus had decreased. However, EU actors failed to view Turkey's perceived interests in Cyprus through the prism of Turkey's specific security culture, discussed in Chapter 2. Although Turkey's military power and technological development reduced the objective importance of controlling Cyprus, the perceived need to prevent Cyprus from becoming a Greek island remained an utmost priority.

This is not to say that EU decisions did not affect Turkish attitudes towards Cyprus. After the perceived rejection at the 1997 Luxembourg Council, Turkey felt freer to support the hardened Turkish Cypriot positions. Instead, after the 1995, 1999 and 2002 'historic compromises' Turkish and Turkish Cypriot reactions to Cyprus-EU relations were more moderate. However, Turkey maintained its support for the TRNC following the Greek-Turkish rapprochement and the Helsinki and Copenhagen European Councils. No Turkish politician could afford to explicitly accept a solution in Cyprus with the slightest element of perceived treachery in it for the sake of EU membership; more so, given that the Turkish establishment

---

[5] It is estimated that since 1993, 16,000 Turkish Cypriots have left the island.

viewed as profoundly unjust the gradual strengthening of conditionality on Turkey together with the elimination of conditionality on the Greek Cypriots.

Furthermore until late 2001, most Turkish policy-makers did not believe that the Union would proceed to integrate Cyprus as a divided island as stipulated in the Helsinki conclusions. Their disbelief in the Helsinki provisions was due to their failure to understand why the EU would accept such a problematic island and extend its frontiers to a tense no-man's land monitored by UN forces. Turkey relied on member states such as France, Italy and The Netherlands to block the ratification of the Accession Treaty with Cyprus, given the reservations expressed by these member states back in 1996-98. Turkish elites were also firmly convinced, until late 2001, that the EU would never 'give up' Turkey for Cyprus. Just like EU actors failed to understand the role of Cyprus in Turkish politics, Turkish policy-makers failed to understand why, given Turkey's economic potential and strategic importance, EU member states would opt for Cyprus' accession at the expense of EU-Turkey relations. Many in Ankara failed to appreciate that by 1999, the European choice was not between Turkey and Cyprus, but rather between Turkey and the fifth enlargement, whose importance went beyond Cyprus and Turkey combined.

By the autumn of 2001 the Turkish establishment understood that Cyprus' EU accession was inevitable with or without its consent. Both the government and the military understood that a policy shift was necessary given that the stalemate in Cyprus was harming both the Turkish Cypriot cause and Turkey's EU accession process. In the midst of an acute economic crisis, international pressure on Cyprus harmed Turkish interests. Indeed the re-launch of the direct talks reverberated positively in EU-Turkey relations. The December 2001 Laeken Council concluded that recent developments had 'brought forward the prospect of opening accession negotiations with Turkey' (European Council, 2001, paragraph 12).

But some of those in Turkey who did appreciate the salience of EU deadlines may not have been motivated to find a settlement because of their attitudes towards the Union. The EU factor failed to generate sufficient political will in Turkey to support a settlement also because of the lack of unanimous genuine support for EU membership within the Turkish establishment. The EU's positive 'catalytic effect' was grounded on the assumption that *inter alia* Ankara viewed EU membership as a desirable goal. Yet, while almost all political actors in Turkey paid lip service to the aspiration of EU membership, not all were genuinely committed to it.

The effective divide in Turkey over questions of reform and EU membership came to the fore in February-August 2002. Prior to the Helsinki Council decision, EU membership was presented and discussed in Turkey in prevalently symbolic terms, relating to Turkey's national identity and foreign policy orientation. Only after the acceptance of Turkey's candidacy did the establishment begin to appreciate the implications of the accession process. The first major change occurred when in October 2001 Turkey succeeded in passing a fundamental constitutional reform package, amending 34 articles in the restrictive 1982 Constitution. When the government began pursuing the ensuing EU harmonization legislative packages to enact the changes agreed in the constitutional reforms, deep-rooted disagreements emerged. These included both divisions within the ruling coalition, particularly between the Motherland Party (ANAP) and the National Action Party (MHP), and more widely between liberal pro-EU circles and nationalist euro-sceptic circles, unwilling to pay the 'price' of reform.

With the election campaign heating up over the summer of 2002, the pro-EU camp gained strength. The August 2002 harmonization package indicated a changing balance within the party system. The package effectively initiated an electoral campaign focused largely on attitudes towards reform and EU membership. Apart from the strong support of Mesut Yılmaz's ANAP as well as the more qualified support of Bülent Ecevit's Democratic Left Party (DSP) and Tansu Çiller's True Path Party (DYP), EU membership and reforms were strongly supported both by Deniz Baykal's Republican People's Party (CHP), and most important Tayyıp Erdoğan's Justice and Development Party (AKP).

The AKP's landslide victory at the November 2002 elections tilted the balance within the party system in favour of the reformists. The AKP's commitment to EU membership, as well as the reform path necessary to attain it, was particularly interesting. The AKP refused to define itself as a religious party but rather called for greater religious freedoms, necessary, not least, for its own political survival.[6] In order to carry a consistent political message it advocated personal freedoms in other spheres as well, including cultural and linguistic freedoms. Its support for EU membership therefore was not only viewed as an end in itself to be attained through painful reforms. In the AKP's rhetoric, the EU anchor was portrayed also as a means to attain the objectives of reform, which were as important as membership itself. But while the balance within the party political spectrum tilted dramatically in favour of the pro-European reformists, this was not necessarily the case within the wider establishment, which included the civilian administration, the Presidency, the intelligence community and the military.

Pro-Europeans in Turkey were weakened internally by the lack of credibility of EU policies (Uğur, 1999 and 2001). This was due to the uncertainty and long-term perspective of Turkey's EU membership. The prospect of membership can be a powerful incentive for reform in Turkey. However, the expected delivery of the conditional benefits to Turkey remains in the distant future. The changes that Turkey would have to undergo in order to be ready for EU membership, as well as the adjustments the EU itself would have to make in order to accommodate Turkey in its structures, imply a long time horizon for Turkey's EU membership. Timing affects the value of a promised benefit, and value is critical to ensure that a promised benefit acts as an incentive for immediate reform. Furthermore, a long time horizon adds to the uncertainty surrounding Turkey's future in the Union. What will the Union look like by the time Turkey is ready to join it and what will be the attitudes of its member states and public opinion?

But perhaps the most critical cause of the lack of credibility of the EU's Turkey policy was the underlying mistrust in Turkey of the intentions of EU actors.

---

[6] The AKP's predecessors, the Refah Partisi and the Fazilet Partisi, were successively banned by the Constitutional Court. The AKP's leader, Tayyıp Erdoğan, was imprisoned for a speech made during his mayorship of Istanbul.

What fuelled Turkey's mistrust? First, mistrust arose when European positions re-awakened the 'Sevrès syndrome', i.e., the idea that western powers were inclined to challenge Turkey's territorial integrity. This occurred when member states displayed sympathetic attitudes towards separatist movements in Turkey such as the Kurdish PKK. Turkish officials heavily criticized The Netherlands' acceptance of the 'Kurdish Parliament in Exile' meeting in 1995, Italy's refusal to extradite Abdullah Öcalan in 1998, and the European Council's neglect for Turkish-deemed terrorist organizations (such as KADEK, the successor of the PKK) in its own black-list of organizations in 2001. These positions were interpreted by Turkish policy-makers and the media as evidence of the deliberate European disregard for Turkey's security concerns. As such they triggered defensive and obstinate Turkish reactions, which further reduced trust in the relationship.

Second, Turkish mistrust arose when EU actors displayed a reluctance to accept Turkey irrespective of its compliance with the Copenhagen criteria. Religion, geography, demography, economic development as well as the legitimate concerns over democracy and human rights were cited as obstacles to Turkey's membership. Of the many expressions of European exclusionism, the most cited examples were the 1997 Belgian Christian Democrat declaration and the 2002 statement by EU Convention President Valery Giscard d'Estaing. In March 1997, at a Christian Democrat Congress, the Belgian Wilfried Martens declared that Turkey had no place in European civilization. In November 2002, Giscard d'Estaing stated that Turkey has a 'different culture, a different approach, a different way of life …. its capital is not in Europe, 95 percent of its population lives outside Europe, it is not a European country…in my opinion it would be the end of the EU' (*TDN*, 2002).

Until 1999 Turkey was not recognized as a candidate to membership. Although, on the basis of Article 28 of the Association Agreement, Turkey was considered eligible to full membership, between the 1987 Turkish application and the 1999 Helsinki European Council decision, most member governments expressed strong reluctance to embrace Turkey in the process of enlargement. The Commission's Agenda 2000 and the Luxembourg European Council's conclusions not to include Turkey in the list of candidates reminded Turkish officials of what they considered evidence of European racism and double standards. The 1999 Helsinki Council initially appeared to increase clarity concerning Turkey's future in Europe. However uncertainty in the relationship soon resurfaced. In December 2000 for example, when the Nice European Council set the guidelines for voting weights and representation in the enlarged Union, Turkey was excluded from all calculations. While all other candidates had a roadmap for accession and clear indications of their future roles in EU institutions, Turkey had neither.

In December 2002, the Turkish government accepted the decisions taken by the Copenhagen European Council. However, both the intense debate that took place between the member states prior to and at the European Council meeting, and the actual decision taken at the meeting fuelled mistrust in Turkey. The member states both resisted a clear conditional signal to Turkey and refrained from taking a collective position until the eleventh hour in Copenhagen. The reluctance of member states such as France, Germany and Austria to extend a conditional date to

Turkey, in the backdrop of the comments made by Giscard d'Estaing, raised Turkish suspicions. If Turkey's non-compliance with the Copenhagen criteria was the only cause of EU reluctance to start accession negotiations, why was the Union reluctant to give Turkey a clear conditional date (i.e., conditional on Turkey's fulfilment of the criteria prior to the talks)?

Turkish and EU ambivalence about Turkey's EU membership critically and negatively affected the Cyprus conflict. Those in Turkey who were against or sceptical of Turkey's EU membership adamantly denied the link between a Cyprus settlement and Turkey's accession. Nationalists argued that Cyprus was a national issue, which could not be compromised for the sake of the EU. To some, a persisting stalemate in Cyprus could have erected a further barrier in EU-Turkey relations, in turn reducing EU pressure on Turkey to embark on difficult reforms.

Those who genuinely favoured Turkey's full membership were far readier to accept the link between a settlement and EU-Turkey relations. As such they were more willing to exert pressure on the Turkish Cypriot leadership. The coming to power of the AKP led to the clearest change in rhetoric. In sharp contrast to previous administrations, the AKP government was willing to acknowledge the link between Turkey's accession process and a settlement. Then Prime Minister Abdullah Gül explicitly broke the taboo in stating that 'if a concrete date is given to Turkey this will definitely create a positive environment which will also facilitate the settlement of the Cyprus issue' (*Cyprus Weekly*, 2002b).

Yet the lack of credibility of the EU's policies towards Turkey strengthened the arguments of nationalist and eurosceptic forces, who argued against an early settlement within the EU. Moderates in Turkey accepted that because of Turkey's own shortcomings, Cyprus' EU membership would occur prior to Turkey's. However, they could not accept that because of allegedly unchangeable features of the Turkish state and society, Cyprus would mark the borders of a united Europe, keeping Cyprus and Turkey on opposite sides of the European divide. Hence, the more EU attitudes and decisions fed Turkish mistrust of the Union, the less credible were the positions of Turkish moderates, and thus the less forthcoming was Turkey towards a Cyprus solution.

The same was true in northern Cyprus. For example, in opinion polls in the north, support for the centre-left pro-EU parties declined when EU decisions were perceived as harming Turkey's interests (i.e., December 1997). The opposite was true when EU decisions were perceived as being more even-handed towards Turkey (i.e., December 1999 and December 2002). According to the Turkish Cypriot centre-left leaders, the demonstrations in 2002-03 would not have been possible had Turkey's EU prospects not been more credible since December 1999.[7]

Following this argument it is interesting to compare the logic behind Turkish decisions after the 1997 Luxembourg European Council and at and after the 2002 Copenhagen Council. The Turkish interpretation of the 1997 Luxembourg decisions simplified Turkey's policy options on Cyprus. In so far as Turkey was determined not to 'lose' Cyprus, and the Luxembourg decision was interpreted as

---

[7] Interviews with Turkish Cypriot opposition leaders, Nicosia, February 2002.

an EU attempt to separate Turkey from Cyprus, the overwhelming forces in Turkey and northern Cyprus weighed in favour of the recognition of Turkish Cypriot statehood and integration with Turkey. In Copenhagen, the argument was more subtle. If the Union was willing to send Turkey a sufficiently strong signal, the government declared itself willing to seal a deal. Unless Turkey had a realistic prospect of beginning accession negotiations, the government felt that a Cyprus settlement within the EU would amount to 'losing Cyprus'. Judging by events, the Copenhagen offer was insufficient to induce Turkey and the Turkish Cypriots to sign an agreement in December 2002 and in March 2003. This failure was not only caused by miscalculated Turkish bargaining tactics. It was also fundamentally linked to Turkey's mistrust of Europe. Whether a deal would have been reached if Turkey had received an earlier and firmer 'date', or if EU-15 had formulated a more resolute and coherent policy towards Turkey before the European Council, will remain unknown. But what was clear was that the Turkish government considered these conditions as the minimum assurance to hedge against their prevailing mistrust. Pressure alone was insufficient to clinch an agreement.

This is not to say that Turkey incorporated decided against a solution within the EU. Throughout 2003 and 2004 trends in Turkey continued to oscillate. Those sceptical of Turkey's future in Europe, persisted in their opposition to Cyprus' EU membership, and consequently in their opposition to the UN Plan. Those in favour of Turkey's EU membership, but unsatisfied with the Copenhagen decision, proposed a postponement of a settlement until Turkey's EU prospects became clearer (i.e., in December 2004). Other pro-Europeans instead pushed for an early settlement based on the UN Plan. They appreciated - albeit uneasily - that the conflict posed a problem for Turkey's EU aspirations. They also understood the difficulty of reaching a favourable solution after Cyprus' EU entry, given that EU conditionality would be placed exclusively on Turkey's shoulders.

By February 2004, those in Turkey pushing for an early settlement appeared to gain the upper hand. Prime Minister Erdoğan's acceptance that the UNSG could 'fill the blanks' in the final version of the Annan Plan to be submitted to separate referenda, and the Turkish government's commitment to the February-April 2004 peace process, pointed to a new majority view within the Turkish establishment. This new position, while being advocated by the AKP government, was either backed or not forcefully opposed by other segments of the establishment including the influential military.[8] This is not to say that the government's position was accepted by all segments of society. Strong opposition was expressed by the opposition CHP and by President Sezer (Balci, 2004).

This argument suggests that while the stick of Cyprus' accession proved insufficient to generate Turkish willingness to seek a solution, the carrot of Turkey's own accession process together with a change in Turkey's political dynamics triggered a shift in Turkey's policies towards Cyprus. A greater Turkish readiness to settle the conflict under the AKP government was evident. This was largely due to the government's unprecedented commitment to EU accession

---

[8] See for example the statements made by Özkök (*TDN*, 2004).

(manifested also by the perseverance in pursuing domestic reforms). It was also due to the increasing link made by EU actors between EU-Turkey relations and conflict settlement. However, without the more credible EU commitments to Turkey since 1999, and particularly since December 2002, the stick of the linkage (between a settlement and Turkey's accession process) probably would have had limited effect. In other words, without the carrot of a credible Turkish EU accession process, the stick of Cyprus' accession was more likely to consolidate partition rather than catalyse a settlement on the island. As the carrot became more credible (and thus more valuable), the Turkish government position shifted in 2003-04.

The expectation that Cyprus' accession process would catalyse a settlement on the island throughout the 1990s failed because of a flawed EU policy of conditionality that included Cyprus' accession process without an accompanying clear strategy towards Turkey. As the next chapter explores, this does not entail that EU actors deliberately or even knowingly encouraged these negative dynamics.

EU actors (with the singular exception of Greece) paid insufficient attention to the reasons behind the strong Greek Cypriot commitment to join the Union, and the effects that Cyprus-EU relations had on internal Greek Cypriot political dynamics. Political and security interests, specifically related to the conflict, led the Greek Cypriot side to engage in the accession process. These gains were not related to an expectation that the Union would foster the emergence of a post-nationalist Cyprus in which ethnic rivalries would subsume. The attraction was on the contrary that of strengthening the Greek Cypriot national cause against its local enemies. As the receipt of EU-related benefits became free from progress in conflict settlement, the accession process reduced the incentives to seek an early agreement of those Greek Cypriot nationalists who sought considerable changes in UN guidelines, and those who, sceptical of any agreement, concentrated on alternative options to ensure the security and prosperity of the Greek Cypriot community.

However, while during the mid and late 1990s nationalist positions were on the rise in southern Cyprus, by the turn of the century the tide seemed to reverse temporarily. In the last years of his Presidency, Clerides appeared to be more willing to move towards a settlement prior to accession. A greater Greek Cypriot sense of security on the eve of accession and the critical changes in Greek foreign policy since 1999 were important explanations of the former Greek Cypriot leader's increased readiness to reach a deal. Yet Clerides was replaced by the more hardline Tassos Papadopoulos in January 2003, who felt free to openly reject the Annan Plan one month before Cyprus' formal entry in the EU .

Insufficiently attractive gains presented by the EU to the Turkish Cypriot community and the perceived costs that EU membership could entail, together with the general climate of mistrust in northern Cyprus of Greek Cypriot and EU intentions, reduced the Turkish Cypriot leadership's incentives to broker a settlement. In the words of Rauf Denktaş: 'the EU is a carrot offered to us in order to make us fall into this trap and to end up being a minority with no state, no status and no sovereignty' (*Kibris*, 2002). Furthermore, the fact that full membership of a divided Cyprus could consolidate partition or the full integration of northern Cyprus into Turkey was viewed as a desirable outcome by the most nationalist forces in northern Cyprus and Turkey. By 2002-03, the Turkish Cypriot government came under increasing pressure from the public, which instead was more persuaded about the desirability of a settlement within the EU. Indeed when push came to shove during the referendum of 24 April 2004, the majority of Turkish Cypriots voted in favour of the Annan Plan and EU accession.

A final flaw in the EU's expected 'catalytic effect' was the absence of a strategy towards Turkey. More specifically, EU officials overlooked the importance of Cyprus in Turkish politics, the lack of genuine unanimous support for EU membership in Turkey and the lack of credibility of EU policies towards Turkey. Turkey instead failed to appreciate until late 2001 that Cyprus could indeed be accepted as a divided island if necessary. As a result, EU incentives were insufficiently strong to trigger a change in Turkey's Cyprus policy. Following the Turkish elections in November 2002, the domestic dynamics in the country were seriously altered. A more credible EU accession process, together with the rise to power of a government that appeared to be seriously committed to the goal of membership, transformed the internal dynamics in Turkey. Yet, despite the importance of this change, alone it not could secure an agreement on the island.

## References

Bahceli, T. (2001), 'The Lure of Economic Prosperity Versus Ethno-Nationalism: Turkish Cypriots, the EU Option, and the Resolution of Ethnic Conflict in Cyprus', in M. Keating and J. McGarry (eds.), *Minority Nationalism and the Changing International Order*, Oxford University Press, Oxford, pp.203-222.

Balci, K. (2004), 'United Cyprus divides Turkey', *Turkish Daily News*, 19 April 2004.

CEPS (2004), *Turkey in Europe Monitor,* Issue 1, January 2004, CEPS, Brussels.

Christou, J. (2002), 'New Year will be Crucial for Cyprus', *Cyprus Mail*, 2 January 2002.

Christou, J. (2004), 'Verheugen: I feel cheated', *Cyprus Mail*, 22 April 2004.

Clerides, G. (1994), Interview with, 'The Cyprus Problem Twenty Years after the Turkish Invasion', *Hellenic Studies*, Fall 1994, pp.9-17.

Commission of the European Communities (1989), *Opinion on Turkey's Request for Accession to the Community*, SEC(89) 2290 final, 18 December 1989, Brussels.

Commission of the European Communities (1997a), *Press Release*, Speech 97/45, Hans Van der Broek Speech at the North Cyprus Young Businessmen Association, Reuter Briefing, 27 February 1997, Brussels.

Commission of the European Communities (1997b), *Agenda 2000*, 15 July 1997, Extracts available on www.cyprus-eu.org.cy/eng/07_documents/documents003.htm

Commission of the European Communities (1999a), *Regular Report on Cyprus Progress towards Accession*, on www.europa.int

Commission of the European Communities (1999b), *Regular Report on Turkey's Progress towards Accession*, on www.europa.eu.int

Commission of the European Communities (2000a), *Regular Report on Cyprus' Progress towards Accession*, on www.europa.eu.int

Commission of the European Communities (2000b), *Regular Report on Turkey's Progress towards Accession*, on www.europa.eu.int

Commission of the European Communities (2001a), *Regular Report on Cyprus' Progress towards Accession*, on www.europa.eu.int

Commission of the European Communities (2001b), *Regular Report on Turkey's Progress towards Accession*, on www.europa.eu.int

Commission of the European Communities (2002a), *Commission Offers a Fair and Solid Approach for Financing EU Enlargement*, IP/02/170, Brussels.

Commission of the European Communities (2002b), *Regular Report on Cyprus' Progress towards Accession*, on www.europa.eu.int

Commission of the European Communities (2002c), *Regular Report on Turkey's Progress towards Accession*, on www.europa.eu.int

Commission of the European Communities (2003), *Continuing Enlargement: Strategy Paper and Report of the European Commission on the Progress towards Accession of Bulgaria, Romania and Turkey*, on www.europa.eu.int

Council of Ministers of the European Union (1995), General Affairs Council Decision on Cyprus' Accession, 06/03/95C, Presidency Proposal, on www.cyprus-eu.org.cy

Council of Ministers of the European Union (2001), General Affairs Council Decision on the Principles, Priorities, Intermediate Objectives and Conditions in the Accession Partnership with the Republic of Turkey, 24 March 2001, 2001/235/EC, *Official Journal*, L85, 24 March 2001, Brussels.

*Cyprus Mail* (2001),'Papandreou: No enlargement without Cyprus', 13 November 2001.

*Cyprus Mail* (2004), 'Simitis: Turkey's European Course Inconceivable without Solution', 20 January 2004.

*Cyprus News*, October 1996, No.87:3.

*Cyprus Weekly* (2001), 'Cyprus will Join', 30 October 2001.

*Cyprus Weekly* (2002a), 'Parties back the Plan as basis for talks', 22 November 2002.

*Cyprus Weekly* (2002b), 'EU links Cyprus to date for Turkey', 29 November 2002.

Emiliou, N. (1997), 'Knocking on the Door of the EU: Cyprus' Strategy for Accession', in H. J. Axt and H. Brey (eds.), *Cyprus and the EU: New Chance for Solving an Old Conflict*, Sudosteuropa-Gesellschaft, Munchen, pp.125-136.

European Council (2001), Meeting on 14-15 December 2001 in Laeken, *Presidency Conclusions*, SN300/01.

European Parliament (1987), Foreign Affairs Committee, Costé-Floret Report, DOCA2-317/87, 26 February 1987, on www.mfa.gov.tr

European Parliament (1990), Resolution of 15 March 1990, Strasbourg.

European Parliament (1991), Resolution of 17 May 1991, Strasbourg.

European Parliament (1993), Resolution of 20 January 1993, Strasbourg.

European Parliament (2001), *Report on Cyprus' Application for Membership of the EU and the State of Negotiations*, Rapporteur Jacques Poos, A5-0261/2001, 11 July 2001, Brussels.

EU-Cyprus Joint Parliamentary Committee (2000), *Press Statement*, 18 April 2000, Nicosia.

*Financial Times* (1988), 'Cypriot Government will seek EC Membership if UN talks fail', 5 December 1988.

Friends of Cyprus (2003), *Still Time*, Report Issue 46.

*Kathimerini* (2001), 'EU Enlargement with Cyprus or not at all', 25 October 2001.

*Kibris* (2001), 'President Denktaş Stands Firm', Vol.IX. No.3, March 2001.

*Kibris* (2002), 'Denktaş replies to Cassoulides', Vol.X, No.6, June 2002.

*Le Monde* (1996), 'Chypre: un test serieux pour l'UE', 3 August 1996.

Neuwahl, N. (2000), 'Cyprus Which Way? In Pursuit of a Confederal Solution in Europe', *Harvard Jean Monnet Working Paper,* April 2000, Cambridge, MA.

Republic of Cyprus (1998a), *Gains from EU Accession to the Turkish Cypriot Community*, on www.cyprus-eu.org.cy

Republic of Cyprus (1998b), 'Statement by President Clerides Relating to Turkish Cypriot Participation', 12 March 1998, on www.cypruseu.org.cy

Republic of Cyprus (2000a), *House of Representatives Resolution*, 11 October 2000, Nicosia, www.pio.gov.cy/news/special_issues/special_issue034.htm

Rhein, E. (2002), *Turkey and the EU, a Realistic Framework for Accession*, EPC, Brussels.

Robins, P. (1998), 'Turkey: Europe in the Middle East or the Middle East in Europe?', in B.A Robertson (ed.), *The Middle East and Europe*, Routledge, London and New York, pp.151-169.

Stivachtis, Y.A. (2000), *The Enlargement of the European Union: The Case of Cyprus*, Conference Paper, International Studies Association, 41$^{st}$ Annual Convention, Los Angeles, CA., 14-18 March 2000, available on CIAO Conference Proceedings www.cc.columbia.edu/sec/dlc/ciao/isa/sty01/

Stivachtis, Y. (2002), 'Greece and the Eastern Mediterranean Region: Security Considerations, the Cyprus Imperative and the EU Option', in T. Diez (ed.), *The European Union and the Cyprus Conflict - Modern Conflict, Post Modern Union*, Manchester University Press, Manchester, pp. 34-53.

Theophanous, A. (2000), 'Cyprus, the EU and the Search for a New Constitution', *Journal of Southern Europe and the Balkans*, Vol. 2, No.2, pp.213-233.

Tocci, N. (2002), 'Cyprus and the EU: Catalysing Crisis or Settlement?', *Turkish Studies*, Vol.3, No. 2, pp.105-138.

Tocci, N. (2003), 'Incentives and Disincentives for Reunification and EU Accession in Cyprus', *Mediterranean Politics*, Vol.8, No.1, pp.151-159.

Tsardanidis, C. and Nicolau, Y. (1999), 'Cyprus Foreign and Security Policy: Options and Challenges', in S. Stavridis, T. Couloumbis, T. Veremis and N. Waites (eds.), *The Foreign Policies of the EU's Mediterranean States and Applicant Countries in the 1990s*, Macmillan, London, pp.171-194.

*Turkish Daily News* (2002), 'Giscard Remarks cause uproar in Ankara, Brussels', 11 November 2002.

*Turkish Daily News* (2004), 'Özkök: Final say rests with Parliament, Turkish Cypriots', 14 April 2004.

Turkish Republic of Northern Cyprus (2002b), State Planning Organization, *Economic and Social Indicators*, Nicosia.

Uğur, M. (1999), *The EU and Turkey: An Anchor Credibility Dilemma*, Ashgate, Aldershot.

Uğur, M. (2001), 'Europeanization and Convergence via Incomplete Contracts? The Case of Turkey', in K. Featherstone and G. Kazamias (eds.), *Europeanization and the Southern Periphery*, Frank Cass, London, pp. 217-242.

United Nations Secretary General (2004b), *The Comprehensive Settlement of the Cyprus Problem*, Fifth Version, on http://www.cyprus-un-plan.org

Wallace, W. (2002), 'Reconciliation in Cyprus: The Window of Opportunity', *Mediterranean Programme Report*, EUI, Florence.

Chapter 6

# Explaining EU Policies Towards the Cyprus Conflict

*'The Union is a master when it comes to avoiding making choices'*
(Zielonka, 1998, p.1)

Chapters 4 and 5, focusing on the impact of EU policies on the Cyprus conflict, largely treated the EU as a monolithic entity. This is because the emphasis was on the perception of the EU by the principal parties and the effect this had on the conflict. This chapter opens the EU black box, attempting to discern the factors that determined EU actions or inactions. Were these policies part of a planned and deliberate strategy which led to unintended results? Or did the 'catalytic effect' fail simply because the question of how best to contribute to a solution in Cyprus never made it to the top of the EU's political agenda?

### The Starting Point: Passivity and Progressive Imbalance

Let us begin by recounting the EC/EU's involvement in the Cyprus conflict prior to the 1990s. Between 1972 and 1990 Cyprus and the EC articulated their relations through an Association Agreement. Despite the close economic ties that this entailed, the EC deliberately kept out of the conflict. Apart from a brief period in the summer of 1974, European Political Cooperation kept a low profile on the conflict and the member states simply supported UN Security Council resolutions.

Several factors determined this stance. Divisions between the member states together with the insufficiently developed EPC structure were important reasons behind inaction. While Gaullist and post-Gaullist France together with Luxembourg and Ireland supported the Greek Cypriot line, Germany, Britain and The Netherlands were more sympathetic to Turkish concerns and supported US mediation between NATO allies Greece and Turkey. Coupled with this was the reluctance of both the UK, as guarantor power and UNSC member, as well as the US to see a more active European role. Most other member states in turn were content to leave the UN to deal with the problem. The Community's passivity towards Cyprus was also part of its wider neglect of the Mediterranean. The Community became progressively more engaged with the southern littoral states over the decades through the Global Mediterranean Policy (GMP) in 1972, followed by the Redirected Mediterranean Policy (RMP) in 1989, and finally with the 1995 Euro-Mediterranean Partnership (EMP). However, the substance, coherence and thus overall effectiveness of these initiatives have been and remain highly questionable.

Both the Commission and the Council were keen to retain an even-handed approach to the Cyprus conflict. The Association Agreement stated that 'the rules governing trade between the contracting parties may not give rise to any discrimination between ... nationals and companies of Cyprus' (Council of Ministers, 1973, Article 5). This provision was used to justify trade with northern Cyprus until 1994. The agreement also provided for the establishment of a joint Parliamentary Committee, which remained dead letter until 1992, given the Community's rejection of a wholly Greek Cypriot delegation. Also in terms of financial assistance to Cyprus, the EC allocated 20 percent of the aid to the Turkish Cypriot community in the first financial protocol (1977-83), i.e., an amount proportionate to the demographic balance on the island.

The EC's even-handedness evaporated over time. In sharp contrast with the first financial protocol, the second protocol (1984-88) allocated a mere three percent to the Turkish Cypriots. In the third protocol (1989-93) the only aid filtering through to the Turkish Cypriots was for the joint sewage project in Nicosia. In the fourth protocol (1995-98), the Commission set aside €12 million to promote a settlement. But given that the aid had to be disbursed through the RoC authorities, it had minimal impact on the Turkish Cypriots. The same was true of pre-accession aid (2000-04) which set aside one third of the funds for bi-communal projects.

What explains the slide away from even-handedness? Turkish Cypriot refusal to accept European funds transferred to the RoC, the Turkish Cypriot UDI in 1983, Turkey's alienation from Europe during the years of political instability in the late 1970s and of military rule in the early 1980s, as well as Greece's membership of the Community since 1981 all explain the shift in the EC's position. As a result the Community was increasingly perceived as being biased in favour of the Greek Cypriots. Hence the commonly held view in Turkey and northern Cyprus: 'the EU *is* Greece. It has always been used by Greece to fight Turkey'.[1]

## The Changing Role of Greece

*The Early Days of Greek Membership*

While Greece was by no means the only driving force of EU policies, its role was crucial in determining EU positions towards Turkey and Cyprus. Over the course of the last decade, member state Greece was also critical in providing the dominant definition of the conflict and of the strategy for its settlement within the Union.

Before focusing on the 1990s, let us briefly review Greece's positions and their impact on EU policies in the early period of membership. In June 1975, with the restoration of democracy under the leadership of Constantine Karamanlis (ND),

---

[1] Interview with Turkish ANAP parliamentarian, Ankara, February 2002.

Greece applied for EC membership. Despite the Commission's negative Opinion, the Council overruled the decision in February 1976 and in January 1981 Greece entered the Community. Notwithstanding the fact that both the Commission's second Opinion in May 1979 and the Council's endorsement of it in June 1979 reassured Turkey that Greece's membership would not affect EC-Turkey relations, upon accession Greece (which by November 1981 was led by nationalist Andreas Papandreou) began to use the EC as the primary platform from which to gain political advantage over Turkey. However until 1983, Greece was not the principal obstacle in EC-Turkey relations. Relations had been frozen as the unanimous Community response to the 1980 military coup in Turkey. The Greek government's position was simply in alignment with the general EC stance.

With the restoration of partial democracy in Turkey in 1983 and the Community's desire to re-establish ties with Ankara after 1985, the Greek position became a key obstacle to normalization. The Greek government's obstructionism was further fuelled by the conflict in March 1987 over oil exploration rights in the Aegean Sea. The conflict underpinned a wider dispute over sovereignty rights in the Aegean's continental shelf and territorial waters. Until April 1988 the Greek government blocked the reactivation of the EC-Turkey Association Agreement. Only in the context of the short-lived 'Davos Process' of détente in January 1988 between Prime Ministers Andreas Papandreou and Turgut Özal, did Greece consent to a reactivation of EC-Turkey relations.

However, despite the reactivation of the agreement, as of 1986 the Greek government started to block in the Council of Ministers the disbursement of the fourth financial protocol to Turkey amounting to €600 million. Greece argued that its consent hinged on the withdrawal of Turkish troops from Cyprus. The Greek veto persisted throughout the 1990s, despite several attempts by the member states to circumvent it. Other European funds earmarked for Turkey that were vetoed by Greece included MEDA funds (€365 million in 1983-92) and EIB loans and funds in the context of the customs union agreement (€450 million). Greek governments used the EC as a platform to pursue national interests. By doing so they ensured that the path of EC-Turkey normalization passed through Athens.

*The Encouragement of External Greek Cypriot Demands*

PASOK came to power under the leadership of Andreas Papandreou in 1981. Until the end of its first administration, PASOK was either entirely against EC membership or highly sceptical of it. By 1985-86 its positions had changed, as it became increasingly aware of the political, security and economic gains of membership. This change was pivotal in generating Greek Cypriot demands for membership. Indeed the initial idea of Cyprus' EC membership was a Greek initiative, which may not have materialized without Greece's insistence.[2] As PASOK appreciated the security benefits of membership, it attempted to sway the RoC to apply for precisely those reasons. EC membership would strengthen the

---

[2] Interviews with Greek retired Ambassador, Greek academic and Greek government advisor, Athens, March 2002.

Greek Cypriot bargaining position given Turkey's aspirations to join the Community. This could ultimately lead to a settlement conducive to Greek Cypriot interests. Short of a settlement, membership would safeguard Greek Cypriot security by raising the costs of Turkish expansionism. By championing the cause of Cyprus' membership, Greece felt it would rectify the harm caused to the Greek Cypriots in 1974, triggered in no small way by its dictatorship at the time.

During Greece's second EC Presidency in the second half of 1988, Foreign Minister Pangalos and most notably Yannis Kranidiotis, the Cyprus-born alternate Minister of Foreign Affairs, attempted to persuade President Vassiliou to apply for membership. In September 1988, Kranidiotis sent a letter to his Greek Cypriot counterpart George Iakovou attempting to persuade him to submit the application for membership. However, the Greek Cypriot government refused to apply. At the time AKEL, in power with Vassiliou's EDI, opposed EC membership on ideological grounds. Vassiliou also feared a blunt rejection from the Community. Helmut Kohl's Germany and Margaret Thatcher's UK had made it abundantly clear to Vassiliou, during his tour of European capitals in 1988, that they would reject both a Cypriot and a Turkish application.[3] The last thing the Greek Cypriot government wanted was to be relegated by the EC to the same basket as Turkey. Hence, Greece in 1988 succeeded only in launching a political dialogue between the EC and Cyprus.

*Domestic Instability and the Macedonian Interlude*

Greece's role in determining EU policies towards Cyprus and Turkey is also highlighted by the stalemate in EU-Cyprus relations in 1990-93. In those years the Greek domestic scene was marked by political and economic instability and Greek foreign policy was dominated by the Balkans and Macedonia.

Between 1989 and 1993, Greece lived through a difficult period of domestic instability. By 1988-89 PASOK's popularity was waning, as the party was implicated in a series of corruption scandals and its leadership vacillated with the first signs of Papandreou's illness. In addition the country suffered from a severe economic downturn. The 1989 elections brought to an end PASOK's rule, only to be replaced by an unstable coalition between ND and the communist party. This government collapsed in November 1989, giving way to a caretaker administration. The April 1990 elections were won by ND, led by Constantine Mitsokakis. However, in 1993 the government fell as Foreign Minister Antonio Samaras left the party and formed a breakaway nationalist movement (Political Spring - *Politiki Anokisi*).

In the early 1990s, Greek foreign policy focused on the Balkans. Fearing Macedonian irredentism, Greece openly diverged from the EU majority. Under this perceived threat, Greece acted as a 'Balkan state', effectively siding with Serbia in the Balkan conflicts and adopting a position on Macedonia which contravened the EU consensus (Ioakimidis, 1999). The nadir of the crisis was the February 1994

---

[3] Interview with former Greek Cypriot President, Nicosia, March 2002 and July 2003.

Greek embargo on Macedonia. These positions led to a severe deterioration in Greece's relations with the rest of the EU, exemplified by the Commission's recourse to the ECJ against Greece and the Dutch refusal to ratify Greece's entry into the West European Union.

Weakness in domestic politics, isolation in the EU, and the general inability of a small member state to push for more than one foreign policy dossier at a time, curtailed Greece's ability to influence EU policies towards Turkey and Cyprus. As a result, the 1989-93 period was not marked by any decisive EU initiative or policy shift vis-à-vis these two neighbouring countries. With regards to Cyprus, political dialogue and economic ties under the Association Agreement continued. But the reluctant Commission took three years to issue its Opinion on membership. In EU-Turkey relations, following the Commission's rejection of Turkey's 1987 application, the Council proposed a soft initiative aimed at retaining good relations with Ankara, i.e., the 1990 Matutes package. Despite its reluctance, the Greek government was unable to block the initiative. In 1992 Mitsokakis also accepted the release of Turkey's MEDA funds under the RMP.

The tide turned with the re-election of PASOK in October 1993. Despite the trade embargo on Macedonia in February 1994, Foreign Minister Theodoros Pangalos appreciated that Greece's hardline stance was a lost cause. The embargo itself was a failure, as the Greek private sector found ways to circumvent it. It simply led to a deterioration of Greece's position in the Union, triggered strong pressure from the US and strengthened Turkey's relative position. By 1995 Greece had regained its position within the European family, signing an interim agreement with FYROM in October.

*Greece and Inter-State Bargaining: Linkage Politics*

With PASOK's return to power and the winding down of the Macedonian debacle, Greek foreign policy re-focused on Cyprus and Turkey. On the one hand, the nationalist PASOK reinforced its ties with the RoC. Hence, the Joint Defence Doctrine discussed in Chapter 4. On the other hand, Athens pushed the Cyprus dossier in Brussels. In the words of Yannis Kranidiotis, Alternate Minister for Foreign Affairs in 1993: '(t)he Greek government set two immediate goals. The first was to secure a firm political commitment as a full member state on the part of the EU for the accession of Cyprus and try to disassociate the accession process from the solution of the Cyprus problem. The second was to agree on a precise date for the commencement of accession negotiations'.[4]

However, as a government party and as the gains of EC membership started filtering through the system, PASOK's ideology and mode of operation transformed, legitimizing the notion of compromise and alliance-building. Furthermore, Greek policy-makers slowly learned how to operate within the EU decision-making process, using it to their advantage. They realized that as a small and relatively weak member state, Greece could not determine independently

---

[4] Speech delivered at the Canon Newham Memorial Lecture, 18 December 1995, Nicosia.

Council positions towards both Turkey and Cyprus. Hence, unlike the early years of membership, the government no longer simply blocked EU-Turkey relations. It rather made its consent conditional on EU steps to further Cyprus' membership, or on increased EU pressure on Turkey regarding Greek-Turkish issues.

Greece encouraged firm EU pressure on Turkey regarding a settlement of the conflict. On the eve of the EC-Turkey Association Council (frozen since the 1980 military coup) in April 1988, the Greek government persuaded the German Presidency to insert a reference to the conflict. At the December 1988 Rhodes European Council, the Greek Presidency added a sentence in the Conclusions stating that the Cyprus conflict affected EC-Turkey relations. As put by Mitsokakis in 1988: 'the Turks must be made to understand that it will be impossible to make progress in Greek-Turkish relations, as well as in Turkey's attachment to the European Community, if they do not solve the Cyprus issue first, and then address Greek-Turkish differences' (Zervakis, 1997, p.143).

Perhaps the most effective means Greece used to encourage Cyprus' EU membership was by linking its consent to EU-Turkey initiatives to progress in Cyprus' accession. Officially the Greek government rejected the linkage between the integration of the two countries. Explicitly admitting support for linkage would have entailed an admission of Greece's own weakness within the EU. In practice however, in the 'historic compromises' of March 1995 and December 1999, the Greek government was well aware of the growing consensus within the EU to develop relations with Turkey and that it could not reverse the tide. So it opted to influence decisions by linking its consent to progress in Cyprus' accession course.

In 1995, following the Commission's negative Opinion on Turkey in 1989, the 1990 Matutes package and the 1994 Corfu European Council, a majority of member states felt that a step in EU-Turkey relations was necessary. The Greek government could not resist for long. At the December 1994 Essen European Council, Greece stood alone in its opposition to the implementation of the final stage of the EU-Turkey customs union. So in March 1995 it consented to the customs union and the release of the fourth financial protocol funds. However, its consent was linked to the Council's commitment to begin accession negotiations with Cyprus six months after the completion of the 1996 Intergovernmental Conference (IGC). The Greek government insisted that the decision specified that negotiations 'will start' rather than 'can begin' after the IGC. The Greek government's consent to the customs union also strengthened its position in demanding that the member states accepted the acronym FYROM rather than the historic name of Macedonia.

A similar story can be told of the 1999 Helsinki Council. EU-Turkey relations were under severe strain in the aftermath of the December 1997 Luxembourg Council. Most member states were keen to re-establish political ties with Ankara. At the Cardiff Council in June 1998 the British Presidency, strongly encouraged by the US administration, proposed to re-shape the Luxembourg Council conclusions. Thirteen other member states were in favour. Most notably Germany had begun to alter its stance (a policy shift later consolidated with the election of Social Democrat Gerhard Schroeder in September 1998). Yet Greece remained staunchly opposed. At the time, Greek-Turkish relations were particularly strained over the

S-300 missiles incident. Yet the Cardiff Council showed that the Greek government could not hold its opposition for long. Its efforts to enter the eurozone also meant that it could not afford to stand out against the rest. In the context of EMU accession, France and Holland explicitly referred to Greece's stance on Turkey in view of the disproportionately high levels of Greek defence expenditure (approximately seven percent GDP in 1999). The Greek-Turkish rapprochement in the aftermath of the August-September 1999 earthquakes provided a propitious atmosphere for a policy shift. By December 1999, the Simitis government was willing to accept Turkey's EU candidacy. Nevertheless it strived to obtain significant concessions in return. The most important was the explicit removal of conditionality on the Greek Cypriots. In addition it obtained a clause providing for possible referral of the Aegean disputes to the International Court of Justice if these were not solved by 2004.

Another way in which Greek negotiators used their leverage to pursue Cyprus' accession was to link the Greek ratification of EU enlargement to progress in Cyprus' EU accession. This form of leverage was first exerted successfully at the 1994 Corfu European Council, when the Greek government persuaded the member states also to include Cyprus in the fifth enlargement by threatening not to ratify the accession of the Scandinavian countries and Austria. It was exerted again in 1997-98, this time linking Greek consent to the fifth enlargement to Cyprus' inclusion in it.

The dispute began when, in February 1997, several member states and most notably Germany called for a settlement prior to negotiations with Cyprus. The Greek government vetoed this formulation, arguing that it amounted to making Cyprus hostage to Turkey's whims and designs. In Deputy Foreign Minister George Papandreou's words: 'if Germany's objective is to offer a political gift to Turkey, it will have attained its goal today' (*Agence Europe*, No.6922, 26 February 1997). Yet Greek opposition went further, taking the form of a threat. Greek Foreign Minister Pangalos bombastically stated that 'it is Greece that will determine when Cyprus will join the EU', by threatening not to ratify both the Amsterdam Treaty and enlargement at a later date (Mortimer and Hope, 1997).

The dispute flared up again on the eve of accession negotiations in the autumn of 1998. In October-November, France led the EU opposition to the accession of a divided Cyprus, insisting that despite accession negotiations, a settlement should be reached before actual membership. The Greek government branded these statements as 'immoral', 'logically baseless' and 'products of political and moral confusion' (*Kathimerini*, 1998c). Again the government threatened to block progress in all accession negotiations and finally the deadlock was resolved. In 1998-99 many officials in the Commission and the member states doubted the likelihood of Cyprus' membership as a divided island. But given that the decision-making moment was still a long way away, they acquiesced to Greek threats. As put by a Commission official: 'will we say no to a divided island? Perhaps. But why say it now? If we do the Greeks will say that's it, and stop the accession negotiations' (Peel and Wagstyl, 1998).

*Greece's Support for a 'European Turkey' and the Greek-Turkish Rapprochement*

In analysing Greece's impact in the formulation of EU policies towards the Eastern Mediterranean, it is fundamental to understand the profound transformation (or europeanization) that Greece itself underwent as an EU member state, and particularly PASOK as a governing party since the late 1990s. This had profound implications in shifting Greek attitudes towards Turkey, both in the context of bilateral relations and of EU-Turkey relations.

While being an ongoing process since 1981, PASOK's transformation accelerated with the replacement of the late Andreas Papandreou by Costas Simitis in 1996. Since then, the government has demoted the Macedonian question from the political agenda, normalized its relations with Albania and upgraded its ties with Bulgaria. During the 1999 Kosovo crisis the Greek government, while cautious in its approach towards the Kosovars and the Albanians, eventually converged with the EU consensus. Subsequently it began to play a constructive role in the establishment of cooperative structures in the Western Balkans (Coloumbis, 1994). With the 1996 Imia/Kardak crisis, the government was driven back to the well-charted waters of Greek-Turkish affairs. Yet the approach was no longer that of direct confrontation. Instead, the Greek government deftly transferred its tensions with Turkey from the bilateral Greek-Turkish domain to the multilateral EU-Turkey domain, and focused on the desirability of Turkey's 'europeanization'. In March 1997, in response to the Belgian Christian Democrats' rejection of Turkey's future in Europe, Foreign Minister Pangalos stated: 'Turkey of course belongs to Europe. If Turkey is not part of European history, then Greece is not part of European history' (Brewin, 1999, p.151).

In terms of the Greek government's position on EU-Turkey relations, the turning point came with the December 1999 Helsinki Council, in which Greece supported Turkey's EU candidacy. As put by Foreign Minister George Papandreou 'we want a candidacy for Turkey that is a real one … that means they have all the privileges of a candidate, and all the responsibilities'.[5] Other factors affected the Greek government's position in Helsinki. The determination both to ensure the lifting of conditionality on Cyprus and to secure Greek entry into the eurozone was crucial. However Greece's new approach towards Turkey persisted in the period after the Helsinki Council, in spite of the fact that most European leaders increasingly echoed the Helsinki conclusions on Cyprus and that Greece qualified for entry to the eurozone at the Feira European Council in June 2001. In the run-up to the Nice European Council in December 2000, Greece insisted on including Turkey in the calculations of voting weights and representation in the enlarged Union. In the autumn of 2001, Greece lobbied for Turkey's participation in the Convention on the Future of Europe, arguing that the mistake made in Nice should not be repeated.

The most striking example of this turnaround in the Greek government's Turkey policy was in the run-up to the December 2002 Copenhagen Council. Both

---

[5] Interview with Greek Foreign Ministry official, Athens, March 2002.

the Commission and the majority of EU member states were largely sceptical of Turkish demands for a 'date' to begin accession negotiations. By September of 2002 Simitis and Papandreou stood out as the sole vocal supporters of the Turkish request, attempting to articulate Turkey's case within EU circles. They were later joined by Italy, Spain and the UK. In the autumn of 2002, Greek diplomacy had turned 180 degrees from the early days of Greek membership, when Greece stood firm against pressure from other member states to advance EC-Turkey relations.

The transformation of Greece's attitudes towards EU-Turkey relations was also linked to the Greek-Turkish rapprochement since August-September 1999. The seeds of rapprochement were sown during the spring of 1999. Foreign Minister Papandreou in particular increasingly felt the need to engage in constructive dialogue with arch enemy Turkey, following the period of rising brinkmanship in 1996-99 over Imia/Kardak, followed by the S-300 incident, followed by the Kosovo war and the capture of Öcalan in the Greek embassy in Kenya. The earthquakes in Greece and Turkey in August-September 1999 and the reciprocal support between the two countries in the light of these humanitarian crises, provided the pretext or the trigger for a major policy shift, which George Papandreou, son of the late Andreas Papandreou, succeeded in endorsing. The earthquake diplomacy led to the groundbreaking reciprocal visits of Foreign Ministers Ismail Cem and George Papandreou to each other's countries in January-February 2000. Rapprochement then filtered through the system. By the autumn of 2002, Greece and Turkey had signed ten bilateral agreements on 'low politics' issues. Joint Task Forces were established to explore how Greek know-how could help Turkey's harmonization with the *acquis*. By April 2003, Greece and Turkey had not yet resolved any of their long-standing disputes in the Aegean and Cyprus. But on the Aegean, Greece and Turkey agreed to engage in talks on the continental shelf in March 2002. The policy of rapprochement has persisted despite the government change in Athens with the election of Costas Karamanlis' ND in March 2004. Indeed Greek-Turkish relations were not a matter of dispute during the 2003-04 election campaign. Both PASOK and New Democracy pledged to persist and intensify the rapprochement with Turkey.

The Greek-Turkish rapprochement and Greece's policy shift on EU-Turkey relations are intricately linked. The rapprochement facilitated Greece's shift on EU-Turkey relations. By the autumn of 2002 the developing relationship with Turkey allowed the Greek government to act as the main supporter of Turkey's EU bid. In turn Greece's policy shift on EU-Turkey relations, while initially met by Turkish scepticism, gradually became a major confidence building measure between the two countries.

Greece has had considerable input in the determination of EC/EU policies towards Turkey and Cyprus. However, this section has showed that Greece's role underwent a considerable transformation since 1981. The replacement of one position by another has been gradual as one approach merged into and gradually gave way to another. The seeds of moderation have existed since the late 1980s. At the same time, confrontational attitudes have persisted throughout the years. During the 1994 Greek Presidency for example, EU-Turkey relations were almost completely neglected, triggering a visit by British and German Foreign Ministers

Douglas Hurd and Klaus Kinkel to reassure Ankara that an EU initiative towards Turkey was on the way. Up until 1999, Greece continued to block the ratification of the fourth financial protocol. An effective Greek-Turkish dispute blocked the development of an ESDP until December 2002. However, a fundamental shift undeniably occurred and is still in the making.

## The Other Member States: The Policy Vacuum

Turkey and the Turkish Cypriots externally viewed EU policies towards the Eastern Mediterranean as being driven by member state Greece. Indeed the (changing) role of Greece was pivotal in the EU policy-making process regarding Cyprus and Turkey. But how could Greece, as a small member state, play such a key role in both driving EU decisions on Cyprus and providing the dominant reading of the conflict and its resolution? Greece's role was determined by the interaction between the Greek government's positions and those of the other member governments. EU policies affecting the conflict were driven to a large extent by Greece *because* of the general neglect of the issue by the other member states. Neglect of the conflict and ambivalence towards Turkey created a policy vacuum which enabled Greek policy-makers to play a pivotal role in the Union's approach towards the conflict and Cyprus' EU accession.

### Positions on the Accession of a Divided Cyprus

When in 1990 the RoC applied for EU membership, eleven member states did not envisage the accession of Cyprus as a divided island. In May 2004 a divided Cyprus entered the EU. How could one small member state have pushed through its views over the course of the decade? An important part of the explanation lies in the effective neglect of the conflict by the rest. Interest in Cyprus was half-hearted and sporadic, and when it emerged it tended to be in the form of a Greek-demanded compensation for enhancing EU-Turkey relations. The following section reviews the key steps in EU decision-making leading to the removal of conditionality on Cyprus.

The first key decision concerning Cyprus' accession was the June 1993 Commission Opinion, endorsed by the Council in October. In the period leading up to the Opinion, the member states were deeply divided about the application. The Commission and the member states (excluding Greece) were reluctant to enter into the dynamics of the intractable conflict by giving a green light to the accession process. Arguments in favour of non-involvement were particularly compelling given that at the time the UN was engaged in an unprecedented effort to unblock the impasse. However, the RoC was an eligible candidate for accession and was already well placed to accede to the Union, both in economic and political terms (setting aside the existence of the conflict). The resulting Opinion reflected these contrasting forces. The largely uninterested member states gave in to Greek pressures, but ensured that the Opinion included a fairly explicit form of conditionality on the Greek Cypriot Republic.

The next key step was taken at the Corfu European Council in 1994, in which the member states unanimously agreed to include Cyprus in the fifth enlargement. In Corfu, the member governments made their bids. Germany and Belgium supported Poland, the Czech Republic, Slovakia and Hungary; the UK and Denmark supported the Baltic states; France supported Romania; Italy supported Malta and Slovenia. And Greece slipped Cyprus into the list of new candidates. In Corfu, there was not a coherent enlargement strategy or a full awareness of the wider strategic implications of EU actions. There was rather a problem-solving atmosphere in which the member states cast their bids and bargained over an overall package. Enlargement was still a long way away and the member states paid insufficient attention to the specificity of Cyprus to raise serious objections to the Corfu decision. Raising objections would have imperilled the entire bargain.

Then came the March 1995 Council decision. In 1995 most member states, encouraged by the US, were interested in deepening relations with Turkey through a customs union after years of impasse. In order to gain Greece's consent, the member states had to make a move on Cyprus as well. Hence, the 6 March 'historic compromise'. The French Presidency pushed for the compromise principally as a means to enhance EU-Turkey ties. Cyprus was the 'price' to pay for Greek consent. Greece was only partially satisfied with the compromise. The member states had consented to accession negotiations with Cyprus, but they had not committed to its full membership. In fact member states such as France, Germany, Italy and The Netherlands did not hide their reservations. It was no coincidence that, upon French insistence, the 1995 wording referred to 'Cyprus' rather than the 'Republic of Cyprus'. Whether 'Cyprus' referred to a post-settlement island or to the RoC was left unspecified. French Prime Minister Alain Juppé went further, stating that *'ces resolutions prevoient la creation d'une Federation bizonale et bicommunautaire…'* (Brewin, 2000, p.28). Greece was aware of these reservations, but felt that the 1995 decision was a sufficiently strong signal for the time being.

Following the 1995 decision, Cyprus effectively came off the EU agenda until January 1997 when, supported by the majority of the member states, the Dutch Presidency stated that accession negotiations with Cyprus should also include Turkish Cypriot representatives. Greece initially resisted these demands, until at an informal Council in Apeldoorn in March 1997, Greek Foreign Minister Pangalos accepted to persuade the Greek Cypriot government to extend an invitation for participation in accession negotiations to Turkish Cypriot officials. By September 1997 an agreement had been reached amongst the member states on the need for Turkish Cypriot participation. Yet little thought was given to what kind of participation this should be. Hence, the invitation was rejected by the Turkish Cypriots who felt that participation under the RoC would undermine their claims to political equality. Member state France hinted at the inadequate terms of the invitation. Yet confronted by Denktaş's blunt rejection, French unease was easily set aside.

Cyprus resurfaced on the EU agenda only one year later, once again at the instigation of the French and under the British Presidency. Britain and France were concerned about the possibility of Cyprus' accession without a settlement. At the

14 March 1998 Foreign Ministers Meeting in Edinburgh, held on the eve of the formal launch of accession negotiations, French Foreign Minister Hubert Vedrine made it abundantly clear that while the EU accepted negotiations with the RoC, it was not committed to the membership of the conflict-ridden island. Vedrine also added that negotiations could be stalled in the event of a persisting impasse in Cyprus. In the autumn of 1998, a few weeks before the launch of substantive negotiations, France again warned that Cyprus' accession was not automatic and questioned the legitimacy of negotiations without the Turkish Cypriots. The French government then tabled a declaration under the Common Foreign and Security Policy chapter of negotiations together with the Germans, the Dutch and the Italians, stating that a settlement must be urgently found, not least because 'the process of negotiations will give rise to serious problems for the functioning and coherence of the Common Foreign and Security Policy' (Council of Ministers, 1998). Implicit in the declaration was the concern that accession negotiations would severely strain EU-Turkey relations.

But EU-Turkey concerns were set aside when the Greek government deftly linked its consent to the entire enlargement with Cyprus' membership. As soon as enlargement as a whole came into play, the Greeks created strong German incentives to settle the deadlock. Indeed in October 1998, the German government unblocked the impasse. Insisting that 'under no circumstances is there an issue of blocking enlargement', the German government persuaded the French to lift their reservations, which were never particularly strong (*Kathimerini*, 1998d). In its place another sentence was added, stating that although the Turkish Cypriots had rejected participation in negotiations, President Clerides' invitation remained open.

Over the next two years, as negotiations proceeded with the candidate countries, the remaining reservations were swept aside. Indeed at the December 1999 Helsinki Council when, at the eleventh hour, the Dutch Premier Will Kock objected to the lifting of conditionality on Cyprus, it was French President Jacques Chirac who stood firm in opposition to the Dutch. The Dutch government was concerned about Turkey's reaction to the European Council's conclusions on Cyprus, keeping in mind the presence of two million Turks in Holland and the strong business links with Turkey. France, which two years earlier had led the opposition to the accession of a divided Cyprus, persuaded the Dutch to lift their objections, arguing that the entire package involving Turkey's candidacy would be at stake otherwise.

In the immediate aftermath of the Council, Turkey was tempted to reject the Helsinki offer, outraged by the decision taken on Cyprus. This triggered a lightning visit by EU High Representative Javier Solana to Ankara, to deliver and explain a letter from the Finnish Prime Minister Lipponen, which attempted to ease Turkish concerns by implying that account for 'all relevant factors' meant that Cyprus' membership was not automatic. However, in reality there was no consensus between the fifteen on the specific meaning of the Helsinki communiqué's wording. The clause was not inserted as a result of an EU strategy grounded on an appreciation of the need to exert pressure on both parties. Those familiar with the Cyprus conflict, like British Special Representative Lord Hannay, referred to the need for Greek Cypriot as well as Turkish Cypriot goodwill following the Helsinki

Council (*CNN Turk*, 12 June 2002). Yet in reality many of the unspecified 'relevant factors' had nothing to do with the conflict. The clause was inserted to forge internal EU consensus. In July 2002 during the Danish Presidency, Danish Ambassador to Turkey Christian Hoppe, when asked about the 'relevant factors' replied that 'the main factor is that nine other countries are at the doorstep of membership. We cannot ask them to wait until there is a solution in Cyprus... we have our own internal factors which might affect enlargement such as the Irish referendum, agricultural policy...' (Örüç, 2002).

Since December 1999 one last factor that reduced resistance against the accession of a divided Cyprus was the decision that member states would ratify enlargement as a package, i.e., as a single Treaty of Accession for the ten new members. The decision was not taken for Greece-Cyprus reasons. It was taken to have the greatest possible assurance that ratification of the historic eastern enlargement would proceed smoothly. The idea of resisting the accession of Cyprus thus became highly unlikely. Member state reservations were certainly not strong enough to forsake the entire fifth enlargement.

*Positions Towards Turkey*

The EU's impact on the Cyprus conflict was also closely connected to EU-Turkey relations. Setting aside Greece, all member states were keen to retain strong economic, political and security relations with Turkey, as a large, growing and strategically located NATO ally. Yet most member states did not support Turkey's full membership. An appreciation of Turkey's strategic importance was insufficient to persuade the member states to embrace Turkey as a full member of the EU.

This did not entail that the member states decided against Turkey's membership and merely used the Copenhagen criteria as a pretext to fend Turkey away. The debate within EU-15 on Turkey existed for years behind the scenes. However, since the late 1990s, as Turkey slowly progressed along the path of reform and Greece no longer acted as the alibi for the hidden scepticism of other member states, the debate on Turkey's future in Europe was increasingly forced into the open. In the build-up to the December 2002 Copenhagen Council Convention President Giscard d'Estaing and a group a Christian Democrats in the EP openly spoke against Turkey's accession. However, Giscard d'Estaing's remarks were harshly criticized by many European leaders, and the Christian Democrat proposal to replace Turkey's candidacy with the offer of a 'special relationship' was rejected by most member state governments. But regardless of the relative strength of the different views in this debate, the fact that an unresolved debate existed explained the absence of a clear and consistent medium/long-term EU strategy towards Turkey.

In practice, this implied that EU-Turkey relations since the late 1980s developed in ebbs and flows. In 1989 Turkey's application for membership was rejected by the Community. By 1994, with the lack of progress in EU-Turkey relations, Turkey's reaction to Cyprus' accession process, and its apparent drift towards political Islam, the majority of member states felt that a positive step towards Turkey was imperative. Germany, France, the UK, Italy, Spain and The

Netherlands, strongly supported by the US, felt that a customs union, foreseen in the 1963 Association Agreement, was the natural candidate for such a step. The customs union would embed Turkey more deeply within the European sphere, lessening its tendencies to drift to the 'East'. At the same time, it would not entail full membership and would not cover agricultural goods. Furthermore, the large and growing Turkish market of over 60 million people was an attractive prospect for European trade and investment.

Turkey was not content with the customs union, and persisted in seeking full integration in the EU. It received a cold shower in Luxembourg in 1997 when the European Council refused to include Turkey in the enlargement process. The concept in Luxembourg was that in view of Turkey's deficiencies, Greece's resistance, European public opinion and the further reservations of several member states (most critically Helmut Kohl's Germany), Turkey should be kept within the orbit of enlargement in principle, but in practice the member states should seek closer ties through alternative means. This concept was met by extreme Turkish resistance. But what made matters worse was the EU's mishandling of the situation. The member states, principally preoccupied with the CEECs, failed to prepare the ground for the Luxembourg decision. The reasons behind the decision were not explained to Turkey before the meeting, and in turn Turkey felt deeply insulted seeing itself surpassed by countries that also failed to comply fully with the Copenhagen criteria, and that were not long standing NATO allies with long-term structured relations with the Community. Immediately following the Luxembourg Council, the EU President Jacques Poos failed to limit the damage by not engaging in dialogue with Ankara to explain the logic behind the decision.

Indeed it is interesting to compare the roles of Javier Solana in 1999 to that of Jacques Poos in 1997. Also in the case of the Helsinki European Council, a consensus within the EU on whether to extend candidacy to Turkey was not taken until a few months before the meeting. Also in the case of the Helsinki Council, the decisions taken (i.e., regarding Cyprus) created unease in Turkey. However, in sharp contrast to Poos' relative passivity in 1997, on 13 December 1999, EU High Representative Javier Solana flew to Ankara and successfully eased Turkish concerns over the Helsinki package.

Under strong American pressure and in view of the change in Greece's position, the member states accepted Turkey's candidacy at the 1999 Helsinki European Council. However, this did not entail a shared willingness of the member states to develop a consistent strategy towards Turkey, and to recognize the long-term implications of their decisions. The debate that took place in the run-up to the 2002 Copenhagen Council, i.e., three years after the Helsinki decision was taken, illustrates this point. Much of this discussion was labelled as 'surreal' by Belgian Foreign Minister Louis Michel in so far as it pretended to ignore the decision that had been taken back in 1999.

In the autumn of 2002, there was no consensus between the member states on the decision to be taken in Copenhagen. The absence of a unified EU position was due to the schism between the Franco-German axis supported by Austria and the Scandinavian countries on the one hand, and Greece, Italy, Spain and the UK on the other. The former group of countries resisted a clear conditional signal to

Turkey, and preferred a rendezvous clause to decide the next steps in Turkey's EU accession path. The latter group instead were more supportive of Turkish demands. Greece supported Turkey in the light of its policy of rapprochement, while Silvio Berlusconi's Italy, José-Maria Aznar's Spain and Tony Blair's UK focused on the importance of EU-Turkey relations in the context of transatlantic relations and the looming war in Iraq. However these countries' support for Turkish demands was more vocal in public than in private (Dempsey, 2002). Hence, the ultimate decision in Copenhagen converged on a variation of a Franco-German proposal advanced a few days earlier.[6] Once again the final decision indicated a process of drift and postponement of key decisions highlighting the absence of a consistent strategy towards Turkey.

## EU Institutions and Decision-Making

This section seeks to complement the analysis of member state attitudes with an examination of EU institutions. What effect did the structures and modes of operation of EU institutions have on the EU's default policies towards the conflict? Given the national positions analysed above, how did their articulation within the EU institutional setting affect EU decisions towards Cyprus and Turkey?

In analysing the impact of institutions on the Cyprus conflict, it is crucial to bear in mind that very few officials in the institutions dealt with the conflict. This, together with the fact that EU institutions act in a remarkably autonomous and uncoordinated way, led to key decisions being taken without an overall strategy towards the conflict. Exacerbating the situation was the fact that this was not appreciated by the principal parties, and particularly by the Turkish and Turkish Cypriot sides (which had far less contact with EU actors than member state Greece as well as the Greek Cypriots involved in accession negotiations).

### The Council of Ministers, the European Council and the Presidency

Cyprus was rarely the focus of high-level discussions within the Council of Ministers or the European Council. Since 1974, the conflict was seldom discussed beyond working group level in the Council, apart from when EPC statements supported UN resolutions, plans and positions. Even following the effective launch of the accession process in 1990, the conflict was not upgraded on the General Affairs Council's political agenda, less still in European Council discussions and communiqués. No member state, with the exception of Greece and to a lesser extent Britain, had a foreign policy towards Cyprus. Neither were the member states willing to exert sufficient effort to enable the Council of Ministers or the European Council to have a view on the matter. Since the establishment of the High Representative's post, no-one in Javier Solana's policy planning unit dealt

---

[6] On 06 December 2002 during a bilateral Foreign Ministers' meeting, France and Germany decided to support the initiation of accession negotiations in July 2005, if by December 2004 Turkey fulfilled the Copenhagen criteria.

specifically with Cyprus or the Eastern Mediterranean. The Council simply left the matter to the Commission, without giving it either a mandate, or the resources, or the expertise to act outside the confines of the first pillar and propose an EU stance on the conflict.

The six-monthly Presidency made matters worse. With the exception of Greece, all Presidencies neglected Cyprus. The conflict was far too intractable and entrenched for any Presidency to expect a quick success over the course of six months. Furthermore, the conflict did not present an immediate threat or crisis calling for rapid European action. Despite the desirability of unification before accession, the member states did not consider the stalemate on the island as an immediate threat to peace and stability in the region. Notwithstanding good intentions at the start of each six months, time and time again the Cyprus 'hot potato' was passed on from one Presidency to the next.

The opposite was true for Greece. Like many member states and small member states in particular, Greek governments viewed its Presidencies as opportunities to upgrade Greek national interests on the EU agenda (Tsakaloyannis, 1996). Cyprus was on the top of the Greek agenda in all its Presidencies. The role of the Greek Presidency was crucial both in January-June 1988, when political dialogue with Cyprus was launched and at the 1994 Corfu Council. In 1994 the Greek Presidency succeeded in its bid to include Cyprus in the fifth enlargement. Ideally Greece would have preferred a clear date and timetable for the launch and conduct of negotiations with Cyprus. In a meeting in the EP before the Corfu Council, Alternate Foreign Minister Kranidiotis declared that: 'one of the central priorities of the Greek Presidency is to obtain the agreement of the Council for setting a date for the start of negotiations with Cyprus and Malta and a firm timetable for conducting these negotiations' (Ioakimidis, 1997, p.72). Greece failed to fulfil its maximal aspirations, and indeed waited until March 1995, until it obtained a clearer assurance, to start Cyprus' negotiations.

Yet it did succeed in embedding Cyprus in the enlargement process by framing its positions in the context of a wider agenda. Increasingly aware of the importance of alliance-building in the Council, the third Greek Presidency proposed policies that attracted wider support than those narrowly focused on Greek national interests. Greece pushed for an inclusion of Cyprus in the fifth enlargement not by focusing exclusively on Cyprus, but by couching its demands within a wider approach to the Mediterranean. The Greek Presidency argued that the eastern enlargement had to be coupled with an EU re-engagement with the south. By concomitantly pushing for the inclusion of both Cyprus and Malta in the enlargement process, and by supporting the drive for the emerging EMP, the Greek Presidency won the support of Italy, Spain and France for its approach. In addition, the Greek Presidency gained the support of the UK, keen to retain good relations with Cyprus, not least because of its military bases on the island.

*The Commission*

Between 1993 and 2004, the Commission dealt with Cyprus' accession. The Council of Ministers and the European Council, while empowering the

Commission to deal with enlargement, did not call upon it to actively promote a settlement in the context of accession. What effect did this have on the Commission's positions?

The Commission's technical role to manage accession negotiations explained its (initially) rigid approach towards the implementation of the *acquis,* which accentuated Turkish Cypriot suspicions of EU membership. Although towards the end of the accession negotiations the candidate countries secured exemptions to the *acquis,* in the early period of negotiations the Commission was keen to give the impression that the *acquis* was not up for negotiation, and the Commission was simply there to give technical guidance and verify compliance with its progressive adoption. The Commission certainly did not consider it its role to offer exemptions to Cyprus driven by political considerations, which the Greek Cypriot team did not even demand. Such offers would have set a dangerous precedent in negotiations with the other candidates.

The absence of an explicit mandate to deal with the conflict also entailed that the Commission was not called to substantiate how the accession process was intended to catalyse a settlement. When it referred to the 'catalyst' effect, DG Enlargement overplayed the importance of economic incentives. It did so primarily because the Commission had an ideological bias towards economic incentives, in view of the fact that these were the instruments at its disposal. Aid, technical assistance, trade agreements and accession negotiations are the Commission's natural domain, which did have significant impact on reforms in the CEECs (Smith, 1999). But economic incentives of various forms have rarely if ever solved (alone) ethno-political conflicts, especially ones like the Cyprus conflict, centred on an entrenched political-security discourse. Throughout the 1990s, the Commission entirely failed to articulate the 'federal culture' of the Union, as one of the principal advantages of membership.

The absence of a mandate to deal with the conflict also entailed a relative lack of knowledge of it. The Commission's exclusive focus on the accession of a small and relatively unproblematic candidate (once the conflict is completely sidelined) implied that relatively few officials dealt with Cyprus in the Commission. Since accession negotiations were launched, the Cyprus unit in the Commission included eight to ten people, most of whom also worked on 'horizontal issues' covering other candidate countries. While Commission officials dealing with Cyprus certainly informed themselves as best they could about the conflict and its history, their official dossiers kept them away from the issue. The Commission also lacked a professional diplomatic service and so its delegations in Nicosia, Athens and Ankara operated without specific training on the complexities of the conflict.

Relative lack of knowledge about the conflict (in the initial period of the accession process) in turn made officials unaware that many of their statements played into Turkish Cypriot stereotypes and fears of the Union. For example in the 1998 Progress Report, when referring to the institutions of the RoC, the Commission stated that 'the fundamentals of these provisions still apply but without the power-sharing element' (Commission, 1998a, p.8). To Turkish Cypriots, the power-sharing element *was* the core of the 1960s arrangements and the absence of that 'element' was precisely what made the current RoC illegitimate and illegal. So if a reunified Cyprus were to accede to the Union without Turkey, would the Commission brush aside in the same way a hypothetical renewed constitutional breakdown on the island? As the accession process proceeded, the knowledge gap narrowed, but another factor emerged which further complicated the Commission's role.

With the opening of accession negotiations in 1998, Commission officials increasingly accepted the Greek Cypriot discourse. With an exclusive mandate to deal with the accession process, the Commission had minimal contact with Turkish Cypriot officials. Instead, contact with Greek Cypriots intensified, leading to the Commission's increasing acceptance of the Greek Cypriot narrative of the conflict and of its resolution. The more the Commission heard the Greek Cypriot line, the more it became intertwined with its own thinking. These attitudes emerged visibly in the Commission's successive Progress Reports on Cyprus. The reports rightly criticized the status quo in northern Cyprus. Yet they hardly mentioned evidence of Greek Cypriot intransigence. As the Commission accepted the view that the blame fell squarely on the Turkish Cypriots, it espoused the view that a settlement should not be a precondition of Cyprus' accession. On the contrary, pressure on Ankara and Denktaş was imperative, as well as luring the Turkish Cypriots with the prospect of EU prosperity. Commission officials therefore, while refusing official contacts with Turkish Cypriot authorities (fearing these would constitute an act of recognition), sought contact with businessmen and opposition leaders, presenting to them the bounties awaiting for them in Europe, provided they pressured their leadership to alter its stance.

Turkish Cypriot attitudes towards the Commission also accentuated the latter's inclinations towards the Greek Cypriots. The Commission, as a non-state actor responsible for Cyprus' accession negotiations, was the easiest target of Turkish Cypriot disapproval of the EU's approach. To the Turkish Cypriot leadership, the EU in Cyprus was the Commission Delegation in Nicosia, rather than the member state embassies. Hence, it was the Delegation which was subject to the harshest criticism and measures of reprisal. The TRNC's decision to ban all EU information campaigns organized by the Commission in northern Cyprus in December 1997, or the TRNC request in 2001-02 that the Commission Head of Delegation obtained a TRNC visa when crossing the green line, were both incidents that further affected Commission attitudes towards the parties.

The Commission thus proceeded with the accession process of the candidate countries including Cyprus. By doing so, it became increasingly adamant not to see the historic fifth enlargement stall due to the Cyprus impasse. Particularly in the last years of negotiations, Commission officials repeatedly warned Turkish and Turkish Cypriot officials that 110 million people in the CEECs would not await a settlement in Cyprus. Unless the Greek Cypriots simply walked out of the peace process, the Commission did not consider that 'all relevant factors' impaired Cyprus' accession. In addition, as the accession negotiations unfolded without attention paid to the conflict, the accession process became increasingly irreversible. The more irreversible the process became, the less tenable were the weak objections of several member states to the accession of the divided island. Following the launch of accession negotiations in 1998, the Commission's inertial progress in the conduct of negotiations carved an increasingly entrenched path, to which the member states became gradually bound.

## The European Parliament

If relative lack of knowledge and imbalance partly characterized the role of the Commission, the European Parliament was even more acutely marked by these distortions. While the role of the EP as far as Cyprus' accession and the conflict were concerned was far less significant than that of either the Council or the Commission, it was nonetheless significant in accentuating Turkish and Turkish Cypriot perceptions of the Union's bias against them.

In the EP as in other EU institutions, there were very few MEPs concerned with the conflict. Those who were tended to be highly committed to the Greek Cypriot cause. So in almost all its pronouncements concerning Cyprus and Turkey, the EP virulently denounced Turkish Cypriot intransigence, advocated the withdrawal of Turkish troops and supported Cyprus' rapid accession to the Union. Rarely was there any mention of the partial responsibility of the Greek Cypriot side for a continuation of the conflict. On 23 November 2001 in a speech delivered in the RoC parliament, former EP President Nicole Fontaine echoed the position of Greece, stating that the EP would not ratify the eastern enlargement unless it included Cyprus.

In several instances, EP pronouncements were so insensitive to Turkish Cypriot concerns that they were perceived as direct threats to the Turkish Cypriots. For example in a 2000 report on Cyprus, the Parliament stated that 'the Union is capable of making a vital contribution to the security of the Greek and Turkish Cypriot communities ... the Union can help resolve the problem of the controlled return of refugees and the repatriation of settlers' (European Parliament, 2000, point 7). While the statement was acclaimed by the Greek Cypriots, it was regarded as a direct threat by the Turkish Cypriot leadership, that completely dismissed both the complete return of refugees and the repatriation of settlers. In a 2001 report, the EP stated that 'the government of Cyprus is negotiating accession on behalf of *all* Cypriots', a statement which even the most moderate of Turkish Cypriot politicians rejected (European Parliament, 2001, point B).

## The European Court of Justice

The ECJ had virtually no official role in the conflict and therefore minimal knowledge of the situation. Yet this does not mean that the ECJ had no effect on the conflict and on the perceived role of the EU in Cyprus.

The 1994 ECJ case banning Turkish Cypriot exports not bearing RoC certification is a classic instance of how an EU institution, with no official role in the conflict, was induced to act in its sphere of competence, by a party with significant interests in the question, in a manner which seriously affected the conflict. The ECJ, taking a strictly legalistic approach in line with its very nature and mandate, ruled in favour of the Anastasiou plea, brought forward by member state Greece. As such it contributed to weakening the unrecognized TRNC. Yet by doing so it further reinforced Turkish and Turkish Cypriot perceptions of the EU's bias against them.

The ECJ judges may well have ignored the serious effects of their decision on Turkish Cypriot perceptions of the Union. Turkish Cypriots did not delve into the reasons behind the ECJ decision, but simply took it at face value, i.e., yet another step in the EU's progressive slide towards the Greek Cypriot position. The Turkish Cypriot leadership mistakenly saw the ECJ decision on the one hand and Commission proposals for the economic development of northern Cyprus on the other as being closely coordinated, and both part of a monolithic EU structure. This raised further suspicions of the Union by legitimizing a narrative whereby the EU deliberated crippled the Turkish Cypriot economy and then offered economic carrots to force the Turkish Cypriots to comply with Greek Cypriot demands.

**External Factors**

So far this chapter has focused on the internal factors affecting EU policies towards the conflict. As discussed extensively in Chapters 4 and 5, the result of these policies fundamentally affected developments in the region. However, closing the circle, it is equally important to assess how external developments interacted with internal EU elements determining EU policies towards the region.

*Greek Cypriot Diplomacy and Preparation for Membership*

In the early and mid-1990s, the Commission and the member states were highly sceptical of the prospect of Cyprus' EU membership. Many felt that the presence of 'two Greeces' in the Union would have complicated the delicate EU-Turkey ties. However, as time elapsed, noting the RoC's preparation for membership and Greek Cypriot signs of goodwill in peace efforts, the Commission and the member states felt increasingly uncomfortable at the prospect of excluding Cyprus from the fifth enlargement.

Under the Vassiliou and Clerides Presidencies, the RoC made rapid and remarkable progress in its preparation for membership. As soon as Cyprus applied for EC membership, the government launched an internal reform process to comply with the *acquis*. In 1990 it set up its first competition authority, in 1991 it adopted the European Energy Charter and in 1992 it introduced VAT taxation and anchored the Cypriot pound to the deutschmark. Following the 1993 Commission Opinion, the government pursued energetically the harmonization with Community law. In late 1993, the Ministry of Foreign Affairs set up twenty sectoral working groups to harmonize legislation with the *acquis*. The government also set up training courses in EC law. Once accession negotiations began, Cyprus was consistently amongst the best performing candidates. In December 2002 it was the first candidate to formally close all negotiation chapters. Greek Cypriot performance won the support and sympathy of many EU policy-makers. As put by

MEP Mechtild Rothe: 'Cyprus is the best in the class of candidate countries and there is no reason why it should be left to wait'.[7]

Particularly between 1999 and 2003, the Greek Cypriot government also succeeded in presenting itself as the compromising party in the conflict. In November 2000, proximity talks had not ended out of Greek Cypriot will. In the year that elapsed before direct talks were launched, Greek Cypriot diplomacy successfully portrayed its side as the party seeking a solution. When in December 2001 Denktaş invited Clerides for direct talks, the latter readily accepted the invitation and throughout 2002 the Greek Cypriot team never hinted at abandoning the process. With the failure of the talks, the UN Secretary General praised the Greek Cypriot team for its constructive positions (UNSG, 2003, paragraphs 35 and 136). Indeed the Greek Cypriot leadership's negative stance in April 2004 towards the Annan Plan came as an unpleasant shock to many within the EU.

*Turkish and Turkish Cypriot 'Intransigence' and the Views of the UN*

Particularly since the mid-1990s, the Turkish Cypriots were labelled as the 'intransigent' party by the UN Secretary General. As a result, the consensus within the Union on the apportionment of blame for the status quo drifted closer to the positions of the Greek Cypriots. This simplified the task of the Greek and Greek Cypriot governments of garnering support for their views on conditionality towards Cyprus and Turkey. EU actors were gradually persuaded that conditionality on the RoC could hamper the search for a settlement, in so far as it would give Turkey the power to prevent both a settlement and Cyprus' EU membership. Following the Greek Cypriot line, it was considered unjust to make the Greek Cypriots 'hostage' to Turkish intransigence.

When negotiations in June-November 1992 over the 'Set of Ideas' failed to produce an agreement, UNSC Resolution 789 called the Turkish Cypriot side to alter its stance, which it considered to be against the terms of the agreement. In 1994, with the failure of negotiations on the CBM package, the lion's share of the blame was on the Turkish Cypriot side, with the Secretary General concluding that: 'the Security Council finds itself faced with an already familiar scenario: absence of agreement was due essentially to a lack of political will by the Turkish Cypriot side' (UNSG, 1994).

Again, Denktaş was blamed for failure in Glion in August 1997. Denktaş's attitudes were closely linked to the Commission's positions in Agenda 2000. Yet this did not alter EU reactions to his stance. On the contrary, the Glion failure was considered an additional factor affecting the Luxembourg decision to begin accession negotiations with Cyprus while barring the way to Turkey (European Parliament, 1998).

The perception of Turkish Cypriot intransigence was reinforced when Denktaş, supported by Turkey, abandoned proximity talks in November 2000. When talks restarted in January 2002 and the parties failed to meet the June 2002

---

[7] Speech delivered during *Cyprus and the EU* conference organized by the University of Kingston, 10 May 2001.

deadline for an agreement, again the UN and subsequently the EU deemed the Turkish Cypriots predominantly responsible for the failure. With the ultimate failure of the direct talks in March 2003, the UNSG's condemnation of the Turkish Cypriot leadership was unequivocal: '(i)n the case of the failure of this latest effort, I believe that Mr Denktaş, the Turkish Cypriot leader, bears prime responsibility' (UNSG, 2003, paragraph 129).

*The Limits of US Pressure*

A final external factor affecting EU attitudes towards Turkey and Cyprus was the role of the United States. The principal preoccupation of the US was that of anchoring Turkey to Europe. American administrations pressed EU member states to engage Turkey in the integration process and raised Turkey's expectations of the EU. Yet while the US encouraged the member states to be more forthcoming towards Turkey, it could not pressure the Union to accept Turkey as a member state. In pursuing its aims, US administrations displayed insufficient understanding of the importance of fulfilling the Copenhagen criteria as a prerequisite of membership. It was one thing to push the member states to accept a customs union with Turkey, and quite another for the US to persuade the Europeans to accept Turkey as a member.

The US played a key role in affecting EU-Turkey relations in 1995, 1999 and 2002. In 1995, the Clinton administration successfully pressed EU member states to extend the customs union to Turkey. In 1997, it failed to persuade the member states to upgrade Turkey's status to that of EU candidate, and contributed to Turkey's over-reaction to the Luxembourg European Council's decision by having raised hopes in Ankara prior to the Council. Thereafter, American officials pressed EU member governments to reverse their stance. The pressure mounted in 1998, when, relying on their closest European ally, the Americans pressed the British Presidency to enhance EU-Turkey ties at the June 1998 Cardiff European Council. Due to Greek resistance, the Cardiff Council failed to mark a categorical turn in EU-Turkey relations. Greece remained firmly opposed despite heavy American pressure (*Kathimerini*, 1998b). However, by the autumn of 1999, US pressure was critical in securing the decision to extend candidacy to Turkey.

However, while pressure contributed to the 1999 decision to extend candidacy to Turkey, excessive pressure at times proved detrimental to Turkey-EU relations. The starkest example was in the run-up to the December 2002 Copenhagen Council, when the US was particularly keen to further Turkey's cause also because of its own war plans in Iraq. In October 2002, White House Spokesman Richard Boucher criticized the Commission's Progress Report for not having proposed a 'date' to launch Turkey's accession negotiations (*TDN*, 2002). The Danish Presidency responded by calling on the US not to interfere in internal EU affairs. In November-December 2002 the US Ambassador in Ankara incessantly argued that Turkey should be extended a date in so far as its August 2002 harmonization package meant that Turkey fulfilled the Copenhagen criteria, a position that was not shared by the Commission and the member states. Finally, on the eve of the Copenhagen Council, US Secretary of State Colin Powell sent a letter to the

Danish Presidency, again calling on the Union to extend a close and firm 'date' to Turkey in order not to foster a 'clash of civilizations'. Particularly in view of US policies in the aftermath of '9/11', Powell's remarks were met by harsh criticism by several high-ranking European officials including External Relations Commissioner Chris Patten and German Foreign Minister Joshka Fischer. As widely reported in the news on the 13-14 December 2002, excessive American pressure and aggressive Turkish tactics proved counterproductive to Ankara's cause (Psyllides, 2002; Dempsey, 2002).

Throughout the 1990s, American involvement in the Cyprus conflict was sporadic and largely a function of its interests in Turkey as well as in the stability of the island, not least because of the importance of the British bases. The US supported Cyprus' EU accession, while at the same time emphasizing the link between progress in EU-Turkey relations and a settlement in Cyprus. In 1998 for example, US Special Envoy Richard Holbrooke strongly supported closer EU-Turkey relations as a measure to unblock the Cyprus impasse (*Kathimerini*, 1998a). Only in 1996-97 was there a more visible US effort in mediation, through Holbrooke's intervention both to ease tensions between Greece and Turkey (during the Imia/Kardak crisis) and to promote inter-communal negotiations in view of the EU's decision to launch accession negotiations with Cyprus (in Troutbeck and Glion).

These US attitudes were reinforced during George W. Bush's Presidency since 2001 and most critically since the 11 September 2001 attacks. American appreciation of Turkey's importance rose until the 2003 war in Iraq. However, this did not entail greater American attention to Cyprus. There was no high-level American input in the 2002-03 mediation efforts. Indeed unlike his predecessor, Bush did not send a high-ranking Presidential Envoy to Cyprus like Richard Holbrooke in 1996-98. In the run-up to the war in Iraq, American attention to Cyprus reduced further, to the extent that some defined Cyprus as the first casualty of the war.[8]

The EU failed to contribute positively to the search for peace in Cyprus in the 1990s because it was not a single and coherent actor. While the official rhetoric suggested that a well-thought-out policy towards Cyprus and Turkey was designed to catalyse and complement the UN mediation efforts, in practice the EU's decisions were the result of an aggregation of internal and external actors and factors. Policy outcomes were based on the interaction between strong Greek national interests and the neglect of most other member states in a context in which different institutions, paying limited or no attention to Cyprus, often took uncoordinated decisions. External factors in turn interacted with internal EU national interests and institutional predispositions. As the 1990s proceeded, these different forces crystallized into an increasingly irreversible 'default strategy'.

But could the EU have encouraged a settlement of the conflict? Bearing in mind the causes of the failed catalytic effect and the fundamental needs and

---

[8] Contribution by Christos Stylianides in *Cyprus' EU Accession and the Greek-Turkish Rivalry* conference organized by Yale University, 4-6 April 2003.

interests of the conflicting parties, did the EU framework have the potential to offer strong incentives to the two communities and to Turkey to settle the conflict?

## References

Brewin, C. (1999), 'Turkey, Greece and the EU', in C. Dodd (ed.), *Cyprus: the Need for New Perspectives*, Eothen, Huntingdon, pp.148-173.

Brewin, C. (2000), *The European Union and Cyprus*, Eothen, Huntingdon.

*CNN Turk*, 'Interview to Lord David Hannay by Mehmet Ali Birand', 12 June 2002.

Commission of the European Communities (1998a), *Regular Report on Cyprus' Progress towards Accession*, on www.europa.int

Couloumbis, T. (1994), 'The Impact of EC Membership on Greece's Foreign Policy', in P. Kazakos and P. Ioakimides (eds.), *Greece and EC Membership Evaluated*, Pinter, London, pp.189-198.

Council of Ministers of the EC (1973), Council Regulation (EEC) No. 1246/73, 'Agreement Establishing an Association between the European Economic Community and the Republic of Cyprus', *Official Journal*, L133, 21 May 1973, Brussels.

Council of Ministers of the EU (1998), 'Joint Statement made by Italy, France, Germany and the Netherlands on the Greek Cypriot-EU Membership Process during the EU General Affairs Council, 9 November 1998', extracts available on www.mfa.gov.tr/grupa/ad/add/doc19.htm

Dempsey, J. (2002), 'Tough Talk by Ankara and Washington Misfires', *Financial Times*, 13 December 2002.

European Parliament (1998), *Report on the Communication from the Commission to the Council and the EP on the Further Development of Relations with Turkey and on the Communication from the Commission to the Council on a European Strategy for Turkey*, Rapporteur Hannes Swoboda, 19 November 1998, Brussels.

European Parliament (2000), *Report on Cyprus' Application for Membership of the EU and the State of Negotiations*, Rapporteur Jacques Poos, A5-0249/200, 19 September 2000, Brussels.

European Parliament (2001), *Report on Cyprus' Application for Membership of the EU and the State of Negotiations*, Rapporteur Jacques Poos, A5-0261/2001, 11 July 2001, Brussels.

Ioakimidis, P. (1997), 'The Role of Greece in the Development of EC Mediterranean Policy', *Mediterranean Politics*, Vol.2, pp.67-81.

Ioakimidis, P. (1999), 'Greece, the EU and Southeastern Europe: Past Failures and Future Prospects', in V. Coufoudakis, H.J. Psomiades and A. Gerolymatos (eds.), *Greece and the New Balkans: Challenges and Opportunities*, Pella, New York, pp.169-194.

*Kathimerini* (1998a), 'US Fails to Unblock Cyprus Talks', 5 May 1998.

*Kathimerini* (1998b), 'Simitis Tells Clinton "No"', 17 June 1998.

*Kathimerini* (1998c), 'FM blasts France, Italy', 12 September 1998.

*Kathimerini* (1998d), 'EU talks put on fast track', 6 October 1998.

Mortimer, E. and Hope, K. (1997), 'Greece in EU Veto Threat if Entry of Cyprus Blocked', *Financial Times*, 27 July 1997.

Örüç, S. (2002), 'Danish Ambassador Christian Hoppe: It Takes Two to Tango', *Turkish Daily News*, 1 July 2002.

Peel, Q. and Wagstyl, P. (1998), 'Journey into the Unknown', *Financial Times*, 9 November 1998.

Psyllides, G. (2002), 'Crunch Time in Copenhagen', *Cyprus Mail*, 12 December 2002.

Smith, K.E. (1999), *The Making of EU Foreign Policy, The Case of Eastern Europe*, Macmillan, London.

Stavridis, S., Couloumbis, T., Veremis, T. and Waites, N. (eds.) (1999), *The Foreign Policies of the EU's Mediterranean States and Applicant Countries in the 1990s*, Macmillan, London.

Tsakaloyannis, P. (1985), 'Greece's First Term in the Presidency of the EC: A Preliminary Assessment', in C. O'Nuallain (ed.), *The Presidency of the European Council of Ministers*, Croom Helm, London, pp.101-118.

Tsakaloyannis, P. (1996), 'Greece: The Limits of Convergence', in C. Hill (ed.), *The Actors in Europe's Foreign Policy*, Routledge, New York and London, pp.186-207.

*Turkish Daily News* (2002), 'US Shows Impatience with EU Delay on Turkey', 11 October 2002.

United Nations Secretary General (1994), *Report of the Secretary General to the UN Security Council*, 25 May 1994, New York.

United Nations Secretary General (2003), *Report of the Secretary General on his Mission of Good Offices in Cyprus*, 7 April 2003.

Zervakis, P. (1997), 'The Accession of Cyprus to the EU: The Greek Viewpoint', in H.J. Axt and H. Brey (eds.), *Cyprus and the EU: New Chance for Solving an Old Conflict*, Sudosteuropa-Gesellschaft, Munchen, pp. 137-150.

Zielonka, J. (ed.) (1998), *Paradoxes of European Foreign Policy*, Kluwer Law International, The Hague.

# Chapter 7

# The EU's Potential to Encourage a Solution in Cyprus

*'The EU factor in particular offered a framework of incentives to reach a*
*settlement as well as the deadlines within which to reach it'*
(Kofi Annan, UNSG, 2003, paragraph 6)

Irrespective of the actual evolution of the conflict, this chapter argues that the EU framework had the potential to contribute to conflict settlement and resolution in Cyprus. The UN Secretary General, as the official mediator in the conflict, could only bring the parties together and seek convergence by presenting bridging proposals. It could not alone generate the incentives to reach a solution. Some scholars argued that the EU was the only third party with the necessary influence to positively alter the incentive structure underpinning the conflict (Joseph, 2000).

The first aim of this chapter is to explore the potential of the EU *framework* to transform the structure of the conflict, so as to facilitate its settlement and resolution. In order to do so, it does not take as a starting point the positions of the parties in 2002-04, given that these were inextricably linked to the EU's own policies during those years. Instead it accounts for the fundamental needs of the principal parties and their negotiating positions in the late 1980s and early 1990s. Second, it analyses the extent to which the principal parties were aware of the potential in the EU framework? Could changes in any of the EU's policies in 1993-2004 have affected the parties' perceptions of the EU, in particular reducing the mistrust of the Union amongst the Turkish and Turkish Cypriot elites? Could this have increased their incentives to reach an agreement?

## The EU's Potential to Alter the Framework of a Settlement

Since 1974 different yet not necessarily incompatible security, identity and justice objectives (or basic needs) were articulated through largely contrasting negotiating positions over constitution, territory, rights and freedoms, and security arrangements. The inherent incompatibility of these positions was primarily due to their elaboration within the prism of state independence, sovereignty and territorial integrity. Both parties believed that if they held absolute sovereignty they would fulfil their underlying aims. Neither party genuinely accepted the logic of federalism. Moreover, as the parties became locked into negotiations, statehood and sovereignty became ends in themselves, rather than possible means to address their underlying aims.

The UN, itself a product of the international system of sovereign states, also operated within the same logic. Its bridging federal proposals in 1992 sought a compromise by splitting the differences between the positions of the parties. They left both communities equally unsatisfied and could not generate the necessary commitment to a solution. Furthermore, several proposals were vaguely articulated precisely because of their attempt to meet halfway the inherently contradictory positions of the parties. For example, sensitive to Greek Cypriot demands, the UN agreed to retain a 'single' sovereignty on the island. Yet sovereignty was also divided in so far as it would 'emanate equally' from the two communities. The UN also argued in favour of a 'new partnership', hinting at the idea of the establishment of a new state. Yet it adamantly denied any recognition of the TRNC, easing Greek Cypriot fears.

To what extent could the EU framework provide an alternative context in which mutually compatible satisfiers could be sought? Much has been written about the role of European integration in securing peace in Western Europe in the post-World War II era. Most of this literature focuses on the search for peace *between* member states through integration and the ensuing creation of dependable expectations that disputes would be settled in peaceful ways (Deutsch, 1957; Haas, 1968; Mitrany, 1966). There is also a growing body of literature that describes the European Union as a multi-level framework of governance, a three-level system in which the inter-dependent European, national and sub-national levels of government interact and as a whole embody the European system of governance (Marks et. al., 1996b; Hooghe and Marks, 2001). In what follows, insights from the multi-level governance literature and from studies of federal systems in the EU are explored to argue that the Union, because of its structure and policies, represented an alternative framework that could have facilitated an agreement in Cyprus. While many differences between the parties would have persisted, the EU dimension could have encouraged an agreement by mitigating some of the divergences on each of the key headings of the conflict settlement agenda.

*The Constitution*

Since partition, the status and constitution of the future state/states in Cyprus has been the most contentious issue in inter-communal negotiations. Absolutist views of sovereignty and statehood prevented the parties from reaching common ground. Yet within the EU, the difference between monolithic and shared sovereignty is fundamentally blurred. Decision-making and implementation is determined by a particular allocation of competences between levels of government. While the different levels remain legally distinct, they become practically inter-related and inter-dependent through channels of communication and policy procedures. As such the notion of sovereignty is essentially transformed. A UN official shared this intuition when stating that 'the vast gap that separates the positions of the two sides on the issue of sovereignty could be narrowed by applying EU norms, something that could give Annan a way out of this maze' (*Cyprus Weekly*, 2002b).

Although the Union is predominantly shaped and constituted by its member states, through its policies and its institutions it mitigates the black-and-white 'differences between single and divided sovereignty. The role of the second (state) level within the EU is fundamentally transformed. While remaining fully-fledged 'states', EU member states delegate several competences to 'Brussels'. Predominantly in the economic domain and increasingly in the justice and home affairs sphere, the first (supra-national) level of government lies at the fore of policy-making. And at the EU level, decisions in most domains are taken collectively on the basis of majority rule. The EU framework also increases the scope for third (sub-national) level roles in EU policy-making (Harvie, 1994; Hooghe, 1996; Scharpf, 1994). As a result EU integration is developing into a multi-tiered process extending above as well as below the state.

However, it would be incorrect to conclude that EU membership necessarily upgrades the role of the third tier (Jeffrey, 2000). It rather enhances opportunities for the development of an inter-dependent (rather than independent) third level. Whether these opportunities are seized depends on the internal structure of the member states, i.e., on the extent to which regions already have pronounced roles within their state (Jeffrey, 2001b, p.217; Bullman, 2001, p.18). In other words, the emerging system of multi-level governance, rather than developing into a homogenous system throughout the Union, is shaped by the internal features of each member state. According to some authors, the opportunities open to sub-state levels of government in the EU are also far too circumscribed (Liable, 2001; Wouters and de Rynck, 1996). Nevertheless, they are considerably more extensive than those within the international system at large. In this respect, the EU could have offered a more propitious framework for a solution in Cyprus on the basis of a decentralized yet single EU member state.

*The participation of sub-state actors in the Council of Ministers*   The case of Belgium illustrates the potential of the EU framework to facilitate an agreement on the future constitutional status of Cyprus (Emerson and Tocci, 2002). While the detailed provisions of a settlement would probably differ from those in Belgium, Belgium shares important structural features with Cyprus. Like Cyprus, Belgium is a small state with two main cultural communities. As Cyprus is striving to achieve, Belgium has restructured its political system in several stages from being a centralized unitary state to a very decentralized federal one, which displays confederal features as well (Jans, 2001). Due to the rising tensions between the Flemish and Francophone communities, Belgium embarked on a slow process of federalization in the 1960s. Belgium's federalization includes three regions dealing with territorial matters (Flanders, Wallonia and Bruxelles-Capitale) and three communities dealing with matters affecting individual citizens (Flemish, Francophone and Germanophone) (see Table 7.1). However, as in Cyprus there are two principal communities: the Flemish and the Francophone. Today Belgium is by far the most loosely federalized state in the EU. For this reason, the Belgian case offers important insights to the search for a Cyprus settlement within the EU.

**Table 7.1     Multi-tier Governance in a Bi-ethnic EU Member State: Belgium**

| 1. | EU level |
|---|---|
| 2. | National EU member state level |
| 3A. | Sub-national territorial entities (Flanders, Wallonia and Brussels) |
| 3B. | Sub-national communities (Flemish, Francophone and Germanophone) |
| 4. | Municipalities |

Moreover, Belgium adopted several principles and provisions that resemble those that were either agreed upon or discussed in Cyprus. Since the 1977-79 high-level agreements, the principal parties accepted that a future state would be bi-zonal and bi-communal, with each region being administered by one community. Belgian federalism also created two major regions of Flanders and Wallonia, administered by the Flemish and Francophone communities respectively. Belgium also includes the region of Bruxelles-Capitale. This region, located in Flanders, was established because of the mixed population in the capital city (85 percent Francophone).

Both Belgian federalism and Cyprus' peace talks emphasized the importance of the lack of hierarchy (or political equality) between the communities and levels of government. In the 1992 'Set of Ideas', the UNSG stated that 'one community cannot claim sovereignty over the other community' and that 'the federal Government cannot encroach upon the powers and functions of the two federated states' (UNSG, 1992a, points 11 and 21). Likewise, the Belgian constitution also endorsed the concept of political equality. This was expressed in terms of the absence of legal hierarchy between the central and sub-national levels of government. All levels enjoy sovereign powers in their areas of competence.

Another interesting parallel is the idea of shared powers in foreign policy-making. The Set of Ideas stipulated that while foreign affairs would be a federal competence, the federated states could enter into agreements with third parties in their areas of competence (UNSG, 1992a). Since 1993, the Belgian constitution endorsed the principle of *in foro interno, in foro externo*, i.e., the Constitution divides treaty-making powers between the levels of government according to the division of internal competences. Each level has limited international legal status to conclude and ratify international treaties in areas of exclusive internal policy competence. For matters falling under shared competences, the constitution calls for inter-ministerial coordination followed by the separate ratification of all the legislative bodies involved. Regions are thus free to engage in external relations provided they adhere to the general principles of Belgian foreign policy.

The principle of *in foro interno, in foro externo* had extremely important implications on Belgium's participation in EU institutions. This was because it affected the manner in which Belgium abided to Article 146 of the 1991 Treaty of Maastricht. Article 146 read: 'The Council shall consist of a representative of each Member State at ministerial level, authorized to commit the government of that Member State.' The significance of this article was that it replaced a former provision stipulating that only ministers of national governments could represent member states in EU Councils. The change in the text was negotiated at the insistence of Belgium and Germany, in order to permit their governments to be represented by ministers from sub-national levels. These demands had resulted from the increasing tendency of the EU to legislate in areas that were mostly or exclusively sub-national competences in federal member states. When Belgium and Germany pressed for this provision, the other member states acquiesced on condition that there could be only one representative who could speak and vote in the Council, and that he/she would be authorized to commit the member state as a whole. The application of Article 146 became more interesting in Belgium than in Germany, both because of Belgium's greater degree of decentralization and because it has only two large federated entities, whereas Germany has 17 *Länder*.

Given these provisions and the absence of legal hierarchy in Belgian federalism, elaborate rules were developed on who would represent Belgium depending on the agenda of the Council (Kerremans, 2000; Kerremans and Beyers, 2001). They were formalized in the 1994 Cooperation Agreements. The decision on whether the leader of the Belgian delegation should be from the federal or sub-national level would depend on which level had the main competence for the policy area of the particular Council in question. For this purpose six categories were set up (see Table 7.2). Two categories identified the exclusive competences of the federal and sub-national levels respectively, in which case only that level of government would be represented. Two categories concerned shared competences. In one case the federal level had the main responsibility and the sub-national level a lesser involvement, and the other case was vice versa. Since 2001, two additional categories have been introduced. Agriculture was considered a separate category in which the federal minister would lead the delegation accompanied by both regional ministers. Fisheries was also dealt with as a separate category, dealt with exclusively by the Flemish government. In categories II, III and IV, only one sub-national representative would attend the Council meetings. The representatives would rotate by half-yearly rotation, coinciding with the EU Presidency.

**Table 7.2  Belgian Model for Representation in EU Councils**

| Type | Division of competences | Leader | Assisted by ... |
|------|-------------------------|--------|-----------------|
| I | Exclusively federal | Federal | None |
| II | Mainly federal, partly sub-national | Federal | Region or community |
| III | Mainly sub-national, partly federal | Region or community | Federal |
| IV | Exclusively sub-national | Region or community | None |
| V | Agriculture | Federal | Flemish and Walloon ministers |
| VI | Fisheries | Flanders | None |

As a result of its use of the opportunities under Article 146, Belgium established an elaborate system of coordination between the levels of government. When the Commission issues a proposal, it is sent to the Belgian Permanent Representation, which sends it to all the levels of government. Each of these governments defines its position and expresses them at weekly meetings of a committee (P.11 Committee) convened at the Ministry of Foreign Affairs. These meetings determine Belgium's position in the Council, and instructions are given to whoever represents Belgium there. There has to be unanimity on the part of the federal and regional governments, since there exists no legal hierarchy between the levels. There are approximately twenty P.11 meetings per month, many of which take place exclusively between community/regional levels of government.

If agreement is not possible, the issue is referred to the Inter-Ministerial Conference for Foreign Policy in which the Ministers themselves are present. If they fail to agree, the issue is passed to the top level: the Concertation Committee of the Prime Minister of Belgium and the Ministers-Presidents of the sub-state entities. If there is still a failure to reach agreement, then Belgium abstains from participating in the negotiations, and also abstains if a vote is taken. However, there are strong incentives to avoid an abstention, given that an abstention never has a neutral effect. When an abstention is cast in a context of qualified majority voting, it counts as a negative vote. The party/parties in Belgium advocating a positive vote therefore have strong incentives to reach a consensus in which their concerns are at least partly reflected. The opposite is true when decisions are taken on the basis of unanimity, i.e., an abstention counts as a positive vote. Indeed Belgium has rarely abstained from a Council vote.

Once the Belgian position and representation within the Council are determined, there is then a division of labour between the 'leader' of the Belgian delegation and an 'assessor' who comes from a different level of government in categories II, III and V. The leader represents the level of government with the larger share of responsibility for the competence discussed in the Council. The assessor assists the leader and takes the floor when the aspect under discussion falls under the competence of the level of government he/she represents. The assessor also has the task of keeping in contact with the non-participating governments at that particular Council meeting as negotiations proceed, thus arranging 'live coordination' by phone from the Council chamber.

The Belgian case demonstrates how, within a highly decentralized EU member state, sub-state actors can play a direct role even in the most inter-governmental institution of the Union, the Council of Ministers. It illustrates how the notion of indivisible internal and external sovereignty is blurred within the EU. Concomitantly, the concept of legal and political equality is bolstered. The roles of second and third-level players in Belgium's participation in EU decision-making have become far less distinct. In a set of policy areas (i.e., categories III, IV and VI), the sub-state level effectively enjoys second-level player status.

Regardless of the specificities of a Cyprus settlement, the Belgian example highlights how notions of sovereignty and statehood can acquire a different meaning within the EU, provided sub-state levels of government already play important roles within their member state. Indeed the concept behind Belgium's representation in EU institutions was included in the 2002-04 Annan Plan and was accepted by the principal parties.[1] The Annan Plan aimed to raise the appeal of a settlement within the EU to the sceptical Turkish Cypriot side by endorsing the Belgian mode of domestic coordination on EU matters. The Plan stated that: 'constituent states shall participate in the formulation and implementation of policy in external relations and EU affairs on matters within their sphere of competence in accordance with Cooperation Agreements modeled on the Belgian example' (UNSG, 2004b, Main Articles, Article 2.2). Thus as in Belgium, the Annan Plan stated that levels of government would need to coordinate their stances in order to reach common positions to be presented at the EU level.

However, while the formulations of the Annan Plan on domestic coordination were modeled on the Belgian example, those on representation in EU Councils were rather vague, thus departing from the Belgian model. Article 19.3 of the Constitution, making use of the possibilities allowed for under Article 146 of the EU Treaty stated: 'Cyprus shall be represented in the EU by the federal government in its areas of competence or where a matter predominantly concerns an area of its competence. Where a matter falls predominantly or exclusively into an area of competence of the constituent states, Cyprus *may* be represented either by a federal government or by a constituent state representative, provided the latter is able to commit Cyprus' (my italics). This meant that Cyprus, together with the Belgian, German and Austrian federations, would belong to the limited number of member states that could be represented at the EU level by federated entities (Kovziridze, 2002). However, unlike Belgium – where in their areas of competence the Federation must be represented by the federated entities – the Annan Plan merely allowed for the possibility of sub-state representation in EU Councils, without making it mandatory. In this respect the regulations in the Plan resembled the German and Austrian models of representation rather than the Belgian one.

Under the Annan Plan, as in the case of Belgium, the implementation of EU laws and regulations would be shared in accordance with the internal division of powers (UNSG, 2004b, Constitution, Article 19.4). If, however, the constituent states defaulted on their EU obligations, the federal level would be called upon to ensure the implementation of EU laws and regulations, irrespective of the policy matter in question. The Plan also stipulated that any new EU treaty or agreement would be ratified by Cyprus unless rejected by both the federal and by the two constituent state legislatures (UNSG, 2004b, Constitution, Article 19.7).

*Direct links between the sub-state and supra-state levels of government*   The EU framework can also encourage the transformation of absolutist views of sovereignty in virtue of the direct links that exist between the sub-state and the EU level of government. These direct links may enhance the role of sub-state actors. The supra-national level has developed policy competences in several areas that affect or are domestically dealt with by the regions, even in states which are not internally federalized. These include environmental protection, technology and

---

[1] In what follows, reference to the Annan Plan refers to the fifth and final version, presented to the parties on 31 March 2004.

R&D, regional policy, social policy, education and culture. They also include financial instruments and most notably, structural funds. These regional policy arenas in turn created the potential for direct links between the sub and supra-state levels of government (Hooghe, 1996). In so far as specific EU policies directly affected EU regions, the Commission established direct contacts with the third level. The two main channels for supra-sub-state relations are the Committee of the Regions and direct regional representation in Brussels.

The Committee of the Regions (CoR) was founded in 1991. The Committee acts as an advisory body that must be consulted by the Commission, the European Parliament and the Council of Ministers on all matters relevant to EU regions. The Committee also has the right to issue its own opinions. However, its recommendations are not binding. Since the 2000 Treaty of Nice, the members of the CoR must be elected representatives of European regions. They are appointed every four years by the member states. Under the provisions of the Nice Treaty, Cyprus is entitled to six seats in the CoR, shared between the two communities in the context of a settlement.

The importance of the CoR should not be exaggerated, given the non-binding nature of its opinions. The Committee has not yet become the 'upper house' of a federal Europe. Nor has it spearheaded a significant development of the 'Europe of the Regions'. It is a highly heterogeneous body given the wide-variations in the characteristics of the regions it represents (Wagstaff, 1999). Nonetheless, while in theory each EU region has the same *de jure* representation in the Committee, in practice the regions from member states with the most decentralized structures have acted as the motors of the institution. For example the amendments made in the Nice Treaty were spearheaded by a declaration of 20 constitutional regions of Europe in September 2000. In so far as a Cyprus settlement would entail a highly decentralized system, its regions could also be expected to play an important role in the Committee. The CoR thus represents an additional, albeit not principal, means to enhance the role of EU regions in a reunited Cyprus.

Since the mid-1990s, there has been a rising number of regional offices in Brussels (Jeffrey, 2001a). These offices were established to lobby European institutions, to secure a greater portion of European funds, to acquire information on European policy-making as well as to provide EU decision-makers with information regarding regional positions.

Again, representation tends to be prominent amongst regions which already enjoy a relatively autonomous status within their member state (Marks, Nielsen, Ray and Salk, 1996a). Given their greater internal powers within the state, these regions are the ones with a higher stake in the European policy process and as such with greater incentives to establish regular contact with European institutions. Functional objectives are often also supplemented by political aims. Regions with greater policy competences tend to be those with a greater sense of distinctive identity. Representation in Brussels and thus the establishment of direct sub-supra-state links is viewed by some regions as a route to enhance their status and by-pass the state. The same could be true in the event of a Cyprus settlement within the EU.

*The growing sphere of EU competence*  The EU could have increased the potential for a Cyprus settlement not only because of the nature and structure of its institutions, but also because of the growing number and salience of EU policies. The transfer of sovereign competences from the national (as well as sub-national) levels of government to the supra-state EU level could have eased the competition for the allocation of competences in Cyprus.

Cyprus' monetary policy at the macroeconomic level – control of interest rates and money supply –would be set in its fundamental aspects 'in Frankfurt' rather than in Nicosia. Cyprus could join the eurozone two years after EU accession provided the country respected the Maastricht criteria. If so, the Central Bank of Cyprus would become part of the European System of Central Banks and its governor would become a member of the Governing Council of the European Central Bank. Monetary union would not automatically settle all divergences over monetary policy. During past negotiations over the Set of Ideas, while the two community leaderships accepted that monetary policy would be a federal competence, they had been at odds over questions of representation and institutional structure, with the Turkish Cypriot side insisting on the retention of two separate central banks (UNSG, 1992b). However the prospect of monetary union would reduce the salience of discussions on Cyprus' monetary policy. Indeed the national central banks of the euro area now find themselves with spare staff resources given their reduced powers and functions. During the 2002-04 talks, monetary policy was unsurprisingly not a bone of contention between the parties.

The EU's own exclusive competences in external trade could have facilitated convergence in Cyprus. The 1992 Set of Ideas proposed and the parties accepted that customs and trade would be a federal competence. Yet differences remained as the Turkish Cypriots insisted that the federal level should set rules and procedures to be implemented by the constituent states. With external trade competences passing to the EU level, the federal level at most would be left with the management of the customs service and the transfer of all customs duties to the EU. This could have induced the Turkish Cypriot leadership to accept central control of the customs service. It could also have made the Greek Cypriot side readier to discuss coordination mechanisms between the national and sub-national levels. The prospect of EU accession could have increased the palatability of a settlement for the Turkish and Turkish Cypriot leaderships also in view of the Turkey-EU customs union. The inclusion of Turkey and Cyprus in the EU customs union would allow Turkey to retain its trade links with the Turkish Cypriots.

In most areas of the internal market, the EU is responsible for the determination of norms and standards through laws and regulations. The areas covered include transport and energy, competition policy as well as the common agricultural policy. Similarly the field of environment, while not regarded as a single market policy, is also the subject of much EU standard-setting and regulation. These standards are then transposed into national laws and implemented by member states according to their internal division of competences. The Set of Ideas entrusted the central level of government with the powers to set standards on questions such as public health, environment, natural resources, and weights and measures. The centre would also be responsible for airports and ports, communications, patents and trademarks. All other residual areas would be sub-state competences. During the 1992 negotiations, the two leaderships accepted these provisions in principle but with several reservations. The Turkish Cypriot side insisted that the centre would only set minimum standards, while the Greek Cypriot side called for central level policy-making and implementation as well as a uniform commercial and company law (UNSG, 1992b). The Union's own competences and harmonization mechanisms could have facilitated agreement on these questions. They could have eased Greek Cypriot concerns about the need for harmonization as well as increased Turkish Cypriot willingness to allow the centre to legislate in several policy fields given the sharing of powers with the EU level. Indeed, the competences reserved for the centre by the Annan Plan such as natural resources, communications, transport, combating terrorism and organized crime, intellectual policy and antiquities were not contended by the parties.

The EU also sets standards in budgetary policy. All EU member states are required to harmonize their value-added tax base and cede a small fraction of these revenues to the EU budget. In addition according to the Growth and Stability Pact, membership of the eurozone requires that the general budget balance should aim to keep the budget deficit below three percent of GDP. Within the EU this is generally considered a national competence and the EU holds the national authorities responsible for seeing that the internal coordination arrangements with the sub-state levels are adequate. However, federal states such as Belgium have developed internal mechanisms for coordination and verification, through the *Conseil Superieur des Finances*. In past negotiations including the 2002-04 talks, the parties accepted both central and sub-state level budgets. In 1992 however, the Greek Cypriot side called for federal powers in setting Cyprus' overall economic and budget policy (UNSG, 1992b). The standards set by the Growth and Stability Pact could have helped to ease differences on this question. The EU would set requirements and standards which Cyprus as a whole would have to abide to.

Since the establishment of the EU Justice and Home Affairs pillar, the Union has witnessed a growing body of EU law governing the movement and residence of persons in EU member states. In addition there are the rules of the Schengen system, which are increasingly being integrated into EU law. Both the Set of Ideas and the Annan Plan classified citizenship and immigration as federal competences and both sides accepted this. In 1992 however, while the Turkish Cypriot side argued that the central level should only set rules and procedures on these questions, the Greek Cypriot side insisted that implementation should also be carried out by federal authorities (UNSG, 1992b). EU competences in the field of Justice and Home Affairs (JHA) could have facilitated a meeting point between the positions of the parties. For example, the Greek Cypriot side could have viewed more favourably the idea of sub-state technical regulations and implementation in this field.

Concerning citizenship, the additional layer of EU citizenship could have contributed to a de-ethnicization of identity as well as to the acceptance of multiple identities in Cyprus. The major cause for disagreement over questions of citizenship was the fate of the Turkish settlers and their possible repatriation. Both sides viewed identity and citizenship through strictly ethnic and highly politicized lenses, which reduced the scope for agreement. The Greek Cypriots insisted on central level policy-making and implementation so as to ensure that individuals not satisfying citizenship criteria would not be granted such rights in practice. The Turkish Cypriot leadership, wary that the centre would force mainland Turks to leave, called for decentralized implementation (UNSG, 1992b). EU citizenship would not eliminate these tensions. However, within the EU, citizenship is acquiring a different meaning and is being increasingly associated with civic rights, rather than with exclusively national or ethnic affiliations. The additional layer of EU citizenship could also have eased the debate on whether Cyprus should have single or divided citizenship (and thus identity). Citizenship would have three rather than only one or two dimensions.

The Annan Plan provided for a three-layered citizenship. In addition to United Cyprus Republic citizenship, Cypriots would enjoy both EU citizenship and constituent state citizenship. The Plan also attempted to insert civic rather than purely ethnic criteria in the definition of citizenship and identity. For example, representation in the lower house of the federal legislature would be based on constituent state citizenship rather than community affiliation (provided the Turkish Cypriot constituent state held at least 25 percent of the seats). Representation in the constituent state legislature would be based on permanent residency and not on ethnicity. Only in the Senate would representation be grounded on community affiliation (i.e., there would be an equal number of Greek and Turkish Cypriots).

*The option of secession*     Historically, the questions of secession (*taksim*) and annexation (*enosis*) touched the core of the Cyprus problem. Negotiating questions of status with the prospect of EU accession could have facilitated a settlement in Cyprus given the reduced significance of annexation or secession within the Union. If a reunified Cyprus were to accede to the Union, would secession be a realistic or desirable option for the Turkish Cypriots? In so far as the EU would not accept a second Cypriot state, the seceding Turkish Cypriots would exit the Union and be deprived of the advantages of membership. However, even if the EU hypothetically accepted a separate Turkish Cypriot member state, Turkish Cypriot incentives to secede could be low. The secession and statehood debate in northern Cyprus has been articulated as a need for physical (as well as political) separation from the Greek Cypriot community. However, if the Turkish Cypriot state seceded while remaining in the EU, the same freedoms would be granted to Greek Cypriots as fellow EU nationals. The Turkish Cypriots could no longer achieve separation through secession in an EU context. Furthermore, the new Turkish Cypriot state would have to renegotiate the terms of its accession to the Union, with all the costs and problems that this would involve.

This transformed meaning of secession within the EU could have generated moderation and trust in inter-communal negotiations. The Turkish Cypriot leadership could have displayed more flexibility on questions of status and state succession, given the different cost-benefit analysis of secession in the EU. The Greek Cypriot leadership, aware of the reduced Turkish Cypriot incentives to secede within an EU framework, could have been readier to accept some 'confederal' elements to a solution, rejected in the past on the grounds that these would have facilitated Turkish Cypriot independence. Indeed during the 2002-04 negotiations, the parties (and in particular the Greek Cypriot side under former President Clerides and the Turkish Cypriot side in the 2004 talks) accepted that an agreement would result in a 'new state of affairs' (UNSG, 2004b, Main Articles, Article 1.1). This vague provision did not validate the positions of either party on the delicate question of state succession.

*Territory and Economic Development*

A settlement would entail some territorial readjustments with a reduction of the Turkish Cypriot zone. Yet there remained substantial differences between the two sides, with the Turkish Cypriot leadership objecting to the return of the Morphou area given that this was the most agriculturally productive area in northern Cyprus. The prospect of EU membership would not ease significantly the debate on territory. However, the prospect of membership could have transformed the economic rationale informing the negotiating positions on territory. In the EU, the economic development of northern Cyprus would rely less on agriculture. Already in the more developed southern Cyprus, in 2000 agriculture represented 3.7 percent of Gross Value Added and 9.2 percent of total employment (Commission, 2001a, p.105-6). A reunified island within the EU would have allowed northern Cyprus to develop in a similar manner. The prospect of EU membership could have increased Turkish Cypriot flexibility concerning the issue of territory given the rapid economic development expected within the EU.

In addition the Union pledged to assist the development of northern Cyprus through structural funds. The rules and criteria of the EU structural funds would have seen the whole of northern Cyprus recognized as 'Objective 1 Priority Region'. The Commission published in January 2002 indications of the likely scale of financial assistance to Cyprus. The total amounts foreseen in commitments for northern Cyprus through structural funds and pre-accession aid (which northern Cyprus did not benefit from during Cyprus' accession process) were €39 million in 2004, €67 million in 2005 and €100 million in 2006 (Commission 2002a).

A large part of these funds could have been spent on the renewal of economic infrastructures specifically linked to issues of territorial readjustment. Special attention would have been paid to transport and communications infrastructures between north and south. Following the experience of Portugal, the EU could have also made grants for investment in institutions of higher education and public health. Loan finance for private sector investment, as well as public infrastructure, could have also been available from the EIB (for the development of tourism for example). This could have supported the scaling down of the public sector in northern Cyprus. Over and above these funds, in 2004 the EU pledged €300 million to aid Cyprus in the implementation of the Annan Plan (and in particular the re-settlement of Turkish Cypriots due to territorial adjustments), in addition to the $400 million pledged by the US.

Non-economic considerations, namely the displacement of Turkish Cypriots resulting from territorial readjustments, were also at the fore of discussions. In this respect, EU membership could have eased the search for a solution given the transformed meaning of borders within the Union. A map of straight lines would have been even less necessary given the merely administrative nature of both intra and inter-state borders in the EU. The possibly greater acceptability of a non-linear border in turn would have facilitated an agreement on territorial adjustments, by minimizing the number of displaced Turkish Cypriots while maximizing the number of Greek Cypriot returnees.

Indeed the Annan Plan did not provide for a linear border. Territorial readjustments provided for under the Plan reduced the northern zone to approximately 29 percent of the land. This percentage was similar to that proposed in the Ghali map in 1992. However, the far more non-linear nature of the Annan Plan border (see Map 2 in Annex) would have allowed for the return of well over half of the Greek Cypriot refugees under Greek Cypriot administration, while displacing the minimum number of Turkish Cypriots. The remaining displaced persons who wished to return to their properties would have the right to reinstatement of one third of the value and one third of the area of their total property within three to five years. They would receive compensation for the remaining two thirds. They would not have the right of reinstatement (and receive compensation instead) if their properties were currently occupied by other displaced persons or had been significantly improved.

*Security*

On security, the main issue of divergence between the parties concerned the role and rights of Turkey in Cyprus. While discussions on the retention, amendment or abolition of the Treaty of Guarantee would have affected exclusively the principal parties and guarantor countries, the EU and its legal mechanisms could have added a positive new dimension to Cyprus' security system. Chapter 5 analysed the Greek Cypriot security gains from EU membership and the ensuing perceived threats to the Turkish Cypriot community. But could the EU's legal mechanisms have contributed to an increased sense of security of both communities and thus facilitated a win-win agreement?

In addition to hard military guarantees, EU membership would have provided also a non-military guarantee of the rights and constitutional order in Cyprus. Under the Treaty of Amsterdam, mechanisms were established through which the voting rights of a member state could be suspended in the event of serious breaches of rights and constitutional provisions within that member state. In the event of a breach to the principles of 'liberty, democracy, respect for human rights and fundamental freedoms, and the rule of law' (Article 6.1), 'the Council, acting by a qualified majority, may decide to suspend certain rights deriving from the application of the Treaty' to a member state (Article 7.3). In other words, upon Cyprus' accession Articles 6 and 7 of the Treaty of the European Union could have acted as an automatic non-military guarantee both of the constitutional order and of the respect for EU norms in Cyprus.

The prospect of an EU non-military guarantee could have facilitated a settlement on security questions in two ways. First, it would have provided an extra element of security to the Turkish Cypriots against a hypothetical recurrence of the events of 1963-74. Provided the EU guarantee existed in addition to rather than as a replacement for any other guarantee freely agreed upon by the parties, EU membership could have been viewed as an additional provider of security to the Turkish Cypriots, given the strong deterrent force of possible EU reprisals. Second, the inclusion of an EU non-military guarantee could have reassured the Greek Cypriot community and thus increased their flexibility in accepting Turkey's role in Cyprus' security. In the hypothetical situation of a constitutional breakdown or an infringement of rights caused by the Greek Cypriots, the Greek Cypriot authorities would be punished first by the EU and only upon last resort by military means. The disincentives on all parties to infringe the agreements would be sufficiently strong so as to effectively eliminate the prospect of a repeat of the 1963-74 scenario.

*Freedom of Settlement and Property*

Another issue of contention was the freedom to settle and acquire property in Cyprus. As discussed in Chapter 5, the *acquis communautaire* became a major cause of Turkish Cypriot suspicion of the EU. However, the EU with its laws as well as its realities could have facilitated a solution in Cyprus on these very questions.

While the EU *acquis* in principle provides for the full liberalization of the movement of goods, services, persons and capital, and as such was viewed favourably by the Greek Cypriots, in its implementation several types of exceptions already exist within the Union. These exceptions could also have existed also in Cyprus upon accession, provided they were incorporated in the Treaty of Accession, an act of public international law which overrules EC law. As such, the practical implementation of the *acquis* could have met Turkish Cypriot concerns.

In the case of several EU candidates there was acute sensitivity over the risks that a sudden liberalization, alongside big differences in wealth between communities living in close proximity (e.g. around the German-Polish frontier), might have led to the richer community 'buying up' the less rich. The Turkish Cypriot community also had similar concerns. In the last enlargement negotiations, the Commission distinguished between three types of property: agriculture land, second homes and investment, and in the end agreed to medium to long-term transition periods for the acquisition of agricultural land and second homes.

The Commission viewed much more unfavourably the possibility of permanent derogations from the *acquis*. However, some permanent derogations have been accepted within the EU in exceptional cases. In Finland, the Aaland Islands represent an autonomous entity of Swedish-speaking Finnish citizens, approximately 25,000 in number. The right to 'official domicile' on the islands is controlled by the Aaland Islands authorities and is restricted to Swedish-speaking people. All Finnish and EU citizens have freedom of movement in and out of the islands. But without official domicile, the individual cannot participate in elections, stand for local office, own property or exercise trade or a profession without a licence of the Aaland authorities. These special arrangements existed prior to Finland's EU membership and were retained upon Finnish accession to the EU through a Protocol annexed to the Treaty of Accession. In southern Denmark there are still permanent restrictions to the acquisition of second homes by German citizens. In the current round of enlargement, Malta succeeded in negotiating permanent restrictions to the purchase of property by EU citizens not residing in Malta. Following EU membership, only individuals who have been residing in Malta for more than five years can freely acquire property on the island. EU acceptance of the permanent derogation was facilitated by the fact that restrictions were not discriminatory against non-Maltese EU citizens, but affected also Maltese citizens not residing in Malta.[2] In order to guarantee the permanent nature of these arrangements, a Protocol was annexed to Malta's Accession Treaty.

In Cyprus, the menu of conceivable possibilities within the framework of the *acquis* could have ranged from Polish-style transition periods to Finnish/Danish/Maltese-style derogations. This could have acted in the interests of the Turkish Cypriot community. Provided the two communities agreed to a set of restrictions, the EU could have accommodated these demands. As such, the EU framework could have eased Turkish Cypriot suspicions and increased incentives to seek a settlement. It is particularly worth noting that the case of Malta showed that negotiating permanent derogations was facilitated because restrictions were not discriminatory against non-nationals. The Turkish Cypriot community could have viewed this as particularly congenial to its case, given its desire to restrict these freedoms to Greek Cypriots as well as to other EU nationals (and most notably Greek nationals). The general framework of liberalization within the Union could have increased Greek Cypriot acceptance of any restrictions, whose gradual phasing out would be more plausible within an EU context than outside it.

The Annan Plan provided for a wide range of exemptions from the application of the *acquis,* included in the 'Draft Act of Adaptation' annexed to the Plan.[3] In terms of the 'three freedoms', while freedom of movement would be liberalized immediately, there would be restrictions to the freedoms of settlement and property acquisition. The Turkish Cypriot authorities could restrict the rights of persons (who have been residents for less than three years) to acquire property in northern Cyprus either for 20 years or as long as the Turkish Cypriot state's GDP per capita did not reach 85 percent of that of the Greek Cypriot constituent state (UNSG, 2004b, Draft Act of Adaptation, Article 1.1). This would constitute a transition period in the application of the *acquis*.

In another temporary exemption from the *acquis,* residence rights for citizens hailing from the other constituent state would be limited according to a specified formula (UNSG, 2004b, Draft Act of Adaptation, Article 2). In the first five years

---

[2] Interview with Commission official, Brussels, January 2002.

[3] In the first three drafts of the Annan Plan, published before Cyprus' signature of the Treaty of Accession in April 2003, the exemptions from the *acquis* were included in Annex V of the Plan, that should have been included in a Protocol attached to the Treaty of Accession. In so far as the Treaty was signed prior to a settlement, UN mediators proposed instead that the Draft Act of Adaptation would be adopted by the European Council.

there would be a moratorium.[4] In years six to nine, residence rights could be restricted if residents hailing from the other constituent state represented over six percent of the population of any given village or municipality. The quotas would rise to twelve percent in years ten to fourteen, and eighteen percent of the population of a constituent state until the nineteenth year (or until Turkey's EU membership). Thereafter the constituent state could apply residency restrictions on a non-discriminatory basis to preserve its 'identity' (to ensure that no less than two thirds of their permanent residents spoke the official language of that constituent state). These safeguard measures would not necessarily entail permanent derogations to the *acquis*, in so far as the latter allows for restrictions to the implementation of the EU's four freedoms if these are motivated for reasons of public security and are non-discriminatory in nature.

In addition to the exemptions regarding intra-island freedoms, the Turkish Cypriot constituent state could adopt temporary economic 'safeguard measures' during the first six years of EU membership, if EU internal market laws threatened the economic development of northern Cyprus (UNSG, 2004b, Draft Act of Adaptation, Article 4.1).

## Creating Incentives to Settle: Flaws in EU Policies

While not eliminating the differences between the principal parties, the EU, with its institutions, policies and laws could have facilitated an agreement in the context of accession. The following section addresses EU policies during the 1990s arguing that, up until late 2001, EU actors failed not only to convey the potential of the Union, but also to eliminate the misconceptions of the EU in Cyprus and Turkey. This, coupled with the Union's policy of conditionality towards these two candidate countries, reduced the incentives to settle the conflict throughout the decade. By late 2001, i.e., almost a decade after the initiation of the accession process, the Commission and the European Council attempted to allay Turkish Cypriot concerns. Most critically, the UN Plan showed in detail how many of the concerns about EU membership could have been averted, and how the EU provided a conducive framework for a solution.

*Presenting the Gains of EU Membership: the Lack of Adequate Information*

Between 1993 and 2001, the presentation of costs and benefits of EU membership in Cyprus was frequently based on misinformation about the EU or about existing practices within the Union. The gains to the Greek Cypriots were presented as political and security losses to the Turkish Cypriots, and as such reduced the incentives of both leaderships to reach an agreement before membership. Until late 2001, EU actors did little to avert these misconceptions. Not only did they fail to present how EU structures, laws and policies could help to satisfy the needs of both

---

[4] After the second year, the moratorium would not apply to former displaced persons over 65 years of age, nor to displaced persons from four villages in the Karpass peninsula.

communities. Officials also did little to inform the Cypriots about the true nature of the EU and how anomalies within the Union already existed and were designed to satisfy the specific concerns of the member states. Particularly Turkish Cypriot civil servants complained bitterly about the absence of adequate information from Commission officials, which led to the manipulation and misrepresentation of the accession process by those unwilling to see an agreement on the island.

Confirming the relevance of this argument was the importance attributed by the Turkish Cypriot leadership to the signals given in 2001-02 by Commission officials concerning the EU's willingness to accommodate the terms of an agreement. As put by Turkish Cypriot negotiator and Undersecretary Ergün Olgun: 'the assurance that the terms of the agreement between the two parties would be taken on board by the EU has helped to ease some of the concerns that the Turkish Cypriot party had'.[5] For the first time, the leadership appreciated that EU actors were willing to meet their concerns rather than simply force on them a settlement along Greek Cypriot lines through 'economic bribes' and 'blackmail on Turkey'. These EU statements also raised Turkish Cypriot public support for EU membership before Turkey.

*Myths concerning the status of Cyprus* A common argument made on both sides of the 'green line' was that EU membership would necessitate a strongly centralized constitutional system. The state of Cyprus should be able to speak with one voice in the Council of Ministers and would be held accountable under the EC law. Therefore, it should be endowed with all the constitutional power necessary to ensure compliance with its EU obligations. The incorrect conclusion that many Cypriots drew from this was that all (of the many) policy areas over which the EU had some jurisdiction would have to fall under the competence of the central level in Cyprus. Until 2002, the official rhetoric in both north and south appeared oblivious to the realities of federal states within the EU, in particular of Belgium. This flawed argument was manipulated by the least compromising factions in Cyprus. Nationalist Greek Cypriots claimed that EU membership prevented the RoC from accepting any solution that provided for a high degree of decentralization. Turkish Cypriot nationalists used the same arguments to the opposite effect. Precisely because EU membership entailed an unacceptable solution, the status quo was preferable to a solution in the EU.

Until late 2001, EU officials did little to rectify these misconceptions. Rather than presenting the EU framework's considerable potential to blur the differences between full-fledged statehood and highly autonomous federated entities, several EU decisions, such as the 1994 ECJ ruling on the Anastasiou case, paradoxically highlighted the significance of recognized statehood. Reinforcing this argument was the positive effect of Commission statements since the Denktaş-Verheugen meeting in Zurich in August 2001. For example, during his visit to southern

---

[5] Speech delivered at the European Parliament and organized by the European Centre of International and Strategic Studies on 9 January 2002. The argument was also frequently mentioned in interviews with a Turkish Cypriot negotiator, a Turkish ambassador, and a Commission official, Nicosia, February-March 2002.

Cyprus, Commission President Romano Prodi stated that 'the EU never seeks to determine the constitutional arrangements of its member states. Such matters are up to them. I am confident that the EU can accommodate whatever arrangements the parties themselves agree to in the context of a political settlement' (*Cyprus Weekly*, 2001). The same position was endorsed by the 2001 Commission Progress Report, which stated that 'in the pursuit of a settlement it should be borne in mind that a member state is free to determine its own constitutional arrangements provided that it is able to speak with one voice in the EU decision-making process and to ensure the fulfilment of its EU obligations' (Commission, 2001a, p.23). These statements were made almost a decade after the 1993 Opinion on Cyprus. Had they been made earlier, they could have worked towards addressing the mistrust in Turkey and northern Cyprus about the EU and its intentions.

The precedent of Belgian federalism also contributed towards deconstructing the myth that EU membership necessitated a tightly-knit federation. Immediately following electoral victory, Tayyıp Erdoğan publicly announced his party's support for a Cyprus solution based on the 'Belgian model' (*Cyprus Mail*, 2002). The Turkish Cypriot leadership was more cautious in its assessment, only arguing in favour of particular aspects of the Belgian constitution. In particular Denktaş warmed to the mode of Belgian representation in EU institutions (Denktaş, 2002).

The Annan Plan was the ultimate confirmation that a settlement within the EU could entail a highly decentralized federal system. Constitutionally, the Plan endorsed several aspects of the Swiss and Belgian federal constitutions. While the United Cyprus Republic would enjoy single sovereignty and international personality, like in Switzerland, sovereignty would not lie exclusively in one level of government. Rather both the federal level and the two constituent states would 'sovereignly' exercise the powers attributed to them by the Constitution in a non-hierarchical fashion as in Belgium (UNSG, 2004b, Main Articles, Articles 2.1 and 2.3; Constitution, Article 3.2). Most powers would be attributed to the constituent states, which would coordinate policies in their spheres of competence. The constituent states could be responsible also for the implementation of some federal policies, including the implementation of international treaty obligations. The constituent states could conclude commercial or cultural international agreements, but these would have to be concluded through the federal foreign ministry.

Federal institutions would be marked by political equality between the parties. Rather than a Presidency and a Cabinet, there would be a five-year term Presidential Council comprising nine members (including at least two Turkish Cypriot voting members, and one Turkish Cypriot non-voting member), within which there would be a rotating Presidency (with a President and a Vice-President from different constituent states rotating every twenty months). The idea of a Presidential Council (modeled on the Swiss constitution) was an ingenious way of escaping the deadlock on whether there should be a rotating Presidency or not. The Plan took up the idea of rotation, called for by the Turkish Cypriots, but by introducing the idea of a Presidential Council it diminished the importance of the President itself. The Council would strive to reach decisions by consensus (although only six of the nine members would be allowed to vote). It would otherwise take decisions by majority vote, provided decisions were supported by at least one member from each constituent state (i.e., one of the two Turkish Cypriot voting members).

The federal parliament would be composed of two houses, where the lower house would reflect the demographic balance, while the upper house would reflect the equality between the constituent states. Decisions would require the approval of both houses by simple majority, including one quarter of voting Senators from each constituent state. Minority blocking power was not envisaged either in the executive or in the legislature. However, for specified matters a two-fifths majority of both Greek Cypriot and Turkish Cypriot Senators would be required. The Supreme Court would be represented by an equal number of Greek Cypriots and Turkish Cypriots and would serve as a dispute-resolving mechanism if federal institutions became deadlocked.

*Myths concerning the acquis communautaire*   The EU's *acquis* was consistently referred to by the two Cypriot communities in a manner that reduced the scope for settlement in Cyprus. In the Republic, the acquis became the banner behind which uncompromising positions concerning the liberalization of the 'three freedoms' were presented. In north Cyprus, the acquis was a principal reason for considerable scepticism about a solution within the Union. Yet as the discussion above has highlighted, the Union is rife with exceptions and qualified applications of EC law.

Yet up until mid-2001, EU statements did nothing to alter the view that accession would set the guidelines for a settlement in favour of the Greek Cypriot side. In its 1993 Opinion, the Commission, referring to the *acquis,* stated that 'these freedoms and rights would have to be guaranteed as part of a comprehensive settlement restoring the constitutional arrangements covering the whole of the RoC' (Commission, 1993, paragraph 10). At the time of the Opinion, the *acquis* was presented as the reason explaining the need for a settlement prior to EU membership. However, as conditionality was gradually removed over the 1990s, the need for *acquis* compliance contributed to a shift in the discourse on the three freedoms in favour of the Greek Cypriots. As put by a EP report in 2001: 'a political solution has to be in accordance with the EU's *acquis communautaire*' (European Parliament, 2001, explanatory note, point 10). Statements such as this bolstered the positions of hardliners in both northern and southern Cyprus.

Perhaps even more seriously, Commission officials did nothing to discredit the view in northern Cyprus that because of the *acquis,* a bi-zonal settlement necessitated a confederal agreement. This position was based on a misreading of the *acquis*. The Union guarantees freedoms between member states. Hence, paradoxically EU membership would be more prone to guarantee the 'three freedoms' between member states than within a member state. So if hypothetically the two leaderships were to agree to restrictions only within Cyprus and accede to the EU as a single member state, strictly speaking this would not necessarily require *acquis* derogations. EC law allows for the discrimination against a state's own nationals so long as this does not violate secondary EC law or human rights law (Usher and Greenwood, 2000). Such restrictions could be considered an internal state matter and would only be a matter for the laws and constitution of Cyprus. Restrictions of this type apply within certain EU member states such as

Austria, where there are inter-regional restrictions for the acquisition of second homes. If instead the Union were to accept the membership of two Cypriot states, which in turn requested restrictions to the freedoms within the island, the two states would have had to negotiate derogations to the application of the *acquis*.

Again only at the meeting between Denktaş and Verheugen in August 2001 did an EU official explicitly mention the possibility of exemptions from the *acquis*. The position was announced in public, when in Nicosia, Prodi declared that: 'the EU, with its *acquis* will never be an obstacle to finding a solution in Cyprus' (*Cyprus Weekly*, 2001). This position, mentioned also in the 2001 Commission Progress Report on Cyprus, was then elaborated during a Commission mission to northern Cyprus in February 2002. During the mission, Director Michael Leigh stated: 'the EU has already indicated very clearly that it could accommodate such arrangements, which may be agreed by the leaders themselves in the political process which is now underway ... there is a general principle that such transitional periods should be limited in time and scope, but if you look at the history of the EU you should see that the EU is a flexible body that has always shown understanding for the needs and requirements of the member states' (*Cyprus Weekly*, 2002a). The same position was espoused by the European Council. The June 2002 Seville Council concluded that the EU 'would accommodate the terms of ... a comprehensive settlement in the Treaty of Accession in line with the principles on which the EU is founded ...' (European Council, 2002a, paragraph 24).

Notwithstanding these political assurances, the issue of exemptions from the *acquis* re-emerged as an obstacle to a solution in the re-launched talks in February-March 2004. The Turkish Cypriots insisted on an assurance that an agreement would not be undermined by future rulings of the ECJ, given that the Accession Treaty was signed in 2003 without an accommodation of the terms of the Plan (that had not been agreed upon yet). In their eyes, unless EU actors provided adequate legal assurances, the whole edifice of the Plan would crumble to their disadvantage. Indeed this question almost became a deal-breaker in March 2004, as the Turkish side remained largely unsatisfied with proposals advanced by the European Council. The European Council proposed that the Council of Ministers would adopt an 'Act of Adaptation' in accordance with the UN Plan. The proposal did not amount to a readiness of the European Council to include the terms of the Plan into EU primary law (through an amendment and re-ratification of the Accession Treaty).

*Myths and realities concerning Turkey's relations with Cyprus* A legal argument made against Cyprus' EU membership by the Turkish and Turkish Cypriot sides was that Cyprus' EU membership before Turkey's would contravene Article 170(1) of the 1960 Constitution, which stated that 'the Republic shall, by agreement on appropriate terms, accord most-favoured-nation (MFN) treatment to the Kingdom of Greece, the Republic of Turkey and the United Kingdom of Great Britain and Northern Ireland for all agreements whatever their nature might be' (Mendelson, 2001, paragraph 40). The EU and the Greek Cypriot side rejected this legal argument (Crawford, Pellet and Hafner, 1997). However the joint membership of Cyprus, Greece and Turkey in a customs union (as part of the Turkey-EU customs union) would automatically eliminate Turkish and Turkish Cypriot concerns that Cyprus' EU membership before Turkey's would grant Greece and not Turkey MFN treatment in Cyprus.

Another myth concerning Cyprus' membership prior to Turkey's was that the EU would make any future Turkish guarantee on Cyprus obsolete and that the Rapid Reaction Force could be mobilized to expel Turkish troops from northern Cyprus. Because of these concerns, Cyprus was presented as one of the factors determining the Turkish (op)position on the development of a European Security and Defence Policy (ESDP). It was not until the November 2001 Progress Report that the Commission explicitly stated that 'member states of the EU are free to decide on their own security arrangements. Therefore security arrangements agreed by the parties in the framework of a settlement of the Cyprus problem would not be affected by EU accession' (Commission, 2001a, p.23). However, during the two years of controversy over ESDP, little was done to ease Turkey's misperceptions over what ESDP entailed. The idea of a hypothetical EU military intervention in Cyprus against Turkey was a myth that EU officials for too long failed to invalidate.

One last area affecting Turkey's ties with Cyprus was the Schengen *acquis*. Questions concerning the movement of persons could have been a potential cause of concern for Turkey and the Turkish Cypriots. EU membership of a reunified Cyprus could have strengthened the border between northern Cyprus and Turkey. Turkey is on the EU's list of countries for which visas are required to enter the Union. Introduction of visas for Turkish citizens who are not legally resident in Cyprus could have been an unfortunate consequence of re-unification and EU accession given the large movement of persons between Turkey and northern Cyprus (including students and seasonal workers).

While the Schengen *acquis* could have posed a real obstacle to Turkish-Turkish Cypriot relations, channels could have been found to mitigate the negative effects. One approach could have been to build upon existing precedents in the EU for territories separated from the continent by sea. These include not only Ireland and the United Kingdom, but also the Spanish provinces of Ceuta and Melilla enclaved in Morocco. Similarly, one could have considered a transitional provision to permit Cyprus to remain visa-free for Turkish citizens, until Cyprus itself was accorded complete freedom of movement within the Schengen system, or until Turkey acceded to the EU's visa-free list. During the transitional period, Turkish citizens would still have had to obtain a Schengen visa to travel to the rest of the Schengen area. Air and sea connections from Cyprus to the rest of the Schengen area would have been subject to control of passport or identity cards upon arrival. However, citizens of Cyprus would still enjoy full access and citizenship rights in the EU, like Spanish citizens arriving from Ceuta or Melilla, or British and Irish citizens arriving on the continent. Ireland and the UK have these arrangements as non-Schengen member states, while Spain is a Schengen member state.

The Annan Plan attempted to reassure Turkey and the Turkish Cypriots that the external balance would be respected despite Greece and Cyprus' EU membership and Turkey's temporary exclusion. In the economic sphere, the agreement stipulated that Cyprus would accord both Greece and Turkey MFN status and apply the rules of the EU-Turkey customs union.

In terms of security, there would be an equal number (6,000) of Greek and Turkish troops until 2011, to be scaled down to 3,000 until 2018 (or until Turkey's EU membership). Thereafter figures would be scaled down to 950 and 650 for Greek and Turkish contingents respectively (as provided for in the 1959 Treaty of Alliance) with the objective of complete demilitarization (UNSG, 2004b, Main Articles, Article 8.1b). The 1959 Treaty of Guarantee would remain in force but would be amended so as to allow the guarantors to protect the constitutional status and territorial integrity not only of the United Cyprus Republic, but also of the two constituent states (UNSG, 2004b, Main Articles, Article 8.1a). The UN Plan further stipulated that Cyprus would not put its territory at the disposal of international military operations (including ESDP operations) without the consent of both constituent states and of both Greece and Turkey until the accession of Turkey (UNSG, 2004b, Main Articles, Article 8.4, Constitution, Article 53).

The Plan also attempted to retain a balance between Greece and Turkey in the spheres of property acquisition, residence and movement of persons, proposing similar rights to Greek and Turkish nationals vis-à-vis Cyprus (UNSG, 2004b, Draft Act of Adaptation, Article 3). For nineteen years or until Turkey's EU membership, the right of Greek (Turkish) nationals to reside in Cyprus would be restricted if this figure amounted to more than five percent of the number of resident Greek Cypriot (Turkish Cypriot) constituent state citizens. The Plan also stated that Greek and Turkish nationals would receive equal treatment in their movements to and from Cyprus. The Plan did not specify whether this entailed Cyprus' non-participation in the Schengen system, or whether additional benefits would be extended to Turkey in Cyprus, despite its non-membership of the EU (and non-inclusion in the EU visa-free list).

*The economic development of northern Cyprus: 'buying' Turkish Cypriot consent*
The principal argument presented by the EU to convince the Turkish Cypriot community of the benefits of EU membership was that of economic development. Economic gains were an important means to increase Turkish Cypriot incentives to reach a settlement, particularly in the light of the deteriorating economic situation in northern Cyprus. However, not only were economic incentives inadequate to generate sufficient attraction to the idea of EU membership within a reunified island, but also the way in which EU actors presented the Union's economic appeal created resentments, particularly amongst the Turkish Cypriot leadership.

Economic incentives were rarely presented in a way that was intrinsically linked to the issues of the conflict. Throughout the accession process (up until the 2002-04 talks), the EU never argued that through its economic input it could facilitate an agreement on questions such as territorial adjustments, reconstruction and compensation. Economic incentives and structural funds in particular were offered by the EU to the Turkish Cypriots essentially on condition that they altered their negotiating positions. They were offered when at the same time the 1994 ECJ judgement crippled further the Turkish Cypriot economy. This allowed the Turkish Cypriot leadership to argue that the EU was attempting to 'buy them off' by 'bribing' them. Hence their reaction, arguing that security was their first priority that could not be bargained over for the sake of economic bonuses.

*Presenting the Costs of Non-Agreement: EU Policies of Conditionality*

Previous chapters analysed EU conditionality towards Turkey and Cyprus. During the 1990s conflict settlement was gradually abandoned as a condition for Cyprus' membership. With it, conditionality on Turkey was strengthened. The logic justifying this approach was that presenting conditional sticks and carrots to the Turkish and Turkish Cypriot sides depended on Cyprus' unconditional accession.

Turkish inflexibility (even prior to the 1990s) was certainly one of the causes of the absence of a settlement. But Greek Cypriot rigidity was also responsible for the failure of the talks in the 1990s, as showed by the ultimate failure of the peace process in 2004. Therefore a successful EU policy of conditionality should have addressed intransigence on all sides, particularly given that a one-sided approach obtained the opposite results by fuelling uncompromising attitudes on both sides of the green line.

Yet given the lag in the expected accession of Cyprus and Turkey, EU decision-makers were faced with a dilemma and the potential for imbalance. If a settlement was a condition for Cyprus' membership, then the burden of conditionality would have fallen predominantly on the Greek Cypriots, given Turkey's longer path to membership. In other words, the principal stick presented to Turkey and the Turkish Cypriots was inextricably linked to the removal of the stick on the Greek Cypriot side (i.e., Cyprus' EU membership before a settlement if necessary). Could EU policy have exerted conditionality effectively on all parties? In order to do so, two principal ingredients were necessary.

On the one hand, sufficiently valuable benefits had to be offered to all sides. Chapter 5 discussed the value of accession to the Greek Cypriot side but pointed out the problematic aspects of the EU's role vis-à-vis Turkey and the Turkish Cypriots. The importance of a concerted EU strategy towards Turkey, as and when the Union consolidated its approach towards Cyprus (i.e., through an accession process) cannot be overemphasized. It is no coincidence that the prospects for a settlement rose when EU policy towards Turkey took shape after December 1999. To embark upon an accession process with Cyprus without an accompanying strategy for Turkey was a key mistake at the heart of the failed 'catalytic effect'.

On the other hand, EU policies had to retain an element of pressure on both sides. The only way to do so would have been to use the provisions in the 1993 Opinion and also in the Helsinki conclusions, i.e., that in taking its decisions, the EU would assess the good will of all sides. How could EU actors assess 'goodwill' without adopting a relatively well-defined position on what the contours of a solution should look like? EU actors repeatedly stated their support for a settlement based on a bi-zonal and bi-communal federation. But the Union never went into further detail concerning what these vague outlines could consist of. However, support for and close coordination with the UN Secretary General's pure mediation could have been sufficient. EU actors could have acted as principal mediators by supporting the more detailed proposals set forth by the UN particularly since the late 1980s. Most notably, the 1992 Set of Ideas, which up until 2002 represented the most detailed set of proposals endorsed by the Security Council, defined vague terms such as 'new partnership', 'political equality' and 'federation'. EU actors could have embraced these positions more explicitly, elaborating what their meaning within the EU could have entailed. Doing so would have allowed for a more balanced policy of conditionality towards the parties. By lifting conditionality on the RoC and failing to convey to the Greek Cypriots the potential repercussions of entering the Union as a divided island, EU actors were partly responsible for the Greek Cypriot rejection of the Annan Plan on 24 April 2004.

This chapter has not argued that the EU framework could have eliminated automatically all sources of friction and disagreement in Cyprus. Nor do the above arguments intend to underestimate the complexity of operating complex ethno-federations, within or outside the EU.

Yet, this chapter has sought to demonstrate that the EU framework, with its institutions and policies, could have offered the opportunity to draw on new and mutually compatible satisfiers, which could have increased the political will necessary to agree to and operate a federal agreement. It could have provided an alternative context within which to forge a win-win settlement, opening the way for the gradual resolution of the conflict.

But EU policies throughout the 1990s failed to present this potential in Cyprus. On the contrary, several EU decisions generated misconceptions about the role and importance of recognized statehood within the Union. These decisions also fuelled greater mistrust, particularly on the Turkish Cypriot and Turkish sides. This in turn entrenched negotiation stances and bolstered the positions of the least compromising elements on all sides of the conflict.

The Annan Plan was critical in using much of the potential provided by the EU framework to draft proposals accounting for the basic needs of the principal parties. By doing so, it also worked towards eliminating many misperceptions in Cyprus and in Turkey concerning what reunification within the EU would entail. What UN, British or American mediators could not do was redress the fundamental mistrust of the EU in Turkey and northern Cyprus. And as previous chapters have analysed, misconceptions and mistrust lay at the heart of the failed 'catalytic effect' during the 1990s. Indeed with the turn of the century, momentum towards reunification rose as and when EU policies towards Turkey in particular became more credible. However, insufficient attention to the incentives of the Greek Cypriot side entailed that an increased Turkish and Turkish Cypriot readiness to reunify the island were insufficient to seal an agreement.

## References

Bullman, U. (2001), 'The Politics of the Third Level', in C. Jeffrey (ed.), *The Regional Dimension of the European Union*, Frank Cass, London, pp. 3-19.

Commission of the European Communities (1993), *Opinion on the Application for Membership from Cyprus*, COM(93) 313, EC Bulletin 6-1993, Brussels.

Commission of the European Communities (2001a), *Regular Report on Cyprus' Progress towards Accession*, on www.europa.eu.int

Commission of the European Communities (2002a), *Commission Offers a Fair and Solid Approach for Financing EU Enlargement*, IP/02/170, Brussels.

Crawford, J., Pellet, A. and Hafner, G. (1997), *Republic of Cyprus: Eligibility for EU Membership*, A/52/481, S/1977/805, 17 October 1997.

*Cyprus Mail* (2002), 'Papandreou: Greece will stand by Cyprus even if it rejects plan', 6 November 2002.

*Cyprus Weekly* (2001), 'Cyprus will join', 30 October 2001.

*Cyprus Weekly* (2002a), 'Danish Foreign Minister "very optimistic"', 8 February 2002.

*Cyprus Weekly* (2002b), 'Tough task for Annan', 6 September 2002.

Deutsch, K. et al. (1957), *Political Community and the North Atlantic Area: International Organization in the Light of Historical Experience*, Princeton University Press, Princeton.

Denktaş, R. (2002), Letter of Appreciation to the Centre for European Policy Studies for the study by M. Emerson and N. Tocci (2002), *Cyprus as Lighthouse of the Eastern Mediterranean*, CEPS, Brussels, dated 4 May 2002, Nicosia.

Emerson, M. and Tocci, N. (2002), *Cyprus as Lighthouse of the Eastern Mediterranean*, CEPS, Brussels.

European Council (2002a), Meeting on 26-27 June 2002 in Seville, *Presidency Conclusions*, SN 200/02.

European Parliament (2001), *Report on Cyprus' Application for Membership of the EU and the State of Negotiations*, Rapporteur Jacques Poos, A5-0261/2001, 11 July 2001, Brussels.

Haas, E. (1968), *The Uniting of Europe: Political, Social and Economic Forces*, Stanford University Press, Stanford, California.

Harvie, C. (1994), *The Rise of Regional Europe*, Routledge, New York.

Hooghe, L. (1996), *Cohesion Policy and the European Union*, Clarendon Press, Oxford.

Hooghe, L. and Marks. G. (2001), *Multi-level Governance and European Integration*, Rowman and Littlefield, Lanham.

Jans, M.T. (2001), *Leveled Domestic Politics - Comparing Institutional Reform and Ethnonational Conflicts in Canada and Belgium*, Mimeo, VUB, Brussels.

Jeffrey, C. (2000), 'Sub-National Mobilization and European Integration: Does it Make Any Difference?' *Journal of Common Market Studies*, Vol.38, No.1, pp.1-23.

Jeffrey, C. (2001a), 'Regional Information Offices in Brussels and Multi-Level Governance in the EU: a UK-German Comparison', in C. Jeffrey (ed.), *The Regional Dimension of the European Union*, Frank Cass, London, pp.181-203.

Jeffrey, C. (2001b), 'Conclusions: Sub-National Authorities and European Domestic Policy', in C. Jeffrey (ed.), *The Regional Dimension of the European Union*, Frank Cass, London, pp.204-219.

Jeffrey, C. (ed.) (2001c), *The Regional Dimension of the European Union*, Frank Cass, London.

Joseph, J. (2000), 'Can the EU Succeed where the UN Failed? The Continuing Search for a Settlement on Cyprus', *CIAO Papers*, September 2000, ISA, 41st Annual Convention, March 2000.

Kerremans, B. (2000), 'Determining a European Policy in a Multi-Level Setting: The Case of Specialized Coordination in Belgium', *Regional and Federal Studies*, Vol.10, No.1, pp.36-61.

Kerremans, B. and J. Beyers (2001), 'The Belgian Sub-National Entities in the EU: Second or Third Level Players?', in C. Jeffrey (ed.), *The Regional Dimension of the European Union*, Frank Cass, London, pp.41-55.

Kovziridze, T. (2002), 'Europeanization of Federal Institutional Relationships: Hierarchical and Inter-dependent Relationship Structures in Belgium, Germany and Austria', *Regional and Federal Studies*, Vol.12, No.3, pp.128-155.

Laible, J. (2001), 'Nationalism and a Critique of European Integration: Questions for the Flemish Parties', in M. Keating and J. McGarry (eds.), *Minority Nationalism and the Changing International Order*, Oxford University Press, Oxford, pp.223-245.

Marks, G., Nielsen, F., Ray, L. and Salk, J. (1996a), 'Competences Cracks and Conflicts: Regional Mobilization in the European Union', in G. Marks et al. (eds.), *Governance in the European Union*, Sage, London, pp. 40-63.

Marks, G., Scharpf, F., Schmiter, P., and Streek, W. (eds.) (1996b), *Governance in the European Union*, Sage, London.

Mendelson, M. (2001), *Why Cyprus' Entry into the EU would be Illegal*, Embassy of the Republic of Turkey, London.

Mitrany, D. (1966), *A Working Peace System: An Argument for the Functional Development of International Organization*, University of Chicago Press, Chicago.

Scharpf, F.W. (1994), 'Community and Autonomy: Multi-level Policy-making in the EU', *Journal of European Public Policy*, Vol.1, No.1, pp.219-242.

United Nations Secretary General (1992a), *Set of Ideas for the Reunification of Cyprus*, S/24472 English, New York.

United Nations Secretary General (1992b), *Summary of the Current Positions of the Two Sides in Relation to the Set of Ideas*, 11 November 1992, S/24472 English, New York.

United Nations Secretary General (2003), *Report of the Secretary General on his Mission of Good Offices in Cyprus*, 7 April 2003.

United Nations Secretary General (2004b), *The Comprehensive Settlement of the Cyprus Problem*, Fifth Version, on http://www.cyprus-un-plan.org

Usher, J. and Greenwood, C. (2000), *Re Accession of Cyprus to the EC: Restrictions on Residence and Acquisition of Property and Related Issues*, Mimeo, Joint Opinion, London.

Wagstaff, P. (1999), 'The Committee of the Regions of the EU', in P. Wagstaff (ed.), *Regionalism in the EU*, Intellect, Exeter, pp.188-193.

Wouters, L. and de Rynck, S. (1996), 'Subnational Autonomy in the European Integration Process: the Belgian Case', in J. Hesse (ed.), *Regions in Europe*, Nomos, Baden-Baden.

# Chapter 8

# Lessons for European Foreign Policy in Ethno-Political Conflicts

*'The European Union is both a curse and a blessing for Cyprus'*
(Former Turkish Foreign Minister, Istanbul, May 2002)

The island of Cyprus has witnessed one of the most intractable ethno-political conflicts of the 20th century. For decades the conflict has been frozen in a stage of segregation, as the principal parties, while engaged in negotiations, failed to reach a comprehensive agreement. A major element in the explanation of this state of affairs has been the parties' negotiating positions (or satisfiers). These chosen satisfiers focused on absolute notions of sovereignty and statehood, making the reconciliation of subject positions almost impossible. Linked to this was the fact that the parties (and their leaderships in particular) appeared to be relatively content with the status quo. In other words, their perception of their own BATNA (Best Alternative to a Negotiated Agreement) has been high and so the bargaining range has been extremely narrow.

Since 1974, the Turkish Cypriot leadership has enjoyed an unprecedented *de facto* status that it has been unwilling to relinquish. With Turkey's support, it has ruled and ensured the physical security of the Turkish Cypriots and controlled 37 percent of the island's territory. By doing so, Turkey has also fulfilled its security interests, as traditionally perceived by its civilian-military establishment. The Greek Cypriot leadership, supported by Greece, on the other hand has benefited from undiluted sovereignty and international recognition. Many Greek Cypriots have been unwilling to give up this status for an effective sharing of sovereignty in a loose federal structure.

In these circumstances, principal mediation, if and when adequately used, can cultivate the ripe conditions for conflict settlement and resolution. It can help to generate political will to settle and subsequently resolve a conflict, by altering the incentive structure underlying it. Through negative incentives or 'threats' the third party can generate sufficient pressure to move away from the status quo by increasing the costs of no-agreement (i.e., reducing the BATNA). But coercing the parties into a deal rarely yields a settlement that opens the way to conflict transformation and resolution. Positive incentives, i.e., gains to the conflicting parties, are also an integral aspect of principal mediation (shifting out the Pareto frontier). However, not all promised gains are appropriate. Positive incentives contribute to conflict resolution if they address the basic needs of the principal parties and contribute to the re-conceptualization of relations between them. The incentives should motivate the parties to seek a solution as an end in itself, rather than as an unpalatable means to access unrelated side-payments.

In analysing the role of the EU in the Cyprus conflict since 1988, the lessons from the literature on principal mediation appear particularly relevant. The EU accession process and the use of conditionality that it entailed affected the incentives of the principal parties, opening the prospect for a constructive shift in positions. However, the impact of the accession process did not correspond to the professed expectations of the member states and the Commission. On the contrary, the major visible development during the 1990s was the hardening of the parties' positions, and those of the Turkish Cypriot side in particular. In 2004 it was the Greek Cypriots that displayed unprecedented inflexibility. It is impossible to determine whether the conflict would have been solved in the 1990s had the EU remained outside it. It is equally impossible to prove that the EU was the principal determinant of the deterioration of the conflict. The hardening of positions was the result of a complex interaction between international, national and sub-national factors, in addition to the EU dimension. However the EU, to a large extent unwittingly, did become an important element in the conflict over the last decade, and perhaps its most important external determinant.

The specific (conditional and unconditional) gains and losses presented to the parties, and the way in which they were presented by EU actors, had unintended and counterproductive effects up until late 2001. This was because they played into the discourse of the most nationalist elements within the principal parties, legitimizing their hardened positions. The conditional gains to the Turkish Cypriots were primarily economic and insufficiently security/identity related. They were thus not valued highly, particularly by the leadership. Moreover, the EU was perceived as a threat by many Turks and Turkish Cypriots, increasing the importance they attributed to separate statehood and closeness to Turkey. This was coupled with the fact that the EU-Turkey relationship suffered from a serious lack of understanding, credibility and trust on both sides. As a result, Cyprus' accession process played into the hands of those opposing reunification both in northern Cyprus and in Turkey. The gains offered to the Greek Cypriots were directly related to the conflict but were gradually made unconditional on an agreement. This fed Turkish and Turkish Cypriot perceptions of the EU's structural bias towards the conflict. It also reduced the incentives to seek an early settlement of those Greek Cypriot nationalists who sought considerable changes in UN guidelines, and those who concentrated on alternative options to ensure the security and prosperity of the Greek Cypriot community.

The tide seemed to reverse by late 2001, and the 2002-04 peace efforts offered the prospects of a final breakthrough. One of the most fundamental insights that emerges from the analysis of the last phase of Cyprus' accession process was the differentiated impact it had on the principal parties. Cyprus' accession process, while not moderating the stance of the Turkish Cypriot leadership, contributed to the creation of a 'hurting stalemate' for the Turkish Cypriot public. In turn this led to an acute split within the elite as well as within the wider public. Indeed, contrary to the view of their leader, the majority of the Turkish Cypriots accepted the reunification and EU accession of Cyprus, as showed by the April 2004 referendum results.

What explains these domestic changes in northern Cyprus? A first important part of the explanation lies in the fact that Cyprus' approaching EU accession coincided with a serious economic decline in northern Cyprus. In turn this was connected to the tightening of the Turkish economy first with the 1999 IMF stabilization programme and then with the Turkish economic crisis in 2001. Economic stagnation, isolation, ensuing emigration and growing dependence on Turkey on the one hand and the prospect of EU membership on the other generated important pro-solution forces amongst the Turkish Cypriot public. Last but not least, the publication of the Annan Plan demonstrated to the Turkish Cypriots that despite important compromises, reunification within the EU would not entail renouncing their security and self-determination aims in return for economic gains.

In Turkey too the tide seemed to turn in favour of a solution after the rise to power of the AKP government. This is not to say that the wider establishment shared the government's views. The approaching deadline of Cyprus' EU accession led to open schisms in the Turkish national consensus on Cyprus. Particularly since the November 2002 elections, different 'Ankaras' have voiced different views on the Cyprus question. These divisions overlapped with the increasingly explicit rifts on the question of Turkey's own EU membership, which in turn reflected the diverging visions on the general development path of the Turkish nation-state. Despite persisting divisions, by 2004 the AKP government appeared sufficiently strong to commit the country to a solution.

The Turkish government could secure a commitment to a settlement both because of its dedication to EU accession, and because Turkey's accession process had become more credible since 2002. In other words, Cyprus' accession process and strong EU pressure on Turkey alone would not have generated sufficiently strong pro-solution forces in Turkey. What generated Turkish incentives was the more realistic prospects of Turkey's own membership (and the imminent decision in December 2004 on whether, when and how to open accession negotiations with Turkey), coupled with the existence of a strong government committed to Turkey's accession course. In turn this highlights the importance of the temporal aspect in the analysis of the failure or possible success of the EU 'catalytic effect'. Chapter 5 argued that the credibility of both the EU's Turkey policy and of Turkey's commitment to its EU path were insufficiently high to generate the necessary momentum in favour of a solution throughout the 1990s. By 2004 changes in EU positions and in Turkish domestic politics were sufficiently strong to secure Turkey's commitment to a solution.

The deadline of accession also appeared to raise the incentives of the Greek Cypriot and Greek sides to reach an agreement under the former leaderships of Glafcos Clerides in Nicosia and Costas Simitis (and George Papandreou) in Athens. Indeed these former leaders and their parties openly backed the 'yes' campaign in the April 2004 referendum. Yet in the case of the Greek and Greek Cypriot sides, domestic changes in the light of imminent EU accession operated against a solution. The flat rejection of the Greek Cypriot leader Papadopoulos and the non-committal stance of the New Democracy government in Athens go far in explaining the Greek Cypriot rejection of the Plan in April 2004.

Up until 2002, an important aspect determining Greek Cypriot positions was the extent of perceived inevitability of Cyprus' EU accession. Chapter 4 analysed how after the 1994 Corfu European Council, Cyprus' EU accession became increasingly inevitable. The EU decisions of June 1994, March 1995, December 1997 and December 1999 set Cyprus on an increasingly irreversible path to EU membership. However, this was not necessarily perceived by the principal parties, particularly in their public discourse. Again the differentiated responses by different domestic actors are of particular relevance. The 2002 Greek Cypriot negotiating team used the remaining uncertainty of EU accession to argue the case for an early agreement before the Copenhagen European Council. Clerides appeared to understand that after accession the momentum for change could dampen and reunification could be delayed until the uncertain day of Turkey's own accession. As such it used the remaining uncertainty to persuade the opposition of the desirability of an early solution. Instead the more nationalist elements within the Greek Cypriot establishment appealed to the irreversibility of accession to argue in favour of postponing a settlement in order to negotiate a more favourable deal from a position of greater strength. Since 2003 not only were these more nationalist forces in power in southern Cyprus, but also nobody (both within Cyprus and the EU) could credibly argue that Cyprus' EU entry on 1 May 2004 was not assured.

The arguments above do not imply that the expected 'catalytic effect' was doomed to fail. In the case of Cyprus, where for decades third parties had failed to mediate an agreement, the introduction of the 'EU dimension' could have been particularly welcome. It could have complemented the pure mediation role of the UN, by raising the political will of the principal parties to reach an agreement. The UN, due to its nature, lacked the necessary leverage to induce the principal parties to settle. UN mediators at most could advance proposals, based on the parties' negotiating positions.

The EU's 'structural diplomacy' on the other hand, i.e., the various forms of association and integration offered by the EU, is potentially well-tailored to induce long-run structural change both within and between countries (Keukeleire, 2000). As the eastern enlargement showed, this potential is strongest when the form of association in question is full membership itself (Smith, 1998, 1999; Grabbe, 2001). Also in Cyprus, accession could have generated new incentives to transform the status quo. The accession process added new and significant material and non-material resources that were intricately related to the EU's very nature as a non-state actor. These resources could have been presented to the principal parties, and made conditional on efforts towards a solution, mediated by the UN. Indeed it is interesting to note that the Annan Plan made extensive use both of the EU framework within which to cast the new Cyprus, and of the deadlines set by the enlargement timetable.

The problem therefore was not in the instruments at the EU's disposal. It was rather in the lack of focus on whether and how to use them, and in service of what strategy. Despite the potential in its 'structure', the Union failed in the realm of 'agency'. The 'catalytic effect' discourse was inspired by the potential complementarity between the roles of the EU and of the UN. However, UN-EU complementarity rested on both the UN and the EU acting collectively and coherently, and on the close and consistent contact between the two actors. While the former would persist in its pure mediation functions, the latter would effectively take on the roles of a principal mediator.

This would have required a collective EU strategy to complement the UN's pure mediation by generating incentives for conflict resolution in the context of accession. The ambition to play such a role existed at the level of EU rhetoric. However, scratching beneath the surface the clearest conclusion drawn was that EU policies were not the product of a unified European strategy towards the conflict. The EU was engaged in *foreign policy activity* in the framework of enlargement (Ginsberg, 1999). Yet it lacked a committed and deliberate *foreign policy* towards the conflict. This was because no EU actor (with the exception of Greece) was interested in a more substantive EU involvement in the conflict. As such, the Commission dealt with Cyprus with an exclusive mission to proceed with the accession process. The external expectations of the EU's ability to act in a state-like fashion complicated matters further, in so far as they led the recipient parties to view EU policies as part of a well-planned course of action. These perceptions and misperceptions reinforced the unforeseen and often unintended negative effects of the EU's role.

Probing into the reasons for the absence of a political strategy leads us to the familiar conclusions introduced in the first chapters of this study, i.e., that the EU was not a coherent, let alone single collective actor in the Cyprus conflict. Chapter 6 analysed the factors driving key EU decisions. What do these conclusions tell us about the formulation and conduct of European foreign policy and in particular about the EU as a third party actor in ethno-political conflicts?

## The Determinants of European Foreign Policy

The discussion in Chapter 6 easily finds its place in the literature on European foreign policy. External demands, national interests, inter-state bargaining, institutional settings and 'Europeanization' are all frequently discussed elements in the theoretical and applied literature on European foreign policy. The rest of this Chapter seeks to contextualize the findings of this study within the wider literature on EU foreign policy.

*External Demands*

In a seminal article in 1993, Hill characterized the deficiencies in European foreign policy by exploring the 'gap' between external expectations and EU capabilities to respond to them (Hill, 1993). External actors expect the EU to act as a joint supervisor of the world economy, as a stabilizer and pacifier of the European continent, as a principal aid donor and interlocutor of the third world and as a second voice in international diplomacy. The specific demands of third countries or regions range from association, aid, trade preferences and membership to recognition and mediation. Although in a later review Hill concluded that external expectations had somewhat lowered from the early 1990s, they nonetheless continued to exceed the Union's effective capabilities (Hill, 1998a). While exceeding capabilities, external demands act as prime determinants of EU external action, or rather reaction. In other words, member states would find themselves compelled to adopt common policies vis-à-vis third countries. Demands from external national, international and sub-national actors induce the Union to respond with some form of common action or position.

These arguments can be easily applied to the case of Cyprus. Encouraged by member state Greece, the Greek Cypriot government applied for EU membership. It applied expecting the accession process to catalyse a settlement favourable to Greek Cypriot interests. Albeit reluctantly, the Union responded favourably to Greek Cypriot demands, and the Council called on the Commission to launch an accession process with Cyprus. Gradually the Commission and the Council assimilated the Greek and Greek Cypriot expectations, and espoused the rhetoric about the 'catalytic effect' of the accession process. In view of Turkey's demands for membership, EU actors overestimated their ability to influence the Turkish and Turkish Cypriot authorities, despite their unwillingness to extend membership to Turkey. Turkey's own uncertain candidacy was only recognized in December 1999, almost seven years after Cyprus' accession process was launched.

*National Interests within Multilateral Negotiation Processes*

The literature also devotes significant attention to the role of member states and their mode of interaction. While there is considerable variation in the emphasis given to national foreign policy, most scholars agree that member state interests and their interaction continues to lie at the core of European foreign policy-making.

The remaining importance of national foreign policy does not exclude the possibility of common European positions or actions. On the contrary, member states frequently deem it in their interests to forge consensus and act in unison precisely to strengthen their individual positions, i.e., the 'politics of scale' (Ginsberg, 1989; Hill, 1997). In other words, European foreign policy allows member states to strengthen and refine their national foreign policies by framing them within an EU framework. The European framework can be a valuable additional instrument of national foreign policy, which can lower the costs and raise the returns of unilateral national action. It can act as a powerful platform for national self-projection, particularly for small member states.

This can occur in different ways. At times, member state interests could simply coincide, and so unified positions would benefit equally all member states. On other occasions, member states could opt for collective positions or actions because espousing individual foreign policies would prove too costly either in domestic or in international realms. On other occasions still, member states could fail to reach common positions. As a result, inaction rather than action would characterize the European stance. Situations calling for punitive measures (e.g. vis-à-vis Israel or China) tend to fall in this category, where historical reasons, commercial interests or security considerations often prevent one or several member states from supporting the deployment of EU 'sticks'.

Finally, common positions may result from the interactions between different national interests. The idea of inter-state bargaining in international politics was articulated through the concept of 'two-level games' (Putnam, 1988). Outcomes are determined by inter-state bargains rather than by clear-cut common strategic aims. The precise bargains are affected by the relative strength of national positions. These in turn are determined by the constraints imposed by and the influence of domestic forces. However, the member state is constrained also by international pressures and commitments. The national negotiator thus lies at the intersection between domestic and external pressures. Decisions are possible when there is an area of overlap between the two sets of constraints.

The relative strength of the member states matters. So in principle small members could be 'bought off' more easily with side-payments than larger states. However, equally important is the relative strength of member states on specific foreign policy questions (i.e., 'issue specific power' as described in Chapter 1), which is determined in part by the different priorities of their national foreign policies. Germany values the stability and development of Poland and the Czech Republic more than Spain. The stability of the Maghreb is more of a French, Spanish and Italian priority than a German or Dutch one (Hill and Wallace, 1996). European foreign policy activity tends to reflect these different prioritizations.

As a result European common positions often reflect the 'median' rather than the 'lowest common denominator' between member states (Nuttall, 1992, pp.314-5). For example, in December 1991, member states reluctantly gave in to the unilateral German decision to recognize the former Yugoslav republics. The European position was not the product of a common foreign policy based on a common assessment of the best possible European response to the Balkan quagmire. On the contrary, the decision was a reflection of the strongly held German views driven by domestic political considerations. The member states valued more the need to forge internal consensus than the desire to pursue the best possible common response to an external problem. Indeed the recognition of Croatia and Slovenia may have precipitated further negative trends in the region.

Following a similar logic, Esther Barbé analyses EU policies towards the CEECs and the Mediterranean as a balancing act between member state interests (Barbé, 1998). EU policies towards the south and the east in the 1990s (i.e., enlargement towards the CEECs on the one hand and enlargement towards Cyprus and Malta, integration with Turkey and the Euro-Mediterranean Partnership (EMP) on the other) were the result of internal EU bargaining between northern and southern member states. The decisions reflected a compromise between the different mental maps and priorities of EU-15. As far as Cyprus was concerned, the southern member states (apart from Greece) were not particularly interested in the island or in the conflict, but simply favoured the concept of greater EU attention to the Mediterranean region.

Hence, EU positions are often determined more by requirements on the inside, i.e., internal consensus formation, than a common strategy to face an external problem. While to some extent all foreign policies are driven more by internal than by external circumstances, in the case of the Union the greater complexity of and potential inconsistency between internal factors accentuates the potential flaws of this mode of foreign policy-making. The predominantly inward rather than outward looking policy-making processes can unwittingly lead to misunderstandings on the outside as well as to inaction or inconsistent, directionless and perverse action. This leads Ifestos to conclude that as long as EU external action is simply the product of a coincidence of interests or inter-state bargains, the 'logic of diversity' would prevail and the Union would not enjoy an effective foreign policy (Ifestos, 1987). A European foreign policy would necessitate coherent and consistent common interests over time, resulting in common strategic priorities and positions on external action. This may require the emergence of truly common interests, which in turn necessitate common identities (Guehenno, 1998).

The Cyprus case study is rich in examples highlighting these features of European foreign policy-making. Greece, a long-time supporter of the internationalization of the Cyprus conflict, activated itself to transfer the conflict into the European domain. An EU platform was significantly more powerful than Greek foreign policy as a means to pursue Greek national interests. The second and third Greek Presidencies were used to further Greek national goals concerning Cyprus. The other member states paid little or no attention to the conflict. Hence, over the course of the decade the EU position converged on the median, determined to a large extent by the Greek government. Despite being a small and thus a relatively weak member state, Greece had strong views on Cyprus, which were consistently advanced within the EU policy-making process (with the marginal exception of the early 1990s when the major Greek preoccupation was Macedonia). Over the course of the decade Greek views were gradually endorsed by the rest of the largely uninterested member states.

Inter-state bargaining is also fundamental in assessing EU-Turkey relations. Again internal rather than external considerations predominantly affected the EU's stance towards Turkey. On the one hand, the Greek rejection of Turkey's full membership (up until 1999), silently backed by other member states, generated considerable EU resistance against Turkey's integration in the Union. On the other hand, all member states, strongly encouraged by the US, appreciated Turkey's importance and were keen not to alienate Ankara. The interaction between these two contrasting internal forces was a crucial determinant of the pendulum effect and frequent inconsistency in EU-Turkey relations since the late 1980s.

*Institutions*

A third factor that emerged as an important element in the Cyprus case study is the role of institutions. The structure and mode of operation of EU institutions considerably affected the nature of EU positions towards the conflict. The role of institutions cannot be disaggregated from that of the member states, in so far as the EU institutional structure is to a large extent a product of member states' views regarding the nature of the Union. So long as the member states resist a truly common foreign policy, they will refrain from empowering institutions with the capability to take on that role. In turn, so long as institutions do not work to forge truly European interests and objectives, different national interests in the member states will prevail.

Beginning with the Council, considerable attention was paid to the role of the Presidency in the Cyprus case study, and most notably the Greek Presidencies of 1988 and 1994 (Tsakaloyannis, 1996). The literature has for decades explored the endemic problems of the rotating Presidency. One such problem is the potential clash between national and collective interests and thus the tendencies of Presidencies to exploit their term in office to further national goals. These tendencies are particularly marked when Eurosceptic or small member states take on the Presidency (Wallace, 1985). Hence, previous Portuguese and Spanish Presidencies concentrated on bringing Africa and Latin America onto the EPC/CFSP agenda, Sweden and Finland insisted on the inclusion of the Baltic states in the fifth enlargement, Austria furthered Hungary's inclusion, Denmark pursued closer EU-Norwegian ties and finally Greece lobbied intensely for Cyprus. Although in 1988 PASOK was far more pro-European than during its early years in office, the second Greek Presidency remained relatively cautious of the Community. As such it used its six-month term in office to focus predominantly on Cyprus in its external relations dossier.

By the time of the third Greek Presidency in 1994, a remarkably transformed PASOK was far better placed to endorse another classic role of the Presidency, that of brokering package deals and building coalitions in order to reach consensus. The case of the Corfu Council is a classic example in this respect. In Corfu, the Greek Presidency, keen to slip Cyprus into the bargain, succeeded in winning the consent of the Mediterranean member states, that favoured a southern counterbalance to the eastern enlargement. The Greek government succeeded in its intent, without defining the implications of this key decision. The Corfu bargain highlights how EU decisions are frequently taken on the grounds of internal needs and demands rather than collective strategies based on common assessments of external realities. Another key issue in this respect is unanimity in decision-making. In order to forge consensus, EU decisions and actions can appear inconsistent and illogical when viewed from outside, simply because their driving logic is often the need to reach internal consensus. Again the predominant use of unanimity in CFSP decision-making (despite the marginal changes made since 1997) remains in itself a clear signal of the persisting divergence between the interests of member states in the foreign policy domain.

The rotating Presidency and the divergence between member state interests and priorities not only creates the potential for incoherence at any given time, but also for inconsistency over time. As member states frequently use their Presidencies to further their different interests without accepting sufficient collective responsibility, the overall result is that a particular dossier risks being treated in different ways and with different intensities on six-monthly intervals.

This was certainly true of the Cyprus dossier. With the exception of the Greek Presidencies and the partial exception of the 1998 British Presidency, no other Presidency in the 1990s paid attention to the Cyprus problem per se, apart from when it was drawn into the logic of EU-Turkey-Cyprus package deals as during the 1995 French Presidency or the 1999 Finnish Presidency. While the rhetoric of all Presidencies stressed the importance of seeking a solution to the conflict prior to accession, none of the fourteen member states paid sufficient attention to how best to contribute to an agreement. The conflict was regarded as far too intractable to be resolved in six months and not pressing enough to justify intense and sustained effort without immediate payoff. So the Cyprus dossier was often on the margins of EU preoccupations, apart from when it was lifted to the core during Greek Presidencies and on a few other isolated occasions.

One last institutional theme discussed at length in the Cyprus case study was the role of the Commission and connected to this the EU pillar structure. The role of the Commission in EU external relations grew in the aftermath of the Cold War and the decision of the July 1989 Western Economic Summit to entrust the Commission with the task of coordinating aid to Poland and Hungary and then to the rest of the CEECs (Nuttall, 1996). Since then, the Commission has played a prominent role in the enlargement process, inducing reform in the CEECs by developing its policies of conditionality.

However the Cyprus case study highlights the limits of this form of conditionality and related to this the defects of the pillar structure. The Commission, due to its nature and mandate, focused on Cyprus' accession rather than on conflict resolution. In turn this meant that Commission officials tended to stress the need for a sufficiently integrated federal system that was capable of endorsing the responsibilities of membership. They did not focus on portraying elements of an EU-embedded solution that would solicit the support of all principal parties. The Commission's mandate also entailed that until late 2001, there was minimal contact between Commission officials dealing with Cyprus and the UN mediators. Indeed only when contacts intensified (in mid-2001, when the prospects of the accession of a divided Cyprus were becoming all too evident) did the Commission and the member governments mention the security and political gains of EU membership to the Turkish Cypriots.

Throughout the accession process the Commission instead emphasized its economic instruments in order to induce a settlement on the island. More precisely, when called upon to substantiate the rhetoric of the EU's 'catalytic effect' on conflict resolution, the Commission overstressed 'pillar 1' economic instruments to attain an essentially 'pillar 2' objective, i.e., the resolution of an ethno-political conflict. As previous chapters argued, the economic dimension of the conflict was important, and became even more so following the grave economic downturn of the Turkish Cypriot economy in 2000-02. Nonetheless, the political/security dimension remained at the core of the conflict and was neglected by the Commission until late 2001. This neglect in turn diminished the value of the 'economic carrot', certainly as far as the Turkish Cypriot leadership was concerned. The leadership actually portrayed the Commission's approach as a 'bribe' to the Turkish Cypriots. However, the structural problem of overemphasizing economic instruments did not derive from a misguided Commission strategy. There was no Commission or indeed no EU strategy to catalyse a settlement in Cyprus. It was the very absence of a common foreign policy towards the Cyprus conflict that led the Commission to focus on the economic instruments that it was most accustomed to using.

## Europeanization

Another element discussed in Chapters 2 and 6 in the context of Greece is 'Europeanization'. Drawing from constructivist approaches, several scholars have emphasized the partial success of European foreign policy in terms of the transformation or Europeanization of the member states and their national foreign policies. Rather than viewing European foreign policy exclusively through realist lenses and thus overemphasizing its shortfalls when measured against national foreign policies, it is important to appreciate the effect that the EU and within it EPC/CFSP mechanisms have had on member states' attitudes and positions. As put by Hill, working within CFSP 'shapes members' perceptions, choices and behaviours not least because it is the only way by which Europeans can have a high political profile in the global system' (Hill, 1998b, p.49).

But member states' positions change not only because of enforcement mechanisms and the costs of non-compliance, but also because of the gradual and genuine transformation of their perceived interests and positions within the EU framework. Working within the Union, and thus slowly but steadily assimilating its written and unwritten rules and norms, affects member state attitudes and preferences. The Union's ideology in support of democracy, soft-edged capitalism and regional cooperation, in addition to the *acquis communautaire* and *politique* are increasingly espoused by the member states as integral to their own ethos.

As such, a process of gradual convergence of views is already underway. Whether these changes will lead to a 'European identity' in future is unclear. Nevertheless, the existence of change within member states, whether minimal such as the emergence of a 'concertation reflex' whereby member states automatically coordinate before taking unilateral external actions, or more far reaching, cannot be denied (Ifestos, 1987, pp.241-242). Transformed agency can then lead to a further transformation of structures, triggering a cyclical inter-relationship between the two. In other words, transformed national positions within the EU framework can in turn affect the institutional setting, making EU institutions better equipped to conduct a truly common foreign policy.

The transformation of Greece within the Union, and more specifically of the PASOK governments, has been a key factor affecting EU policies towards Cyprus and Turkey. Starting from a nationalist and rejectionist platform, PASOK has undergone a radical change since 1981. This transformation impinged critically on its attitudes towards the EU, and subsequently its positions on Cyprus-EU and Turkey-EU relations. As the Greek government appreciated the economic and security gains of membership, it began lobbying intensely for Cyprus' inclusion in the bloc. Greek Cypriot security concerns would be alleviated if not resolved within the European security community, just like Greece itself was experiencing. So the PASOK governments assiduously worked first to persuade the initially reluctant Greek Cypriot government in 1988-90, and thereafter to sway its European partners to assure Cyprus' EU membership.

The government's Europeanization is even clearer in its transformed positions towards Turkey and EU-Turkey relations. From epitomizing in the 1980s the most critical obstacle in advancing closer EC-Turkey ties and the primary scapegoat behind which reluctant member states hid, the PASOK government of Costas Simitis (and in particular former Foreign Minister George Papandreou within it) became the most vocal advocate of Ankara's cause two decades later. While several factors contributed to this change, one if not the most important explanation lies in the transformation of Greece itself as an EU member state. Over the course of its membership, Greece felt sufficiently secure to rationally assess its national security interests and revise those interests by concluding that a 'European Turkey' embedded in a common cooperative structure would represent Greece's strongest security guarantee. Given Turkey's expectations, a 'European Turkey' entailed support for Turkey's EU membership bid. The transformation of Greek foreign policy vis-à-vis Turkey owes much to the previous PASOK administration and in particular to George Papandreou. The current New Democracy government appears more cautious (for example by refraining from openly backing the Annan Plan in April 2004). Nonetheless, the Greek-Turkish rapprochement seems likely to persist and it is highly improbable that we will witness a return to recurrent Greek obstructionism within the Union concerning EU-Turkey relations.

## The Constructive and Destructive Interactions between the Determinants of European Foreign Policy

The Cyprus case study displays several of the oft-mentioned factors determining European foreign policy activity. Yet probably the most important insight from this study is the interaction between these different elements, an interaction which itself becomes the prime determinant of the final outcome. These interactions over time are numerous and complex. In what follows a few are elucidated. In particular some of the links connecting the 'inside' to the 'outside' appear to lie at the crux of the Cyprus case study.

Cyprus' accession process was initiated by Greek Cypriot external demands driven by political and security reasons. Yet had it not been for the close ties between Nicosia and Athens, those external demands may not have emerged. In turn Greece would not have persuaded the Greek Cypriots to apply for membership had its own perceptions of the Union not changed. And this change was the slow result of a decade of membership, in which Greece transformed its ideology and views of the Community through the experience of membership itself. As the Greek governments appreciated the economic, political and security gains of membership, they became keen to expose the Greek Cypriots to the same benefits.

Greek membership also goes a long way towards explaining the resistance of the Turkish and Turkish Cypriot authorities towards Cyprus' accession. Greek positions within the EC in the 1980s, together with the general neglect of the Cyprus conflict and the ambivalence towards Turkey by the other member states, made Turkey and the Turkish Cypriots suspicious of the Union. They automatically resisted the unilateral application of the Greek Cypriots, espousing the mirror image of the same logic that induced the Greek Cypriot government to apply. Their resistance took the form of increased antagonism towards Greece, the Greek Cypriots and the Commission, and intransigence in reunification talks.

Turkish and Turkish Cypriot antagonism and intransigence in turn strengthened the already existing imbalance of EU institutions and member states towards the conflict. The more the Commission was snubbed by Turkish Cypriot officials and therefore the less contact it had with them, the more it tended to sympathize with Greek Cypriot views. The more it sympathized with the Greek Cypriot narrative, the more cautious it was in its contacts with Turkish Cypriot officials. This entailed focusing more on Turkish Cypriot civil society than seeking official contacts with the authorities. In turn, this was interpreted by Turkish Cypriot officials as the Commission's attempt to bypass and undermine them by bribing the impoverished Turkish Cypriot population. In short, dynamics within the EU and the Turkish/Turkish Cypriot sides interacted creating a vicious circle of misconceptions, bias and misunderstandings. As time elapsed these tendencies reinforced each other, generating an effective default EU policy towards the conflict, which operated against its resolution. Hence, while at times the interaction of different factors generated a shift in direction, such as the emergence of Greek Cypriot demands for membership, in other instances it reinforced existing trends, namely Turkish and Turkish Cypriot suspicions of the Union.

The short and medium-term effects of Cyprus' accession process on efforts to resolve the conflict were largely negative. However, the long-term effects, that began to seep through at the turn of the century, may operate in the opposite direction. The slow transformation of states within the Union appears to lie at the heart of the explanation. By operating within the EU institutional setting, the Greek government's perceptions of its own options and preferences transformed. While initially the relevance of the EU institutional setting was principally that of constraining unaltered choices, by the late 1990s the EU setting penetrated deeper, affecting underlying positions and interests.

Nowhere has this been more evident than in the transformation of Greek attitudes towards Turkey. From representing the most critical obstacle to smooth and close EU-Turkey relations in the 1980s, by December 2002, the Greek government appeared to be the most adamant spokesman for Turkey in the Union. This change generated two inter-related effects. First, it slowly began to affect positively Turkey's own perceptions of the Union and in turn it accelerated Turkey's transformation or Europeanization. Turkey increasingly appreciated that, contrary to its long-held views, the EU is no longer endemically against Turkey in view of Greece's inclusion and Turkey's exclusion from the club. The Turkish establishment and public opinion remain sceptical of the Union's willingness to embrace Turkey. However, the reasons behind this scepticism are focused less on Greece. Rather, Greece is increasingly regarded as an asset to Turkey's EU bid.

As such, and with progress in Turkey's EU accession process and its gradual compliance with the Copenhagen criteria, Turkey's own mode of foreign policy-making began to transform. The Copenhagen criteria represent an effective programme for the Europeanization of candidate countries by inducing them to endorse models of governance reflecting the norms and modes of operation of the

Union. As Turkey progressed along this path particularly under the AKP government, its own views on Cyprus altered.

Greece's transformation and the ensuing initiation of Cyprus' accession process also altered the attitudes of the Greek Cypriot elite. Most notably those Greek Cypriot actors that spearheaded and pushed through Cyprus' EU accession over the course of the 1990s (namely George Vassiliou and Glafcos Clerides) had softened remarkably their views on a settlement by 2004, speaking out strongly in favour of the UN Plan. The first signs of change came in the late 1990s, as the Clerides government portrayed itself as being both close to motherland Greece, thus satisfying nationalistic demands, as well as being pro-solution and pro-rapprochement with the Turkish Cypriots. Being a Greek Cypriot nationalist in 2002 did not have the same meaning as it did in 1992. Indeed it was the same Clerides who in 1993 campaigned against the 1992 Set of Ideas, who a decade later called upon the Greek Cypriot public to support the Annan Plan, which in many respects came closer to satisfying Turkish Cypriot concerns than past UN proposals. The process of change has certainly not been linear. Indeed Chapters 4 and 5 discussed the increased antagonism in Greek Cypriot positions particularly in the mid-1990s, both in terms of defence policy and by pursing property restitution cases in the ECHR. In the backdrop of secured EU accession, Greek Cypriot nationalism resurfaced with the election of Tassos Papadopoulos in 2003, and was responsible for the Greek Cypriot 'no' at the 2004 referendum.

There have also been fundamental interactions between internal EU factors and external developments as far as EU-Turkey relations were concerned. On the one hand, the more sceptical were the member states regarding Turkey's future in Europe and thus the less forthcoming were EU policies towards Turkey, the greater was the credibility of Turkish hardliners, who claimed that Turkey would never be admitted to the Union and so Ankara should be cautious in its domestic reforms and foreign policy re-conceptualizations. In other words, the greater was Turkey's mistrust of Europe, the slower was its own process of Europeanization. In turn, the less likely was a change in Turkey's Cyprus policy. In this respect, paradoxically Greece's ongoing Europeanization, having exposed the deep reservations of the other member states towards Turkey, contributed to Turkey's mistrust of the Union.

On the other hand, as and when nationalists in Ankara gained the upper hand in the determination of domestic and foreign policy, EU actors became less forthcoming towards Turkey. Some 'Turkey-sceptics' in Europe, who disapproved of the forthcoming decisions on Turkey taken in December 1999 and December 2002, indeed may have hoped for an impasse in Cyprus in order to cool relations with Ankara. In several instances in the recent history of EU-Turkey relations, 'anti-Turks' in Europe and 'anti-Europeans' in Turkey reinforced each other in a vicious circle of antagonism and lack of reform in Turkey together with European distancing from Turkey.

Yet on other occasions the circle was broken. This has been largely the case since the December 1999 Helsinki European Council and most notably since the rise to power of the AKP government in Ankara. When vicious circles were broken, they gave way to constructive interactions between Turkey and the Union, which in turn facilitated the search for an agreement in Cyprus. In particular, at the critical juncture of April 2004, as Turkey awaited the EU's green-light for the opening accession negotiations, the pro-EU AKP government appeared sufficiently strong to commit the country to a Cyprus settlement. Yet, Turkey's commitment together with that of the Turkish Cypriot public could not alone catalyse a solution before Cyprus' accession.

The interaction between the different determinants of European foreign policy gives rise to what Hill and Wallace have defined as a 'multi-level governance' process leading to a 'system of external relations' (Hill and Wallace, 1996, p.5). The Union still falls short of enjoying a truly common foreign policy as shown by the visible absence of design and strategy in EU external policy. However, European foreign policy is gradually evolving over time into a complex, interactive and dynamic foreign policy system, in which different actors and factors from different levels of government and civil society, internal and external to the Union, interact to produce the overall policy outcomes. This dialectic process is marked by contrasting forces of convergence and of divergence. External demands, globalization and Europeanization may lead to a gradual process of convergence, contrasted by the persisting divergence in national interests and perceptions, driven by different geographical and historical contexts.

Consequently, the outcomes are also mixed. At times the system produces uncertainty, delay and misperceptions. On other occasions it can lead to deep-rooted change and moderation. The Cyprus case study shows that starkly opposite effects can coexist and their relative strength can change over time as some take precedence over the others. The 1990s witnessed a deterioration of the conflict, determined at least in part by the introduction of the EU variable in the conflict. What made matters worse was that the EU framework could have potentially aided the UN's search for an agreement by adding conditional economic, political and security assets, vital to the basic needs of the principal parties.

This leads to a paradoxical conclusion: 'despite its enormous power of attraction the Union has serious problems transforming its normative strength into operational capability' (Zielonka, 1998, p.11). But the possible explanation of the paradox is perhaps more intriguing than the paradox itself. Those very aspects of the EU multi-level governance framework which created the potential for a constructive European role in conflict resolution efforts became the very cause of the EU's failure when confronted with the need to act towards the conflict.

When faced with a typical foreign policy problem such as the need for intervention in an ethno-political conflict a traditional state actor is often more effective at mobilizing its resources, given the greater simplicity in its policy-making process. The complexity of a multi-level framework instead raises the difficulties in effective external action. As put by Allen: 'if Bonn is to be challenged by the Länder, or Madrid by Catalonia, or Rome by northern Italy, or indeed London by Scotland, then the task of foreign policy coordination will become that much more complex' (Allen, 1996, p.300). So the resources offered by a non-nation-state framework like that of the Union, while being potentially of greater value, are rarely exported effectively *because* of their very nature. In the case of Cyprus, this was the case until May 2004.

In 2002-03, while UN drafters of the Annan Plan made considerable use of the EU framework within which to embed a new Cyprus, the EU as an actor remained largely passive. Neither the Commission nor the Council engaged actively in the peace process in order to gain the confidence of the Turkish Cypriot and Turkish sides and induce the Greek Cypriot side to accept an agreement. Their relative passivity was justified by them on the grounds of the existing UN mediation and Turkey's scepticism of the EU's role in Cyprus. Yet this passivity also entailed that little was done to deconstruct the logic which had motivated the hardening of Turkish and Turkish Cypriot positions during the 1990s. As reported by UNSG Annan: '(h)e (Denktaş) seemed to perceive the approaching date of EU accession and the EU's strong preference to welcome a united Cyprus not as an opportunity to achieve a settlement on a favourable basis and, in the process, pave the way for Turkey's aspirations regarding the EU, but as a trap and threat' (UNSG, 2003, paragraph 130). Whether greater coherence and activism in EU policy could have altered these (mis)perceptions cannot be known. Nevertheless, little was done to attempt such a re-conceptualization of external perceptions.

In 2004, EU pressure on Turkey and the Turkish Cypriots, in the light of virtuous circles in EU-Turkey relations and key domestic changes in northern Cyprus and Turkey, secured a shift in their stance. Yet, this time the Greek Cypriot side, on the tide of resurfacing nationalism and bolstered by the imminent entry into the Union, rejected the reunification of the island. Ironically it was the very party that had incessantly argued in favour of the 'catalytic effect' of EU accession that, on 1 May, allowed the 'europartition' of the island.

The short-term conclusions drawn from the Cyprus case study may indeed be dispiriting. However the possible long-term lessons may be far brighter. In the short term or even more acutely in times of crisis, the Union often fails to mobilize its potential precisely because of its very nature. Yet in the long term the opposite conclusions may be drawn. The EU's comparative advantage is in the long-term efforts to change the environments out of which conflicts spring, so as to inoculate against them (Hill, 1992, p.146).

It is still too early to tell whether this conclusion will be vindicated in the case of Cyprus. What can be concluded is that the first signs of transformation in subject positions within Greece, Turkey and Cyprus may be emerging. In Greece this was manifest in the previous government's support for the Secretary General's 2002 proposals and for Turkey's progressive integration in the Union. In southern Cyprus it was most evident in the positions of the previous leadership, while not being shared by the ensuing administration or by the majority of the public. In northern Cyprus, the opposite was true, with a public far ahead of its leadership in terms of revising its positions and attitudes, and in turn triggering key changes in domestic political dynamics. In Turkey, while still far from having reached internal consensus within the wider establishment, the current government succeeded in overturning an entrenched Turkish foreign policy on Cyprus. In these progressive and endemic processes of transformation or 'Europeanization', the role of the EU anchor clearly lies at the heart of the matter.

## References

Allen, D. (1996), 'Conclusions: The European Rescue of National Foreign Policy?', in C. Hill (ed.), *The Actors in Europe's Foreign Policy*, Routledge, New York and London, pp.288-304.

Barbé, E. (1998), 'Balancing Europe's Eastern and Southern Dimensions', in J. Zielonka (ed.), *Paradoxes of European Foreign Policy*, Kluwer Law International, The Hague, pp.117-129.

Ginsberg, R. (1989), *Foreign Policy Actions and the Politics of Scale*, Lynne Reinner Publisher, Boulder.

Ginsberg, R. (1999), 'Conceptualizing the EU as an International Actor: Narrowing the Theoretical Capability-Expectations Gap', *Journal of Common Market Studies*, Vol. 37, No.3, pp.429-454.

Grabbe, H. (2001), 'How does Europeanization Affect CEE Governance? Conditionality, Diffusion and Diversity', *Journal of European Public Policy*, Vol.8, No.6, pp.1013-1031.

Guehenno, J.M (1998), 'A Foreign Policy in Search of a Polity', in J. Zielonka (ed.), *Paradoxes of European Foreign Policy*, Kluwer Law International, The Hague, pp.25-34.

Hill, C. (1992), 'EPC's Performance in Crisis', in R. Rummel (ed.), *Toward a Political Union: Planning a CFSP in the EC*, Westview, Oxford, pp.135-146.

Hill, C. (1993), 'The Capability-Expectations Gap, or Conceptualizing Europe's International Role', *Journal of Common Market Studies*, Vol.31, No.3, pp.305-329.

Hill, C. (1997), 'Chapter 5', in E. Regelsberger, P. de Schoutheete de Tervarent and W. Wessels (eds.), *Foreign Policy of the EU*, Lynne Rienner, London, pp.85-97.

Hill, C. (1998a), 'Closing the Capabilities-Expectations Gap?', in J. Peterson and H. Sjursen (eds.), *A Common Foreign Policy for Europe*, Routledge, London, pp.18-38.

Hill, C. (1998b), 'Convergence, Divergence and Dialectics', in J. Zielonka (ed.), *Paradoxes of European Foreign Policy*, Kluwer Law International, The Hague, pp.35-51.

Hill, C. and Wallace, W. (1996), 'Introduction', in C. Hill (ed.), *The Actors in Europe's Foreign Policy*, Routledge, New York and London, pp.1-16.

Ifestos, P. (1987), *EPC: Towards a Framework of Supranational Diplomacy?*, Ashgate, Aldershot.

Keukeleire, S. (2000), *The EU as a Diplomatic Actor*, Discussion Paper No.71, University of Leicester, Leicester.

Nuttall, S. (1992), *European Political Cooperation*, Clarendon, Oxford.

Nuttall, S. (1996), 'The Commission: the Struggle for Legitimacy', in C. Hill (ed.), *The Actors in Europe's Foreign Policy*, Routledge, New York and London, pp.130-147.

Putnam, R. (1988), 'Diplomacy and Domestic Politics: the Logic of Two-Level Games', *International Organization*, Vol.42, No.3, pp.427-60.

Smith, K. (1998), 'The Instruments of EU Foreign Policy', in J. Zielonka (ed.), *Paradoxes of European Foreign Policy*, Kluwer Law International, The Hague, pp.67-85.

Smith, K.E. (1999), *The Making of EU Foreign Policy, The Case of Eastern Europe*, Macmillan, London.

Tsakaloyannis, P. (1996), 'Greece: The Limits of Convergence', in C. Hill (ed.), *The Actors in Europe's Foreign Policy*, Routledge, New York and London, pp.186-207.

United Nations Secretary General (2003), *Report of the Secretary General on his Mission of Good Offices in Cyprus*, 7 April 2003, New York.

Wallace, H. (1985), 'The Presidency of the Council of Ministers of the EC: Tasks and Evolution', in C. O'Nuallain (ed.), *The Presidency of the European Council of Ministers*, Croom Helm, London, pp.1-22.

Zielonka, J. (1998), 'Introduction' in J. Zielonka (ed.), *Paradoxes of European Foreign Policy,* Kluwer Law International, The Hague, pp.1-14.

# Annex

**Map 1  The 1974 Partition of Cyprus**

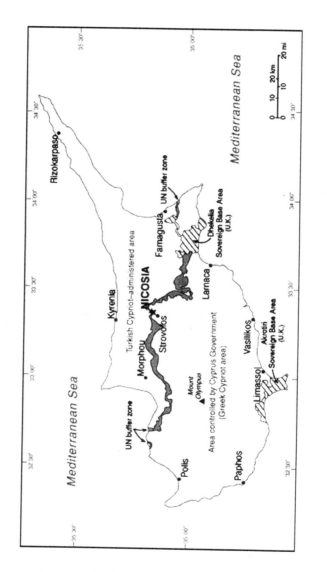

*Source:* The General Libraries, The University of Texas at Austin

188

**Map 2  Map Presented in Annan Plan V**

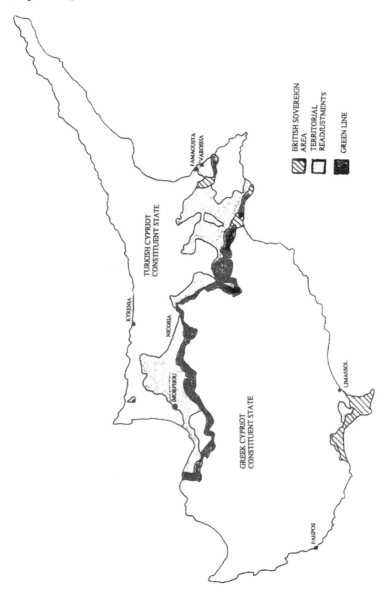

*Source:* The United Nations, Department of Peace-keeping Operations,
Cartographic Section

# Bibliography

**Books and Articles**

Attalides, M.A. (1979), *Cyprus Nationalism and International Politics*, Q Press, Edinburgh.

Attina, F. and Stavridis, S. (eds.) (2001), *The Barcelona Process and Euro-Mediterranean Issues from Stuttgart to Marseilles*, Università di Catania, Catania.

Axt, H.J. and Brey, H. (eds.) (1997), *Cyprus and the EU: New Chance for Solving an Old Conflict*, Sudosteuropa-Gesellschaft, Munchen.

Bahceli, T. (2001), 'The Lure of Economic Prosperity Versus Ethno-Nationalism: Turkish Cypriots, the EU Option, and the Resolution of Ethnic Conflict in Cyprus', in M. Keating and J. McGarry (eds.), *Minority Nationalism and the Changing International Order*, Oxford University Press, Oxford, pp.203-222.

Bercovitch, J. (ed.) (1996), *Resolving International Conflicts - the Theory and Practice of Mediation*, Lynne Rienner, Boulder, Colorado.

Bercovitch, J. and Rubin, J.Z. (eds.) (1992), *Mediation in International Relations - Multiple Approaches to Conflict Management*, Macmillan, London.

Bertrand, G. (1999), 'Vingt-cinq Ans Après, Où en est la Partition de Chypre?', *Les Etudes du CERI*, No.59, SciencesPo, Paris.

Biçak, H.A. (1997), 'Recent Developments in Cyprus-EU relations', in E. Doğramaci et al. (eds.), *Proceedings of the First International Conference on Cypriot Studies*, Eastern Mediterranean University, Famagusta.

Bloomfield, D. (1995), 'Towards Complementarity in Conflict Management: Resolution and Settlement in Northern Ireland', *Journal of Peace Research*, Vol.32, No.2, pp.151-164.

Bölükbaşi, S. (1995), 'Boutros-Ghali's Cyprus Initiative in 1992: Why Did it Fail?', *Middle Eastern Studies*, Vol.31, No.3, pp.460-482.

Borowiec, A. (2000), *Cyprus: A Troubled Island*, Praeger Publishers, Westport.

Borzel, T. and Risse, T. (2000), 'When Europe Hits Home: Europeanization and Domestic Change', *European Integration Online Papers*, Vol.4, No.15 http://eiop.or.at/eiop/texte/2000-015.htm

Brewin, C. (2000), *The European Union and Cyprus*, Eothen, Huntingdon.

Burton, J. (ed.) (1990), *Conflict: Human Needs Theory*, Macmillan, London.

Burton, J. and Dukes, F. (eds.) (1990), *Conflict: Readings in Management and Resolution*, Macmillan, London.

Checkel, J. (1999), 'Norms, Institutions and National Identity in Contemporary Europe', *International Studies Quarterly*, Vol.43, No.1, pp.83-114.

Chrysostomides, K. (2000), *The Republic of Cyprus: A Study in International Law*, M. Nijhoff Publishers, The Hague, London.

Clerides, G. (1989a), *Cyprus: My Deposition*, Volume 1, Alithia Publishers, Nicosia.

Clerides, G. (1989b), *Cyprus: My Deposition*, Volume 2, Alithia Publishers, Nicosia.

Clerides, G. (1994), Interview with, 'The Cyprus Problem Twenty Years after the Turkish Invasion', *Hellenic Studies*, Fall 1994, pp.9-17.

Cortright, D. (ed.) (1997), *The Price of Peace: Incentives and International Conflict Prevention*, Carnegie Corporation, Rowman and Littlefield, New York.

Coughlan, R. (1992), 'Negotiating the Cyprus Problem: Leadership Perspectives from Both Sides of the Green Line', *The Cyprus Review*, Vol.4, pp.80-100.

Crawford, J., Pellet, A. and Hafner, G. (1997), *Republic of Cyprus: Eligibility for EU Membership*, A/52/481, S/1977/805, 17 October 1997.

Curle, A. (1995), *Another Way - Positive Response to Contemporary Violence*, Jon Carpenter, Oxford.

Demetriou, M. (1998), 'On the Long Road to Europe and the Short Path to War: Issue-Linkage Politics and the Arms Build-up on Cyprus', *Mediterranean Politics*, Vol.3, No.3, pp. 38-51.

Deutsch, K. et al. (1957), *Political Community and the North Atlantic Area: International Organization in the Light of Historical Experience*, Princeton University Press, Princeton.

Denktaş, R. (2002), Letter of Appreciation to the Centre for European Policy Studies for the study by M. Emerson and N. Tocci (2002), *Cyprus as Lighthouse of the Eastern Mediterranean*, CEPS, Brussels, dated 4 May 2002, Nicosia.

Diez, T. (ed.) (2002), *The European Union and the Cyprus Conflict - Modern Conflict, Post Modern Union*, Manchester University Press, Manchester.

Diez, T., Stetter, S. and Albert, M. (2004), 'The EU and the Transformation of Border Conflicts', *EUBorderConf Working Papers*, No.1, January 2004.

Dodd, C. (ed.) (1993), *The Political, Social and Economic Development of Northern Cyprus*, Eothen, Huntingdon.

Dodd, C. (1999a), 'Confederation, Federation and Sovereignty', *Perceptions - Journal of International Affairs*, Vol.4, No.3, September-November 1999, on www.mfa.gov.tr

Dodd, C. (ed.) (1999b), *Cyprus: the Need for New Perspectives*, Eothen, Huntingdon.

Dorussen, H. (2001), 'Mixing Carrots with Sticks: Evaluating the Effectiveness of Positive Incentives', *Journal of Peace Research*, Vol.38, No.2, pp.251-262.

Durrell, L. (1958), *Bitter Lemons*, Marlowe & Co., New York.

Emerson, M. and Tocci, N. (2002), *Cyprus as Lighthouse of the Eastern Mediterranean*, CEPS, Brussels.

Ertekün, N.M. (1981), *In Search of a Negotiated Cyprus Settlement*, Ülüs Matbağacılık, Nicosia.

Faulds, A. (1988), *Excerpta Cypria for Today: A Source Book on the Cyprus Problem*, K. Rustem and Brother, Lefkoşa, London.

Featherstone, K. and Kazamias, G. (eds.) (2001), *Europeanization and the Southern Periphery*, Frank Cass, London.

· Fetherston, A.B. (2000), *From Conflict Resolution to Transformative Peace Building: Reflections from Croatia*, Working Paper 4, University of Bradford, Bradford.

Fetherston, A.B. and Parkin, A.C. (1997), 'Transforming Violent Conflict: Contributions from Social Theory', in L.A. Broadhead (ed.), *Issues in Peace Research 1997-98*, Department of Peace Studies, University of Bradford, pp.19-57.

Fisher, R. and Ury, W. (1991), *Getting to a Yes - Negotiating an Agreement without Giving In*, Random House, London.

Galtung, J. (1969), 'Violence, Peace and Peace Research', *Journal of Peace Research*, Vol.3, pp.167-192.

Ginsberg, R. (1989), *Foreign Policy Actions and the Politics of Scale*, Lynne Reinner Publisher, Boulder.

Ginsberg, R. (1999), 'Conceptualizing the EU as an International Actor: Narrowing the Theoretical Capability - Expectations Gap', *Journal of Common Market Studies*, Vol. 37, No.3, pp.429-454.

Grabbe, H. (2001), 'How does Europeanization Affect CEE Governance? Conditionality, Diffusion and Diversity', *Journal of European Public Policy*, Vol.8, No.6, pp.1013-1031.

Haas, E. (1968), *The Uniting of Europe: Political, Social and Economic Forces*, Stanford University Press, Stanford, California.

Habeeb, W.M. (1988), *Power and Tactics in International Negotiation: How Weak Nations Bargain with Strong Nations*, John Hopkins University Press, Baltimore.

Harvie, C. (1994), *The Rise of Regional Europe*, Routledge, New York.

Hill, C. (1993), 'The Capability-Expectations Gap, or Conceptualizing Europe's International Role', *Journal of Common Market Studies*, Vol.31, No.3, pp.305-329.

Hill, C. (ed.) (1996), *The Actors in Europe's Foreign Policy*, Routledge, New York and London.

Hitchens, C. (1997), *Hostage to History: Cyprus from the Ottomans to Kissinger*, Verso, London.

Hoffman, M. (1987), 'Critical Theory and the Inter-Paradigm Debate', *Millennium Journal of International Studies*, Vol. 16, No.2, pp.231-250.

Hooghe, L. (1996), *Cohesion Policy and the European Union*, Clarendon Press, Oxford.

Hooghe, L. and Marks, G. (2001), *Multi-level Governance and European Integration*, Rowman and Littlefield, Lanham.

Hopmann, T. (1996), *The Negotiation Process and the Resolution of International Conflicts*, University of South Carolina Press, Columbia.

Ifestos, P. (1987), *EPC: Towards a Framework of Supranational Diplomacy?*, Ashgate, Aldershot.

Ioakimidis, P. (1997), 'The Role of Greece in the Development of EC Mediterranean Policy', *Mediterranean Politics*, Vol.2, pp.67-81.

Ioakimidis, P. (1999), 'Greece, the EU and Southeastern Europe: Past Failures and Future Prospects', in V. Coufoudakis, H.J. Psomiades and A. Gerolymatos (eds.), *Greece and the New Balkans: Challenges and Opportunities*, Pella, New York, pp.169-194.

Jans, M.T. (2001), *Leveled Domestic Politics - Comparing Institutional Reform and Ethno-national Conflicts in Canada and Belgium*, Mimeo, VUB, Brussels.

Jeffrey, C. (ed.) (2001), *The Regional Dimension of the European Union*, Frank Cass, London.

Jeffrey, C. (2000), 'Sub-National Mobilization and European Integration: Does it Make Any Difference?' *Journal of Common Market Studies*, Vol.38, No.1, pp.1-23.

Joseph, J. (2000), 'Can the EU Succeed where the UN Failed? The Continuing Search for a Settlement on Cyprus', *CIAO Papers*, September 2000, ISA, 41st Annual Convention, March 2000.

Kazakos, P. and Ioakimides, P. (eds.) (1994), *Greece and EC Membership Evaluated*, Pinter, London.

Kerremans, B. (2000), 'Determining a European Policy in a Multi-Level Setting: The Case of Specialised Coordination in Belgium', *Regional and Federal Studies*, Vol.10, No.1, pp.36-61.

Keukeleire, S. (2000), *The EU as a Diplomatic Actor*, Discussion Paper No.71, University of Leicester, Leicester.

Kleiboer, M. (1996), 'Understanding Success and Failure in International Mediation', *The Journal of Conflict Resolution*, Vol.40, No.2, pp.360-389.

Kovziridze, T. (2002), 'Europeanization of Federal Institutional Relationships: Hierarchical and Inter-dependent Relationship Structures in Belgium, Germany and Austria', *Regional and Federal Studies*, Vol.12, No.3, pp.128-155.

Kramer, H. (1997), 'The Cyprus Problem and European Security', *Survival*, Vol.39, No.3, pp.16-32.

Kressel, K., Pruitt, D.G. and Associates (eds.) (1989), *Mediation Research, the Process and Effectiveness of Third Party Intervention*, Jossey-Bass Publishers, San Francisco.

Kriesberg, L. and Thorson, S.J. (eds.) (1991), *Timing the De-escalation of International Conflicts*, Syracuse University Press, Syracuse, New York.

Küçük, F. (1963), *Turkish Reply to Archbishop Makarios' Proposals*, Nicosia n.d.

Kyriakides, S. (1968), *Cyprus Constitutionalism and Crisis Government*, University of Pennsylvania Press, Philadelphia.

Laible, J. (2001), 'Nationalism and a Critique of European Integration: Questions for the Flemish Parties', in M. Keating and J. McGarry (eds.), *Minority Nationalism and the Changing International Order*, Oxford University Press, Oxford, pp.223-245.

Lall, A. (1966), *Modern International Negotiation: Principles and Practices*, Columbia University Press, New York, London.

Lederach, J.P. (1997), *Building Peace: Sustainable Reconciliation in Divided Societies*, US Institute of Peace Press, Washington D.C.

Marks, G., Scharpf, F., Schmiter, P. and Streek, W. (eds.) (1996), *Governance in the European Union*, Sage, London.

Martinelli Quille, M. (2000), *A Response to Recent Critiques of Conflict Resolution: Is Critical Theory the Answer?*, Copri Working Paper, Copenhagen.

Mavratsas, C. (1997), 'The Ideological Contest between Greek Cypriot Nationalism and Cypriotism 1974-1995', *Ethnic and Racial Studies*, Vol.20, No.4, pp.718-737.

Mendelson, M. (2001), *Why Cyprus' Entry into the EU would be Illegal*, Embassy of the Republic of Turkey, London.

Mirbagheri, F. (1998), *Cyprus and International Peacemaking*, Hurst & Co., London.

Mitrany, D. (1966), *A Working Peace System: An Argument for the Functional Development of International Organization*, University of Chicago Press, Chicago.

Neuwahl, N. (2000), 'Cyprus Which Way? In Pursuit of a Confederal Solution in Europe', *Harvard Jean Monnet Working Paper*, April 2000, Cambridge, MA.

Nuttall, S. (1992), *European Political Cooperation*, Clarendon, Oxford.

Olgun, E. (2002a), *Cyprus: Settlement and Membership*, Conference Paper presented at the European Parliament on 3 June 2002, Brussels.

Olgun, E. (2002b), *Some Characteristics of the Belgian State that May Apply to the New Partnership State of Cyprus*, Non-paper dated 26 June 2002, Brussels.

Olgun, E. (2002c), *Significant Openings made by the Turkish Cypriot Side for a Resolution of the Cyprus Issue*, Non-paper dated 11 September 2002, Nicosia.

Papadakis, Y. (1998), 'Greek Cypriot Narratives of History and Collective Identity: Nationalism as a Contested Process', *American Ethnologist*, Vol.25, No.2, pp.149-165.

Peterson, J. and Sjursen, H. (eds.) (1998), *A Common Foreign Policy for Europe*, Routledge, London.

Pijpers, A. (1990), *The Vicissitudes of European Political Cooperation*, CIP-Gegevens Koninkluke Bibliotheek, Leiden.

Polyviou, P.G. (1976), *Cyprus in Search of a Constitution*, Chr Nicolaou & Sons Ltd, Nicosia.

Putnam, R. (1988), 'Diplomacy and Domestic Politics: the Logic of Two-Level Games', *International Organization*, Vol.42, No.3, pp.427-60.

Reddaway, J. (1986), *Burdened with Cyprus - The British Connection*, Rustem & Bro. and Weidenfeld & Nicolson, Ltd., London, Nicosia, Istanbul.

Regelsberger, E., de Schoutheete de Tervarent, P. and Wessels, W. (eds.) (1997), *Foreign Policy of the EU*, Lynne Rienner, London.

Rhein, E. (2002), *Turkey and the EU, a Realistic Framework for Accession*, EPC, Brussels.

Richmond, O. (1998), *Mediating in Cyprus*, Frank Cass, London.

Robins, P. (1998), 'Turkey: Europe in the Middle East or the Middle East in Europe?', in B.A. Robertson (ed.), *The Middle East and Europe*, Routledge, London and New York, pp.151-169.

Rubin, J.Z. (ed.) (1981), *Dynamics of Third Party Intervention, Kissinger in the Middle East*, Praeger, New York.

Rummel, R. (ed.) (1992), *Toward a Political Union: Planning a CFSP in the EC*, Westview, Oxford.

Scharpf, F.W. (1994), 'Community and Autonomy: Multi-level Policy-making in the EU', *Journal of European Public Policy*, Vol.1, No.1, pp.219-242.

Smith, K.E. (1999), *The Making of EU Foreign Policy, The Case of Eastern Europe*, Macmillan, London.

Stavridis, S., Couloumbis, T., Veremis, T. and Waites, N. (eds.) (1999), *The Foreign Policies of the EU's Mediterranean States and Applicant Countries in the 1990s*, Macmillan, London.

Stavrinides, Z. (2001), *Greek Cypriot Perceptions on the Cyprus Problem*, available on http://website.lineone.net/~acgta/Stavrinides.htm

Stedman, S. (1991), *Peacemaking in Civil War: International Mediation in Zimbabwe 1974-1980*, Lynne Reinner, Boulder, Colorado.

Stefanidis, I.D. (1999), *Isle of Discord: Nationalism, Imperialism and the Making of the Cyprus Problem*, Hurst & Company, London.

Stivachtis, Y.A. (2000), *The Enlargement of the European Union: The Case of Cyprus*, Conference Paper, International Studies Association, 41st Annual Convention, Los Angeles, CA. 14-18 March 2000, available on CIAO Conference Proceedings www.cc.columbia.edu/sec/dlc/ciao/isa/sty01/

Suvarierol, S. (2001), 'La Question de l'Adhésion de Chypre à l'Union Européenne et le Problème de la République Turque de Chypre-Nord', *CEMOTI* (Cahiers d'Études sur la Méditerranée Orientale et le monde Turco-Iranien), No. 31, Janvier-Juin 2001, pp.163-188.

Theophanous, A. (2000), 'Cyprus, the EU and the Search for a New Constitution', *Journal of Southern Europe and the Balkans*, Vol. 2, No.2, pp.213-233.

Theophanous, A. (1996), *The Political Economy of a Federal Cyprus*, Intercollege, Nicosia.

Theophanous, A., Peristianis, N. and Ioannou, A. (eds.) (1999), *Cyprus and the EU*, Intercollege, Nicosia.

Tocci, N. (2003), 'Incentives and Disincentives for Reunification and EU Accession in Cyprus', *Mediterranean Politics*, Vol.8, No.1, pp.151-159.

Tocci, N. (2002), 'Cyprus and the EU: Catalysing Crisis or Settlement?', *Turkish Studies*, Vol.3, No. 2, pp.105-138.

Tocci, N. and Houben, M. (2001), 'Accommodating Turkey in ESDP', *Policy Brief No.5*, CEPS, Brussels.

Tsakaloyannis, P. (1985), 'Greece's First Term in the Presidency of the EC: A Preliminary Assessment', in C. O'Nuallain (ed.), *The Presidency of the European Council of Ministers*, Croom Helm, London, pp.101-118.

Uğur, M. (1999), *The EU and Turkey: An Anchor Credibility Dilemma*, Ashgate, Aldershot.

Usher, J. and Greenwood, C. (2000), *Re Accession of Cyprus to the EC: Restrictions on Residence and Acquisition of Property and Related Issues*, Mimeo, Joint Opinion, London.

Wagstaff, P. (ed.) (1999), *Regionalism in the EU*, Intellect, Exeter.

Wallace, H. (1985), 'The Presidency of the Council of Ministers of the EC: Tasks and Evolution', in C. O'Nuallain (ed.), *The Presidency of the European Council of Ministers*, Croom Helm, London, pp.1-22.

Wallace, W. (2002), 'Reconciliation in Cyprus: The Window of Opportunity', *Mediterranean Programme Report*, EUI, Florence.

Wouters, L. and de Rynck, S. (1996), 'Subnational Autonomy in the European Integration Process: the Belgian Case', in J. Hesse (ed.), *Regions in Europe*, Nomos, Baden-Baden.

Young, O. (1968), *The Politics of Force: Bargaining during International Crises*, Princeton University Press, Princeton, New Jersey.

Zartman, I.W. (1989), *Ripe for Resolution, Conflict and Intervention in Africa*, OUP, Oxford.

Zartman, I.W. and Berman, M.R. (1982), *The Practical Negotiator*, Yale University Press, New Haven.

Zartman, I.W. and Rasmussen, J.L. (eds.) (1997), *Peacemaking in International Conflict, Methods and Techniques*, US Institute of Peace Press, Washington D.C.

Zielonka, J. (ed.) (1998), *Paradoxes of European Foreign Policy*, Kluwer Law International, The Hague.

**Official Documentation**

Commission of the European Communities (1989), *Opinion on Turkey's Request for Accession to the Community*, SEC(89) 2290 final, 18 December 1989, Brussels.

Commission of the European Communities (1993), *Opinion on the Application for Membership from Cyprus*, COM(93) 313, EC Bulletin 6-1993, Brussels.

Commission of the European Communities (1997a), *Press Release*, Speech 97/45, Hans Van der Broek Speech at the North Cyprus Young Businessmen Association, Reuter Briefing, 27 February 1997, Brussels.

Commission of the European Communities (1997b), *Agenda 2000*, 15 July 1997, Extracts on www.cyprus-eu.org.cy/eng/07_documents/documents003.htm

Commission of the European Communities (1998a), *Regular Report on Cyprus' Progress towards Accession*, on www.europa.int

Commission of the European Communities (1998b), *Regular Report on Turkey's Progress towards Accession*, on www.europa.eu.int

Commission of the European Communities (1999a), *Regular Report on Cyprus' Progress towards Accession*, on www.europa.int

Commission of the European Communities (1999b), *Regular Report on Turkey's Progress towards Accession*, on www.europa.eu.int

Commission of the European Communities (2000a), *Regular Report on Cyprus' Progress towards Accession*, on www.europa.eu.int

Commission of the European Communities (2000b), *Regular Report on Turkey's Progress towards Accession*, on www.europa.eu.int

Commission of the European Communities (2001a), *Regular Report on Cyprus' Progress towards Accession*, on www.europa.eu.int

Commission of the European Communities (2001b), *Regular Report on Turkey's Progress towards Accession*, on www.europa.eu.int

Commission of the European Communities (2002a), *Commission Offers a Fair and Solid Approach for Financing EU Enlargement*, IP/02/170, Brussels.

Commission of the European Communities (2002b), *Regular Report on Cyprus' Progress towards Accession*, on www.europa.eu.int

Commission of the European Communities (2002c), *Regular Report on Turkey's Progress towards Accession*, on www.europa.eu.int

Commission of the European Communities (2003), *Continuing Enlargement: Strategy Paper and Report of the European Commission on the Progress Towards Accession of Bulgaria, Romania and Turkey*, on www.europa.eu.int

Council of Europe (1974), *Recommendation 573 of the Assembly of the Council of Europe*, Strasbourg.

Council of Europe (1987), *Recommendation 1056 of the Assembly of the Council of Europe*, Strasbourg.

Council of Ministers of the European Communities (1973), Council Regulation (EEC) No. 1246/73, 'Agreement Establishing an Association between the European Economic Community and the Republic of Cyprus', *Official Journal*, L133, 21 May 1973, Brussels.

198     *EU Accession Dynamics and Conflict Resolution*

Council of Ministers of the European Union (1995), *General Affairs Council Decision on Cyprus' Accession*, 6 March 1995, Presidency Proposal, on www.cyprus-eu.org.cy
Council of Ministers of the European Union (1997), *Joint Statement made by Italy, France, Germany and the Netherlands on the Greek Cypriot-EU Membership Process During the EU General Affairs Council*, 9 November 1998, extracts available on www.mfa.gov.tr/grupa/ad/add/doc19.htm
Council of Ministers of the European Union (2001), *General Affairs Council Decision on the Principles, Priorities, Intermediate Objectives and Conditions in the Accession Partnership with the Republic of Turkey*, 24 March 2001, 2001/235/EC, *Official Journal*, L85, Brussels.
European Council (1992), Meeting on 26-27 June 1992 in Lisbon, *Presidency Conclusions*.
European Council (1994), Meeting on 24-25 June 1994 in Corfu, *Presidency Conclusions*, extracts available on www.cyprus-eu.org.cy/eng/07-documents/document004.htm
European Council (1997), Meeting on 12-13 December 1997 in Luxembourg, *Presidency Conclusions*, extracts available on www.cyprus-eu.org.cy/eng/07-documents/document004.htm
European Council (1999), Meeting on 12-13 December 1999 in Helsinki, *Presidency Conclusions*, SN300/99.
European Council (2001), Meeting on 14-15 December 2001 in Laeken, *Presidency Conclusions*, SN300/01.
European Council (2002a), Meeting on 26-27 June 2002 in Seville, *Presidency Conclusions*, SN 200/02.
European Council (2002b), Meeting on 12-13 December 2002 in Copenhagen, *Presidency Conclusions*, SN 400/02.
European Court of Human Rights (1989), Court Case No.15318/89, Strasbourg.
European Court of Justice (1994), *S.P. Anastasiou Ltd. versus the UK*, Case C-432/92, ECR3087, Luxembourg.
European Parliament (1987), Foreign Affairs Committee, Costé-Floret Report, DOCA2-317/87, 26 February 1987, on www.mfa.gov.tr
European Parliament (1990), Resolution of 15 March 1990, Strasbourg.
European Parliament (1991), Resolution of 17 May 1991, Strasbourg.
European Parliament (1993), Resolution of 20 January 1993, Strasbourg.
European Parliament (1998), *Report on the Communication from the Commission to the Council and the EP on the Further Development of Relations with Turkey and on the Communication from the Commission to the Council on a European Strategy for Turkey*, Rapporteur Hannes Swoboda, 19 November 1998, Brussels.
European Parliament (2000), *Report on Cyprus' Application for Membership of the EU and the State of Negotiations*, Rapporteur Jacques Poos, A5-0249/200, 19 September 2000, Brussels.
European Parliament (2001), *Report on Cyprus' Application for Membership of the EU and the State of Negotiations*, Rapporteur Jacques Poos, A5-0261/2001, 11 July 2001, Brussels.

EU-Cyprus Joint Parliamentary Committee (2000), *Press Statement*, 18 April 2000, Nicosia.

Republic of Cyprus (1989), 'Outline Proposals for the Establishment of a Federal Republic and for the Resolution of the Cyprus Problem', Submitted on 30 January 1989, Appendix 20 in *The Cyprus Problem, Historical Review and the Latest Developments*, April 1999, Information Office, Republic of Cyprus, Nicosia.

Republic of Cyprus (1998a), *Gains from EU Accession to the Turkish Cypriot Community*, on www.cyprus-eu.org.cy

Republic of Cyprus (1998b), *Statement by President Clerides Relating to Turkish Cypriot Participation*, 12 March 1998, on www.cypruseu.org.cy

Republic of Cyprus (2000a), *House of Representatives Resolution*, 11 October 2000, Nicosia, www.pio.gov.cy/news/special_issues/special_issue034.htm

Republic of Cyprus (2000b), Department of Statistics, *Economic and Social Indicators*, Nicosia.

Republic of Cyprus (2002), *Observations of Mr Clerides to the Document of Mr Denktaş*, 29 April 2002, Non-paper dated 1 May 2002, Nicosia.

Republic of Turkey (1998), *Background of the Cyprus Problem*, Directorate General of Press and Information, Ministry of Foreign Affairs, Ankara.

Turkish Republic of Northern Cyprus (2001a), *Objectives and Basic Elements of a Cyprus Settlement*, Letter by Rauf Denktaş to the UN Secretary General, Non-paper dated 29 August 2001, Nicosia.

Turkish Republic of Northern Cyprus (2001b), *Rauf Denktaş's Letter to the UN Secretary General*, Non-paper dated 10 November 2001, Nicosia.

Turkish Republic of Northern Cyprus (2002a), *General Remarks on Draft Outline*, President's Office, Non-paper dated 29 April 2002, Nicosia.

Turkish Republic of Northern Cyprus (2002b), State Planning Organization, *Economic and Social Indicators*, Nicosia.

United Nations General Assembly (1974), Resolution 3212 (XXIX) of 1 November 1974.

United Nations General Assembly (1983), Resolution 37/253 of 13 May 1983.

United Nations Security Council (1964), Resolution 186 of 4 March 1964.

United Nations Security Council (1975), Resolution 367 of 12 March 1975.

United Nations Security Council (1983), Resolution 541 of 18 November 1983.

United Nations Security Council (1984), Resolution 550 of 11 May 1984.

United Nations Security Council (1990), Resolution 649 of 12 March 1990.

United Nations Security Council (1991), Resolution 716 of 11 October 1991.

United Nations Security Council (1992), Resolution 750 of 10 April 1992.

United Nations Security Council (1999), Resolution 1250 of 26 June 1999.

United Nations Secretary General (1991), *Report of the Secretary General to the UN Security Council*, S/23300, 19 December 1991, New York.

United Nations Secretary General (1992a), *Set of Ideas for the Reunification of Cyprus*, S/24472 English, New York.

United Nations Secretary General (1992b), *Summary of the Current Positions of the Two Sides in Relation to the 'Set of Ideas'*, 11 November 1992, S/24472 English, New York.

United Nations Secretary General (1994), *Report of the Secretary General to the UN Security Council*, 25 May 1994, New York.

United Nations Secretary General (1999), *Report of the Secretary General on his Mission of Good Offices in Cyprus*, 22 June 1999, S/1999/707, New York.

United Nations Secretary General (2000), 'Secretary General Stresses Equal Status of the Parties in Cyprus Proximity Talks', *Press Release*, SG/SM/7546, 12 September 2000, New York.

United Nations Secretary General (2003), *Report of the Secretary General on his Mission of Good Offices in Cyprus*, 7 April 2003, New York.

United Nations Secretary General (2004a), 'Transcript of the Press Conference by Secretary General Kofi Annan at the UN Headquarters, 13 February 2004', *Press Release*, SG/SM/9159, New York.

United Nations Secretary General (2004b), *The Comprehensive Settlement of the Cyprus Problem*, Fifth Version, on http://www.cyprus-un-plan.org

United Nations Secretary General (2004c) *Secretary General, in Message to Cypriot People, says Reunification Plan will Determine Destiny of Divided Island*, SG/SM/ 9264, 21 April 2004.

## Media and Web Sources

*Agence Europe* (www.agenceeurope.com)
*Anadolu Agency* (www.anadoluajansi.com.tr)
*Athens News Agency* (www.ana.gr)
*Cyprus Mail* (www.cyprus-mail.com)
*Cyprus News* (www.cyprusnews.com)
*Cyprus Weekly* www.cyprusweekly.com.cy)
*Financial Times* (www.ft.com)
*Friends of Cyprus Reports* (www.friendsofcyprus.org)
*Hürriyet* (www.hurriyetim.com.tr)
*Kathimerini* (www.ekathimerini.com)
*Kıbrıs Gazetesi* (www.kibrisgazetesi.com)
*Kıbrıs Monthly* (http://bornova.ege.edu.tr/~ncyprus/mfa/ncmonthly.html)
*Le Monde* (www.lemonde.com)
*Radikal* (www.radikal.com.tr)
*The Guardian* (www.guardian.co.uk)
*Turkey in Europe Monitor* (www.ceps.be)
*Turkish Daily News* (www.turkishdailynews.com)
*TurkishPress.com* (enews@anatolia.com)

# Index